CRIMINAL JUSTICE IN ANCIENT INDIA

Criminal Justice in Ancient India

HARIPADA CHAKRABORTI
M.A.(Double),Ph. D.,D.Litt.

Foreword
RAMARANJAN MUKHERJI

SHARADA

Sharada Publishing House
DELHI - 110052
1996

First Published 1996

ISBN: 81-85616-21-3

Published by B.L. Bansal
for SHARADA PUBLISHING HOUSE
(Publishers on India's Past and Present)
40, Anand Nagar, Inder Lok, Delhi - 110035
Ph: 5117390, 5116763
Typesetting by Neographics
1811 Gyani Bazar, Kotla , New Delhi 110003
Printed at Santosh Offset, Delhi - 110035

Dedicated to
the sacred memory of my wife
(Late) Latika Chakraborti

Foreword

The richness of Indian Culture has left its stamp in all Institutions designed by the mind of ancient India, and the judicial system formulated by ancient India is no exception to this general rule. As a matter of fact, in the Vedic period itself Indian mind could establish a magnificent system of administration of justice, which did contain the highest principles and finest procedures of judicial system, not dreamt of even by the Jurisprudence of Rome and England in ancient times. This system of administration of justice is surprisingly modern, since it upholds the independence of the judiciary, and declares the firm principle that nobody including the supreme monarch is above the prescription of law.

Ancient India employs the important term 'Dharma' to signify the concept of law, and this law is comprehensive in character inasmuch as, it brings under its orbit not only the laws of physical science, but also social laws, which the experience, wisdom and intuition of highly developed personalities could discover as unalterable. Indian Legal Texts always proclaim the supremacy of this 'Dharma', and say that all the exercises of man are to be regulated by the canons of 'Dharma', which is supposed to protect the individual and the society when followed with meticulous care. The Mahābhārata gives a clarion call to posterity to control, all pursuits for attainment of wealth and libidinal satisfaction, as also ventures for having liberation with the canon of this 'Dharma'.

It is astounding that even in the hey-days of monarchy, Indian mind could keep the administration of justice separated from the executive and evolved institutions and systems through setting up of which this independence could be maintained for all time to come. The Vinaya-Piṭaka refers to a beautiful case in which it is reported that a prince and a citizen submitted their case to the law-court and the court was pleased to decide against the prince. The prince accepted the decision in good grace, and he considered that this was binding on him.

Though the body of laws or 'Dharma' was traditional in character and from that point of view could not be altered by direct changes introduced by the state, yet law was continuously being made by the judges through interpretation. In this respect, this interpretation was more or less like the rulings of the modern judicial system and they were quoted by the judges for giving a decision on a particular point. This system followed by the ancient India made the rules, evolved through interpretation the most powerful instruments for administration of justice, and this fact itself testified to the necessity felt by ancient India of interpreting the laws and extending them to meet the challenges of the changing times.

It was extremely significant that the judges including the Chief Justice, technically known as Prāḍvivāka, were required under this system to take the help of the society in administering justice. The king appointed councellors to assist deliberation in the court, and the rule of the assembly was that everybody was required to express his opinion according to the law. The Institution of Justice depended much on the part played by the jury and the jury was appointed from members of the society having divine qualities, command over law and necessary competence to tender advice to the judge. To keep the judiciary free even from the influence of the monarch, the law was that the king alone was not allowed to hear cases, but was required to have Prāḍvivāka or the Chief Justice with him. In describing the qualifications of this Chief Justice, Nārada points out: the judge must be self-controlled, of a respectable family, impartial, not given to excitement, steadfast, afraid of the consequences of a bad judgement, virtuous, energetic and free from passion. While the Chief Justice was appointed by the monarch the subordinate judges were appointed by persons having sovereign authority for administering justice in local areas. There were provisions for making appeals against decisions taken by these subordinate judges, and these appeals used to lie to the court of the Chief Justice, thereafter to the Privy Council or the King-in Council.

The procedure of administration of criminal law was equally significant. No one was exempted from punishment and even a relation of the king was required to undergo punishment as prescribed in texts on criminal law. It was also prescribed that if persons of a responsible position and social status and officers in the administration commit an offence they were required to undergo punishment more severe than that meted out to an ordinary citizen committing the same offence. The Manusaṃhitā declares that where an ordinary man is punishable with a token fine of one Kārṣāpaṇa, the king himself committing the same offence should be punished with a thousand time amount. The punishments in criminal law under this system were carefully graded: it started from censure; rebuke came thereafter: this was followed by pecuniary punishment, which included fine and forfeiture of property: the highest punishment was corporal punishment, which included imprisonment, penal servitude and death sentence. Ancient texts repeatedly proclaim: penalty (Daṇḍas) keeps the people under control, - penalty protects, - penalty remains awake when people are asleep: so the wise consider 'Daṇḍa' as the instrument leading to righteousness. All this indicates that punishment was regarded not only as a deterrent, but also as retributive and reformative.

Though ancient India had stated much about criminal justice and judiciary system, no author has as yet made an attempt to collect all the available materials from ancient Indian texts and give a comprehensive and exhaustive treatment of the system of administration of criminal justice as prevalent in ancient India. In order to make this exhaustive treatment the writer is required to have deep penetration into original Sanskrit texts, an acquaintance with the principles of modern judiciary and legal systems, and above all, thorough command over English idioms and expressions. Dr. Haripada Chakraborti, retired Head, Dept. of AIH and C, Viswa-Bharati University, having deep penetration into Smriti texts and command over both Sanskrit and English idioms and expressions and possessing thorough acquaintance with the modern principles of Judiciary have come forward to remove a long felt want with his *magnum opus* entitled 'Criminal Justice in Ancient India'. Starting from an analysis of the evolution of law and kingship, as recorded in Ancient Indian Smriti Texts and the Epics and the Purāṇas, Dr. Chakraborti has proceeded to expound the theory that was floated by Ancient India, - the Theory, that the King was considered to be the fountain head of justice. In order to administer justice it becomes necessary to have judges and different types of courts, and a full procedure is to be laid down for trial including the exercise to be adopted by the court, which ultimately are to lead to pronouncement of judgement. A detailed treatment of these stages of trial has found place in the Book, enhancing its value as a source-book.

Ancient India did formulate a clear-cut definition of 'Crime' and prescribe different punishments for different types of crimes, beginning from defamation and ending with criminal assault and murder. Different types of courts were required to try different types of cases, and consequently the jurisdiction of different courts were also required to be spelt out clearly. While spelling out the jurisdiction of different types of courts Indian Judiciary System did elaborate the principle to be adopted by different courts for arriving at a decision, and at the same time pointed out the cases, where offenders could be exempted from punishment. The right to private defence was recognised and laws of evidence were formulated in a comprehensive manner. Evidence was broadly divided into three classes (a) document; (b) witness; (c) conduct. Documents were divided into two classes, the official and the private. The witness was tested, and while giving his deposition the witness was placed near both the plaintiff and defendant. The law of evidence enunciated by ancient India, thus, deserves minutest consideration. Dr. Haripada Chakraborti has been successful in analysing all the concepts of the system of criminal justice floated by ancient India with reference to the original texts from which the data have been collected and conclusions drawn.

The second book of the work deals with topics of litigation and describes the various types of crimes and the punishments recommended for them by Indian scriptures. Indian mind has all along pronounced a note of caution in regard to the functioning of the forces of disintegration, and, consequently, has thought it proper to formulate a detailed law of treason. Dr. Chakraborti has described the problem of treason in its manifold aspects and has shown how Indian mind at different stages of human history had tried to combat this problem with spectacular success. The book also deals with the crimes of violence and tries to justify the different types of punishment prescribed for different crimes of violence.

The work 'Criminal Justice in Ancient India' testifies to wide reading on the part of the author, who has quoted excerpts not only from the Mahābhārata and the well-known Smriti texts like Manusaṃhitā and Yājñavalkya Saṃhitā, but also from the Saṃhitās written by the Dharmaśāstrakāras who are less known, but, nevertheless, whose contribution to the development of Indian judiciary system is profound. The author's acquaintance with the entire range of Sanskrit and Buddhist literature, as also his deep penetration into book on modern judiciary and constitutional law, and the comprehensive knowledge which he has acquired through acquaintance with diverse treatises has been able to give comprehensive character to the work. The book 'Criminal Justice in Ancient India' can be described as a source-book containing the entire fund of knowledge deposited in ancient Indian legal texts and can be regarded as a guide book for persons administering justice even in modern times. As a matter of fact, the modern judiciary system is not a gift of contemporary days, but is developed through a continuous process of evolution: and though it is said that the modern system owes its origin to the British system, it is a fact that the ancient Indian system was the richest of all the systems developed by human mind and the British system did draw substantial component from the ancient Indian system. The work 'Criminal Justice in Ancient India', therefore, forms the connecting bridge between the ancient

Indian system and the modern system, and it has been able to show the exact impact produced by the most brilliant ancient Indian Judiciary system on the modern Judiciary system, supposed to rest itself on the British Model. This splendid work, therefore, is sure to enrich the stock of human knowledge particularly in the arena of studies in Dharmaśāstra and Law. It is sure to be appreciated not only by scholars and students of Law and Justice, Sociology and Criminology, Purāṇas and Dharmaśāstras, but by common readers as well who are likely to have a taste of justified pride by knowing the richness of the ancient Indian acumen. I offer my respectful congratulation to Dr. Haripada Chakraborti, who happens to be my learned teacher and welcome this magnificent work to the fold of treatises on Indian Legal Systems.

RAMARANJAN MUKHERJI

Preface

In the following pages an attempt has been made to trace the history of "Criminal Justice in Ancient India". Scholars like Jolly, Bühler, Jayaswal and Kane have discussed some aspects of the subject but nobody has yet given any systematic treatment of it. "Crime and punishment in Ancient India", hitherto done in this field by Dr. R.P. Dasgupta is the only work that deserves mention and I am indebted to this scholar for the light on the laws of other ancient peoples. While civil law of ancient India has received a careful attention from a number of scholars, the criminal law has ever been neglected. But the penal law of a country is the true index of its civilisation, and an enquiry into it gives us an insight into the political, social, economical and religious conditions prevailing in ancient India. Regard being had to the works, already done on the subject the present author may claim to say that he has got to walk along a path, which, though not devoid of light, is mostly untrodden.

The criminal law of ancient India has history of its own evolution from the humblest beginnings to a fairly developed system, though not without defects, through different periods representing thereby various stages of development of India's culture and civilisation. It emerged in its most rudimentary shape, as reflected in the Dharmasūtras, passed gradually through higher and higher stages of development in the periods of Kauṭilya, Manu and Yājñavalkya and reached ultimately the most highly developed stage in the periods of Nārada, Bṛhaspati and Kātyāyana and of the Agni and Matsya Purāṇas and subsequently the importance of commentaries and digests in this connection is also equally great because they try to explain the original texts of earlier jurists and to reconcile the anomalies, if any, by a clever trick of interpretation.

Besides the Smṛtis, the works like Kauṭilya's Arthaśāstra and the Nītiśāstras of Śukra and Kāmandaka have also been properly utilised, because these treatises are mines of information on law and judicature of ancient India. The difference between the Dharma and Artha-laws has been carefully noted. The literary sources and epigraphic records bearing on the subject are equally tapped.

Scholars like Nelson raise a question how far the criminal law was applied in practice. It should be admitted that the Dharma-śāstras often preach the ideal rather than actual facts but they show at least the tendencies of the age and wherever possible, their evidences are corroborated by others of more tangible nature. Dr. Nares Chandra Sengupta's remark in this connection may be quoted here: "Smṛti law was the practical law administered at some time in ancient India, no matter when ...... the evidence of epigraphic records, such as they are, also furnishes some independent corroboration of the theory that smṛti-law was honoured by Hindu kings. In literature too, the trial scenes in Mṛcchakaṭikam and Dhūrta-samāgamam show that in the main smṛti-law was sought to be followed by kings in the times of their authors". (Sources of Law of Society in Ancient India", Introduction, pp. 5 and 6).

Moreover, to render comparative study of criminal laws easier and to create further interest in the subject the laws of other countries in the ancient and medieval world and those of the Indian Penal Code have been treated here.

In Book I of this volume are discussed the various questions relating to law and administration of justice with particular attention to crimes and the function of the state to remove them. Book II treats in different chapters the laws relating to crimes only. The ancient Indian jurists divided the subject-matter of law-suits under 18 titles but only the laws, connected with criminal justice, as noted under a few particular heads have been dealt with here, of course with due attention to the corresponding crimes, treated in the Indian Penal Code.

I have tried to present the views embodied in the works used by me with an eye to chronology. I have accepted the views of recognised scholars like Bühler, Jolly, Jayaswal, Keith, Winternitz and Kane regarding dates. I have spared no pains to give a systematic account of Criminal Justice of Ancient

India and I shall deem my labour amply rewarded, if this essay helps the understanding of the spirit of the subject concerned.

Let me pay my heartful thanks to Dr. Ramaranjan Mukherjee, formerly Vice-chancellor of Burdwan and Rabindra Bharati Universities and at present Chancellor of Tirupati Saṁskṛta Visvavidyalaya, who has, in spite of his various pre-occupations, kindly written the 'Foreword' of this book and I am sure this has much enhanced the value of this work.

Last but not of the least importance is the contribution of Prof. Satkari Mukherjee, a renowned scholar and Director of the Research Institute of the Government of India, New Delhi, who also deserves my heartful thanks for his help in the matter of its publication. Let me pay my thanks to Sri B.L. Bansal as well, for Sharada Publishing House (40, Anand Nagar, Inder Lok, Delhi - 110 035) for his keen interest in its publication.

Naivedya H.P. CHAKRABORTI
P.O. Bolpur
(Birbhum)
15th August, 1995

Contents

Book II

Topics of Litigation

BOOK - I

Law and Administration of Justice

CHAPTER I

Evolution of Law and Kingship

Adjudication presupposes a basis of rules of justice. People must have had an idea of justice in human relations as reflected in the Vedic concept of Ṛta. Ṛta signifies a moral law which sustains and regulates the moral order of the beings. Long before the rise of any adjudication or any juridical law there might have existed a standard of right and wrong which was supported by the opinion of the community and which might be enforced by the aid of the community. The earliest society of the Aryan race was governed not by a king but by a group of men who devoted themselves to the study of superhuman things, as for example, the Magi of Persia, the Brāhmaṇas of India and the Druids of the Celtic races and who derived law from the tradition which represented the custom of the learned men.[1]

There is no doubt that the foundation of the entire system of the administration of justice lies in the instinct of vengeance. A person injured seeks vengeance and he redresses his wrong by self-help or by the help of his family and kindred. In a primitive society fighting between individuals or families was the normal mode of settling disputes. In some places disputes were settled by the entire tribal assembly, somewhere else by the king, e.g., in the Greece of Homer and Rome before the rise of the Republic but in India by the Pariṣad of religious persons whose words were the Āryan-laws but we may guess some of the ways from the institution of Vrātya-stoma,[2] as depicted in the *Pañcaviṃśa Brāhmana*.

Law in the Vedic period covered all fields of human activities and indicated the regulative principles of nature and society. To the Vedic people there was but one Ṛta for nature and man. Ṛta, the moral standard bound all men together with one common string. To Vedic seers Law and Truth came to be regarded as two aspects of one and the same Reality. The

Upaniṣad enunciated the principle that Truth is the one Reality and law and order are its different phases. The *Bṛhad. Upa.* asserts that "Law is the king of kings ..... nothing is higher than Law. The *Bṛhad. Upa.*[3] may be quoted here: "Dharmaṃ tadetat kṣatrasya kṣatraṃ yad-dharmas tasmād dharmāt parataraṃ nāsti atho' valīyān valīyāṃsam-āśaṃsate dharmeṇa yatha rājñaivam yo vai sa dharmaḥ satyam vai tat tasmāt satyaṃ vadantam-āhurdharmaṃ vadatīti dharmaṃ vā vadantaṃ satyaṃ vadatītyetat haiva etad-ubhayaṃ bhavati". This passage shows that law is the power of the Kṣatra, nothing is higher than law. Vidhi helps the weak to rule over the strong, law gives the king power, law and truth are identical and the source of both of them is the human society. The sovereignty of law and its interest in human society is best explained here. The Buddhist conception of law was also moral in nature, because to the Buddhists Dhamma and Law are the same.

The nature of law was in the later period believed to be based on truth and justice. From the sociological standpoint dharma or law represents the privileges, duties and obligations of a man and its main purpose is to promote the welfare of man individually and socially and to make it applicable, it encouraged obedience by reward and discouraged disobedience by punishment. The *Mahābhārata* also conceives of law as being based on the contract between the state and people: "Dharma is created to put a stop to the harm done by the harmful-natured man;" and it assigns a wider power to the king saying, "Whatever a king ordains a dharma is to be considered actual law". The Purāṇic conception is that Dharma is created according to the nature of men and thus it gives us a realistic touch to law. The different purāṇas show how different classes of society should be ruled by different laws. Here we mark the difference between common law and Dharma-law. The culprit must be punished by the king according to the common law and his sins are to be purged out by the dharma law.

An analysis of Āpastamba's *Dharma-sūtra* reveals the fact that the dharma-laws were originally concerned with ceremonial and religious conduct and with infliction of penances as the spiritual counterpart of the administration of criminal law but sometimes we find there the junctions of dharma and artha (royal) jurisdictions: "The spiritual guide shall order those who (whilst) participating according to the śāstras, have gone astray through the weakness of their appetites, to perform penances proportionate to their sinful acts as laid down in the śāstra. If they disobey the śāstra, the Ācārya (Spiritual guide) will take them to the king. The king shall send them to the Purohita,[4] versed in the Dharma and Artha, who shall order the Brahmin culprits to do the penance and reduce them to obedience by methods short of killing and slavery according to their physical strength.[5] In cases of other castes the king after having examined their acts may punish them up to death.[6] Thus we see the closer co-ordination between the Dharma and Artha-laws. Āpas.[7] says that the king had the authority to rule and punish. A man committing a crime was responsible to the king's law or Artha-law. But he had to do penance independently. The penance was prescribed by the spiritual guides who took the help of the king when they were not obeyed.

The concept of law, as noted above (in the Upaniṣad) is that Law is the final ruler of this universe and the laws of the state are meant for guiding the relations of men. The King, Lord of all men was at that time equally subject to it. He was, according to Kauṭilya, (Ch. I, BK III, 150) neither to make nor to alter the law but to carry out its maxims. By doing so, he derived his soul authority : "Catu-r-varṇāśramasyāyaṃ lokasyācārarakṣaṇāt/ naśyatāṃ sarva-dharmānāṃ rājā dharma-pravartakaḥ". Kauṭilya says that Varuṇa is the moral judge par excellence and the king is also like Varuṇa. Hence the king was regarded as the mere custodian of law. He must administer law impartially and reward or punish the good or evil-doers. In case of failure to do so, he was liable to a fine 30 times the amount to be paid by the guilty: "A-daṇḍya-daṇḍane rājño daṇḍa-s-triṃśad-guṇo' mbhasi Varuṇāya pradātavyo Brāhmaṇebhyo tataḥ param" (Ch. 13, BK IV - AŚ).

It is noteworthy that certain principles of Dharma schools were accepted by the Artha Schools as well: "None (brought to the king) shall be punished in case of doubt".[8] The king, Āpas.[9] says, may convict only after searchingly investigated through cross-examination. Thus the equitable doctrine of the Dharma School was followed in the Artha School as well. But the latter never allowed ordeals in their proof. Kauṭilya rejected the ordeals. After the Brahmanical revival under the Śuṅgas and Kāṇvas the cause of ordeals was strongly advocated. The *Mṛcchakaṭikam*[10] shows, however, that later on the courts did not allow the trial of ordeal to a brahmin, accused in a murder case. Āpas.[11] shows how the principles of Dharma School were also desired to be followed by the Artha School. As for example, gambling should be brought under state control, as it was a vice in the eye of the Dharma School. It was the king's duty to protect those who suffer from want in his kingdom and to guard against theft. The administration was held responsible for theft. According to the Dharma School the king would be responsible for theft and he would be liable to penance, if he failed to guard against thieves. Adultery was a sin, according to the Dharma School and this School claimed jurisdiction over it, as marriage was held to be a creation of Dharma law.[12] Āpas.[13] prescribes repressive measures against Śūdras who showed contempt to the members of the Dharma School. Such punishments were needed by the rise of heterodoxy in the society. Aśvaghoṣa says that the Buddhist śūdras were as learned and good as the brahmins. As the Buddhists were beyond the control of the Dharma School, the king's intervention was sought.

According to K.P. Jayaswal[14] "the real and regular civil and criminal laws of the country were in the Artha-śāstras". The Artha laws were known as—'Vyavahāra' in Gautama's *Dh. Sūtra,*[15] and as 'rāja-śāsana' in Kauṭ.'s Arthaśāstra. The supremacy of Artha-laws is proved by Patañjali in his *Mahābhāṣyam*: "Naiva Īśvara ājñāpayati nāpi Dharma-Sūtra-kārāḥ paṭhanti".[16] This is neither ordained by the ruler nor by the authors of the Dharmasūtras. Impartiality was the first criterion of justice and reason was the main factor of judicial administration. The disputes were settled in four ways, (i) by dharma, (ii) by

Vyavahāra (witness to the transaction), (iii) by cāritra (customs) and (iv) by rāja-śāsanam (royal adjudication). "Rājñām-ājñā tu śāsanam". Theoretically the king had no legislative authority but practically he could modify the laws. He could repeal, modify or introduce customary laws. He could, by edict, issue regulations and ordinances which had the force of laws. With the rise of the king's power the king could issue fresh laws where the Dharma code was silent on the punishment of certain crimes. Manu,[17] however enjoins that in judging cases only traditional "dharma" is to be followed. Yāj.[18] recognises the importance of "dharma" in the administration of justice.

It may be pointed out that in the Maurya period when the imperial administrative system was introduced throughout the vast empire, the power of the king was strengthened and the king began to assert his power by issuing new edicts and ordinances which gradually hardened into a code or criminal laws. The Maurya laws had the following aims in view: to preserve the safety of the king's person and the regal rights, viz. incomes from various departments and to check theft or defalcation, to bring all economic sectors under state control and regulate prices, wages etc. for the good of the people and to punish crimes, not covered by the Dharma laws. These laws became too current to be ignored and some of them proved so beneficent as to be quoted even as late as the period of Daṇḍin[19] who speaks of the Maurya law prescribing capital punishment to be executed in cases of merchants found guilty of possessing stolen property. From this we may presume that some merchants had been reputed for fair dealing and they could never be thought of as receivers of stolen property. Again it may be pointed out that in dealing with cases of theft the *Dharmaśāstra* asks the circumstances of the crime to be circulated.[20] Traders may in course of business get the stolen property without knowing and if so, it would be against the spirit of the *Dharmaśāstra* to punish such traders with capital punishment. Hence the example of Daṇḍin here may be taken as a proof that the Mauryas simply enforced the existing law and did not change it.

According to Smṛtis and the *Mahābhārata* law and law of punishment were divine creations as the king and existed independently of the latter who had to respect and enforce them. According to the *Dharmaśāstras* the main source (see Appendix-A) of law were the Śruti (Vedas), Smṛti, Nyāya and Sadācāra and it is interesting to note that except Nārada no other jurists mention the king as the source of law. In ancient India as elsewhere custom was the main source of law and hence the Vedas, the repository of old customs, believed by some to be divinely revealed were accepted as the highest authority on Dharma or Law. The Smṛtis were the codified texts of old traditions. But to meet the need of the society in view of its dynamic nature the conduct of the good and learned men (sadācāra) gained gradually the force and sanctity of law. In course of time various interpretations of the legal texts to justify the new customs under changed circumstances of the society became an additional source of law. In cases of conflict in the interpretation of law the sense of justice, equity or reasoning (Nyāya) was allowed to prevail and so the judge-made laws became another source of law, as the courts flourished under the royal authority. That is why the king is mentioned as the 'Dharma-pravartaka', that is, the king is not the maker or giver of laws but simply an authority to enforce the laws as established by sages.

Now let us examine what Kauṭilya thinks of the king whether or how far he is a source of law. Some scholars think that the king is a source of law and his edicts override even 'dharma', as reflected in *Artha-Śāstra* (3.1): "Dharma-ś-ca vyavahāra-ś-ca caritraṃ rāja-śāsanam / vivādārtha-ś-catuṣpādaḥ paścimaḥ pūrva-vādhakaḥ//". But others differ and take the above verse as referring to the four ways of settling legal disputes,[21] as reflected in and confirmed by the next verse of AŚ.[22] which means that "in truth lies Dharma, in witness vyavahāra, in tradition of the people lies caritra and in the order of the king, śāsana". So 'rāja-śāsana' is to be accepted as the final authority in legal decision and it takes place when the evidence is equally balanced and when the Smṛtis and Sabhyas are at variance.[23]

Such decisions might have become precedents for the future and so rāja-śāsana may be accepted as the indirect source of law only in a derivative sense. It is interesting to note the following verses of Kauṭilya[24] : "Anuśāsad-dhi Dharmeṇa vyavahāreṇa samsthayā/nyāyena yaḥ caturantām mahīṃ jayet// Saṃsthayā Dharma-śāstreṇa śāstram va vyavahārikaṃ/ yasminnarthe viruddhyeta Dharmeṇārthaṃ vinirṇayet // śāstram vipratipakṣyeta Dharma-nyāyena kenacit / nyāya-s-tatra pramāṇam syāt tatra pāṭho hi naśyati //". —"The king who administers justice in accordance with Dharma, vyavahāra, saṃsthā and Nyāya will be able to conquer the world bounded by four quarters. Whenever there is disagreement between saṃsthā and Dharma or between Vyavahāra and Dharma, then the matter should be settled in accordance with Dharma. But whenever Dharma is in conflict with Nyāya, then Nyāya shall be held authoritative, for there the original text loses its force". This shows that in cases of conflict even Dharma is to be bent before equity or reasoning (as understood by the judges). Breloer translates the last line as "For the text underlies the change". He adds that the judge is thus given the opportunity to build up new legal sentences outside of and even contrary to the sacred law. Some scholar is inclined to interpret 'dharma-nyāyena' in the sense of 'a good custom' which is very significant in the sphere of good administration. Yāj.[25] refers to the application of reason (Yuktibhiḥ) in deciding difficult cases of disputes. Bṛhaspati is one of the most powerful advocates of the application of Yukti.[26] ("Yuktyā vibhajanīyam tat anyathā anarthakaṃ bhavet"). He would apply it to determine the preference in cases of conflict of laws: "Dharmaśāstra-virodhe tu yukti-yukto vidhiḥ smṛtaḥ". (IX. 8) He denounces emphatically the mere dependence on the letter of the written law without its critical interpretation through reason (Yukti): "Kevalaṃ śāstram-āsritya na vaktavyo vinirṇayaḥ / yuktihīne vicāre tu Dharma-hāniḥ prajāyate/".

It must be borne in mind that Kauṭilya means by 'Dharma, civil and criminal law and social conduct and attaches due importance to it when he says that the king is 'Dharma-pravartaka', i.e., he is to maintain dharma and punish justly the violaters of dharma. He is not primarily a law-maker but a mere administrator of law by establishing civil (Dharmasthīya) and criminal (Kaṇṭakaśodhana) courts throughout his kingdom. The king's power is thus more judicial than legislative[27]: "Esāpi vidhi yā iyam dhammena pālanā dhammena vidhāna dhammena sukhiyanā dhammena gotī ti'— this should be the rule (of action), viz., administration according to the law (of piety), regulation (or legislation) according to the law (of piety), making men happy etc. according to the law (of piety) and protection according to the law (of piety).

But it cannot be denied that the edicts of the king controlled the market, fixed prices, standardised weights and measures and regulated all economic activities of the land during the Mauryan rule. Kauṭilya[28] says that "kings principally depend on edicts, peace and war being rooted in them". The edicts issued orders for punishment or rewards (ājñālekha) and so they may be taken as regulative laws though not substantive or positive laws. The Kaṇṭaka-śodhana courts decided cases on the basis of such 'rāja-śāsana'. The examination of the list of subjects in the jurisdiction of these courts shows that some cases of Dharmasthīya courts could also be tried in the Kaṇṭakaśodhana courts as well[29] and hence the king-made laws were extending their sphere. 'Rāja-śāsana' may, therefore, be taken as a subsidiary source of law, as it was recognised in law-courts.[30]

It is interesting to point out that N.C. Sengupta admits that the legislative power of the king is not supported by any other scripture than Manu and Medhātithi. (cf. Sources of Law and Society in Ancient India). But this remark is really surprising. Manu and Medhātithi should be carefully examined. Manu[31] says, "Tasmād dharmaṃ yam-iṣṭeṣu sa vyavasyennarādhipaḥ" on which Medhātithi comments—"śāstrācārāviruddhaṃ vyavasyen-niścitya sthāpayen-na vicālayet. Sā tādṛṣī rājño' nujñā nātikramanīyā". To sum up the whole thing Manu and Medhātithi mean to say that the king should prescribe 'just in accordance with the prescription of the Dharmaśāstras and he must not violate the injunctions of Dharma-śastras. Medhātithi explains it further that the king's order in connection with festivals, fairs or slaughter of animals etc. should not be violated because such order is not in clash with the injunctions of the Dharma-śāstras. Thus it appears that the law-making power of the king was never absolute or unrestricted. An inscription,[32] edited by Dr. D.C. Sircar indicates that Viṣṇusena, the king of the 6th cent. A.D., when asked by a group of merchants to state the law by an 'Ācāra-sthiti-pātra', laid down the law, current in his time without claiming to have had any legislative power. This 'sthiti-pātra' is actually a list of customary laws, quoted in the inscription.

REFERENCES

1. *Early Law and Custom,* Ch. II.
2. For the different varieties of Vrātyastoma vide N.N. Ghosh, *Indo-Aryan Literature and Culture,* p. 6.
3. 1.4. 11-14.
4. See Appendix B
5. *Āpas.* II. *Dh. S.*, III, 5.11. 12-16.
6. *Āpas.* II. 5.11.1.
7. II.5.10.6.
8. *Āpas. Dh.S.,* II. 5.11.2.
9. II. 5.11.3.
10. Act, IX.
11. II.10.25-29.
12. "Dharmāddhi saṃbandhaḥ" - *Āpas.* II.10.27.1.
13. II.10.27.14.
14. *Manu and Yājñavalkya,* p. 13.
15. XI. 19-20.
16. On Pāṇ, 1.1.46.
17. "Dharmaṃ śāśvatam āsritya kuryāt kārya-vinirṇayam"—VIII. 8.
18. II. 186.
19. "Mauryadatta eṣa varo vanijām idrśeṣu aparādheṣu nāsti asubhiḥ abhiyogaḥ".—*Dasa. K.Ch.,* Uttara, 2nd Uccha, 44. cf. AŚ. ch.87.
20. Cf. Manu, IX. 261-267.
21. Cf. *I.H.Q.* 28, p. 307 ff.
22. "Tatra satye sthito Dharmo vyavahāra-s-tu sākṣiṣu/caritram saṃgrahe puṃsām rājñam-ājñā tu śāsanam/".

23. Cf. *Age of Imperial Unity,* pp. 354-350.
24. III.I.
25. II. 212.
26. "Yuktyā vibhajanīyam tat anyathā anarthakam bhavet".
27. Cf. Aśoka's R.E., I.
28. II. 10.2.
29. Cf. P.V. Kane, vol. III, p. 257.
30. Cf. *Public Administration in Ancient India,* p. 137.
31. VII. 13.
32. *JRASB,* XVI, p. 113 ff.

CHAPTER II

The King as Fountain of Justice

A definite history of the evolution of law begins with the rise of the king as fountain of justice. The Vedic literature speaks very little of the king's administration of justice. The king was not at that time so powerful as to be a judge, though of course, it was his duty to maintain law and order and enforce people to perform their duties. Disputes were decided by the people themselves who formed Kula-s and guilds. We have already noticed that the ancient Āryans did not look upon the king as either the source or even the repository of law. The law was in the special knowledge of the sages and the Ṛgveda shows that it was the king's duty to choose his Purohita and be guided by him. The king emerged as administering justice in the period of the Sūtra literature.

Gautama speaks of the king as an authority to administer justice and enjoins at the same time that the king has to get his law from the following three sources: (1) Scriptures like Veda, Dharmaśāstras, Vedāṅgas and Purāṇa; (2) Customs or usages of countries, communities and Kulas, not opposed to sacred texts; and (3) laws or customs prevailing among cultivators, traders, herdsmen, money-lenders and artisans, as determined by each community in matters relating to themselves.[1] He adds that the king should decide cases after ascertaining the law from those who are expert on the particular matter (*Ibid.* 22) and if there be any conflict, he must consult with those who are masters of three Vedas. (*Ibid.* 25). Thus the king is, according to Gautama, a judge of disputes and he must know law from competent sources. Elsewhere[2] Gautama speaks also of a brāhmaṇa, learned in Śāstras as an alternative hand to administer justice (Prāḍvivāka). It is interesting to note that no sūtra works other than Viṣṇu mentions the king's "Sabhā", which rises to prominence in later legal literature in connection with the administration of justice. The emergence of the king as judge was thus gradual. In the Vedic age the king was assisted and advised by the learned Purohita like Vaśiṣṭha and Viśvāmitra. In the age of the Dharmasūtras the king was assisted by Prāḍvivāka, the reminiscent of the Purohita of the earlier period and later on, by a 'sabhā' of learned men.

The Jātakas, also refer to the king as judge. The king is repeatedly warned to be impartial in judgement.[3] The beam of justice was even then as it is today, regarded as a symbol of impartial justice.[4] The king used to hear cases and he might have gone to the court-house every morning, as heard of in the epic.[5] Sometimes one or more of his ministers like the Purohita, Senāpati or even the prince acted as judges.[6] The *Jāt.*[7] mentions five judges ("Tassa pana raññо pañca amacca ...... vinicchaye niyutta"). We have no reference to a definite code of law but some passages state: "Execute justice in this way" and the king had righteous judgment inscribed on a golden plate.[8] The king caused a book of judgment to be written and said, "By observing this book you should settle suits".[9] A body of precedents had already grown by this time. Bribery was resorted to in judgment.[10] One who judged rightly was praised by the people and then he would be formally appointed by the king as judge. The king directed the judge as to time and way.[11] Officers with criminal jurisdiction were appointed.

Kauṭilya[12] says that the king must look into the disputes "of both citizens and country people". "When in the court, he shall never cause his petitioners to wait at the door, for when a king makes himself inaccessible to his people, and entrusts his work to his immediate officers, he may be sure to engender confusion in business and to cause thereby public disaffection and himself a prey to his enemies". He shall, therefore, personally attend to the affairs of all, without any discrimination. Megasthenes[13] says how the king passed the whole day in court without any break and thus confirms how Kauṭilya's advice for the wakefulness of the king about litigants was practised in real life. Aśoka's Separate Rock Edict I, shows likewise the king's interest in the judicial administration of the land through the Māhamātras.

The *Rāmāyana*[14] and the *Mahābhārata*[15] show how the king is to suffer, if he offers himself to pleasures and does not take care of litigants. The *Rāmāyaṇa*[16] speaks of the king Nṛga who was cursed to be a chameleon by two brahmins who came to get their disputes over a cow settled by the king but in vain.

Next to Visnu Dharmasūtra, Manu was the first of the Dharmaśāstra writers to mention the 'Sabhā' as assisting the king in judicial matters. Now let us enquire into the function of the 'Sabhā' of the earlier period. The Vedic period witnesses the rise of 'Sabhā' which decided cases of land-disputes, cheating, murder, assault, debts, inheritance and also problems of war and peace.[17] Towards the end of the Vedic age began the rule of justice of the king. The king is heard of as penalising a Śūdra in the *Kāṭhaka Saṃ.* (27.4). The period of the Brāhmaṇas shows the decline of the power of sabhā and rise of kingship, guided by laws of the land. The judicial administration organised by the king had its distinct administration organised by the king had its distinct manifestation in the period of the Dharmasūtras. By this time the power of the king along with that of the local bodies was well-guarded. Kauṭilya mentions two separate courts, Civil (Dharmasthīya) and Criminal (Kaṇṭakaśodhana); and by this time the customs of countries and groups received no less importance than the legal texts in judicial matters.[18] Disputes were settled in village-courts (sabhā) as well, in which no judge was employed by the king but "elders among, farmers, cowherds or outsiders who formerly had possession there" did point out the boundary.[19] Kauṭilya's Kaṇṭakaśodhana courts were so powerful in weeding out the thorns of the society that Megasthenes found India free from crimes.[20] These may be taken as the first courts of Criminal law, which may be called Police courts.[21] N.C. Banerjee rightly remarks: "As time went on, as society became complex, as the royal authority increased and as the administrative body extended its jurisdiction, the necessity of new laws became evident. As there was no legislative agency, the right of issuing ordinances or of making laws devolved on the king and his ministers". Hence these criminal courts exercised the authority and jurisdiction of Police officials and criminal investigators. Monahan thinks that these courts controlled the military organisation and protected the people by cruelly punishing the criminals.[22]

The *Rāmāyaṇa* speaks of 'Sabhā' as a body of people's representatives. It consisted of brahmins and representatives of municipalities as members but no Śūdras were allowed to be in. The Sabhā called by Vaśiṣṭha after the death of Daśaratha, it had no Śūdra members. The Sabhā of Nṛga also had ministers, priests and representatives of trade guilds as its members.[23] The 'rāja-sabhā' is described as the meeting of gods in the *Mahābhārata.*[24] Each member of the court had liberty to express his view, as proved in the case of considering Draupadī-problem.

Manu[25] and Yājñavalkya[26] enjoin that the king administers justice with the members of the Sabhā ("Sabhāsadaḥ"). Manu[27] says that a king, desirous of investigating law-cases must enter his court of justice, together with brahmins and experienced councillors ('Sabhya') and decide everyday the causes of litigants. Medhātithi comments that protection consists in the removal of troubles, secular and spiritual. Vijñān[28] says that the protection of the people, the greatest duty of the king is not possible without punishing the wicked and the finding out of the wicked is not possible without judicial enquiry. Manu[29] says that "if the king does not personally investigate the suits, let him appoint a learned brahmin to try them" and that man shall, accompanied by three assessors, consider as case brought before the king." Thus the court of justice consists of three brāhmaṇas, learned in the Vedas and the learned judge, appointed by the king.[30] Yāj. also says: "Vyavahārān-nṛpah paśyet vidvadbhir-brahmaṇaih saha" and Vijñān. comments—"na kṣattryaiḥ"—not even with the Kṣatriyas, what to speak of others. Manu allows even a brahmin who subsists by the name of his caste, to interpret the law but never a Śūdra.[31] His commentators point out that as the Śūdras as judges are strictly forbidden, Kṣatriyas and Vaiśyas may be taken in, if necessary. Yāj.[32] lays stress on the fact that the king should decide cases with the help of learned brahmins on the basis of the traditional or customary law and without being actuated by anger and avarice. Yāj. insists on the appointment of the jurors (*'sabhāsadaḥ'*) who must be learned in the Vedas, and in religious scriptures, truthful and equal to all, friends and foes. He is silent about the caste of these jurors, though he insists on the assistance of learned brahmins in II.1. It is difficult to read the mind of Yāj. who might have had liberal opinion so as to appoint persons of other castes also being 'sabhāsad', specially in an age when India had reached the height of her material success by the development of trade and commerce and crafts and industries. Vijñān., however, opines that these jurors were to be brahmins alone and quotes for justification Kātyāyana who uses the term "dvijottamaiḥ". But the term 'dvija' might have been equally applied to any of three upper castes, thus not excluding even the merchant class. Manu, of course, mentions at least three jurors of the brahmin class (viprāḥ), as he is believed to have appeared in the age of brahmanical revival. Vijñāneśvara's argument gets strengthened by his quotation from Bṛhaspati who like Manu clearly mentions the term 'viprāḥ'.

The texts of Viṣṇu and Yāj. show that the jurors (sabhāsadaḥ) were appointed by the king as permanent adjuncts to the court and they were duty-bound to give their opinions on the cases heard before them. Besides these appointed members of the court, any learned brahmin who came in, was invited to attend the sabhā and it was his moral duty and right to give his view likewise, as evidenced by an anonymous text quoted by *Mitākṣarā* under Yāj. II.2—"Niyukto vā' niyukto vā dharmajño vaktumarhati". Kātyāyana refers to these two classes of assistants in the matter of judgment of the king, i.e., the brahmins and the Sabhya-s—"Sa-prāḍ-vivākaḥ sāmātyaḥ-sabrāhmaṇa-purohitaḥ / Sa-sabhyaḥ prekṣako rājā svarge tiṣṭhati dharmataḥ//". The brāhmaṇas were noted here as independent members, not appointed for the purpose; whereas the jurors (*sabhāsadas*) are held as appointed, whose responsibility was far greater for guiding the king. The jurors should help the king in determining truth in disputes and should regulate the king, if the latter takes a wrong decision. The brāhmaṇas, again being independent, should help the king by their wise sayings. They were to blame if they remained silent or if they said wrong. But they were not held responsible, if the king took wrong path in decision in spite of their warning. Manu[33] says in this connection: "Sabhā vā na praveṣṭavyā vaktavyaṃ vā samañjasam/avivruvan vivruvan vā naro bhavati kilviṣī//". That the jurors could be selected even from the merchant class is warranted by Vijñāneśvara (on Yāj. II.2) who quotes Kātyāyana to justify it: "Kula-śila-vayo-vṛtta-vittavadbhi-r-amatsaraiḥ/ Vaṇigbhih syāt katipayaiḥ kulabhūtai-r-adhiṣṭhitam/". This means that the sabhā should include a few merchants of good birth and conduct, aged, wealthy and free from greed. Gautama, we have already noticed, classed merchants with cultivators and herdsmen as the sources of law in matters relating to themselves but since then, with economic development of the country the merchants gained good status in the society, as reflected in the Jātakas and in works like the *Mṛcchakaṭikam*.

Besides, trade-disputes on which the earlier law books are quite silent, came to the forefront in the king's vyavahāra in the later period and hence the advice of reliable and respectable merchants was needed in the court. Kātyāyana quoted by Aparāka: "A-lubhdhā dhanavantaśca dharmajñāḥ satyavādinaḥ/sarva-śāstra-pravīṇā-ś-ca sabhyāḥ kāryā dvijottamāḥ//" shows that the jurors should not be greedy and poor, the brahmin 'sabhya' should not only be possessed of other virtues, mentioned in this verse, but also he must be rich enough. The "Vyavahārodyata" states clearly the distinction between the functions of a brahmin and a Sabhya in the Court: "Anenaiva sabhyānāṃ pratyavyāyam vadatā sabhopaviṣṭānām brāhmaṇānāṃ sabhāsadām ca bheda uktaḥ. Sabhyānām-eva pratyavyayaḥ na tu brāhmaṇānām". The Subodhinī, commenting on Yāj. (II. 4) insists on the severe punishment of 'Sabhya-s', if they support the wrong decision and such members are called 'open thieves' ("prakāśa-taskara") in *Daṇḍa-Viveka,* (pp. 105, 337).

Nārada, again says that the unappointed members like the brāhmaṇas should not make any statement in matters of judgment—"nāniyuktena vaktavyam vyavahāra kathaṁcana". This prohibition is explained in *Smṛticandrikā* and *Vyavahāra-prakāśa* as meant for such unappointed heads who are present for a particular cause and thus it is reconciled with other injunctions. Kātyāyana's verse 'Sa-prāḍvivāka—etc.' already noted shows the importance of the priest ('sa-brahmaṇa-purohita' and the 'Prāḍvivāka' along with other members in judicial matters. Yāj.[33] also says that the king should consult first with ministers, then with the brahmin priest and come to decision on any state affair by his own intelligence. ("Taiḥ śārdhaṃ cintayet rājyam vipreṇātha tataḥ svayaṃ").

The position of the Prāḍvivāka was much improved in the later period when Nārada says that the king should accept the view of Prāḍ-vivāka ("Dharma-śāstram puraṣkṛtya Prād-vivāka-mate sthitaḥ") as much as the king of England decides according to the opinion of the Judicial Committee of the Privy Council. This shows that to render justice unbiased or unprejudiced the king was not to decide by himself but to follow the suggestion of the judge. The idea that it is not safe for any man, however clever and intelligent he may be, to decide rightly was so prevalent that Kālidāsa refers to it in the *Mālavikāgnimitram,* Act I: "Sarvajñasyāpi ekākino nirṇayābhyupagamo doṣāya". The king Atithi is also referred to in *Raghu.* (17.39): "Sa dharmastha-sakhaḥ śaśvadarthi-pratyarthināṃ svayaṃ/dadarśa saṃśayacchedān vyavarhārān-atandritaḥ//". The term 'dharmastha' here means, as in Kauṭ's Aś. (III. I) 'the judge'.

The same idea is also expressed in *Sarasvatī-vilāsa* (p. 67): "Tasmānna vācyam-ekena vidhijñenāpi dharmataḥ iti pitāmahena ekasya dharma-kathana-niṣedhāt". It should be noted that it is not a fact that the king was short of knowledge in law of the land but the significance is that the king should always take the advice of others who are masters of law. He must not decide alone or in secret because Śukra says that there is every chance of mistake in such a decision arising out of natural weakness of a human being. In matters of decision the king, the Chief Justice (Prāḍ-vivāka) and the jurors (sabhāsadaḥ) were equally responsible. Kātyāyana thinks that the decision should be declared by the jurors ("Jaye' vadhṛte sabhaiḥ"), while Nārada opines that after the decision of the jurors the king must declare it. ("paścādrājñā śāsyaḥ"). Bṛhaspati, quoted in *Vyavahāra-Mayūkha* says "Vaktādhyakṣo nṛpah śāstā sabhyāḥ kārya-parīkṣakāḥ"—that is, the Sabhā will decide, the Chief Judge is the speaker and the king pronounces the sentence.

If all the judges, the king, the Chief Justice and jurors agree on any decision, it was held as authentic (niḥśalya), otherwise un-authentic (saśalya) "(Nār. 3.17 "Yatra sabhyo janaḥ sarvaḥ sādhvetaditi manyate/sa niḥśalyo vivādaḥ syāt saśalyaḥ syād-ato'-nyathā//". The *Vyavahāra-prakāśa*, on the authority of Jaimini's sūtra[34]—"Vi-pratiṣiddha-dharmānāṃ samavāye bhūyasāṃ syāt sadharmatvam" states that "Saṃkhyāvaiṣamye tu bhūya'lpa-virodhe bhūyasāṃ syāt sadharmatvam—iti nyāyena vipratipattau adhika-saṃkhyā-vacanam-ādaraṇīyaṃ guṇa-sāmye"—in cases of difference of opinion the decision of the majority must be accepted. Aparārka also opines in the same light on the strength of the words of Gautama[34]—"Vipratipattau traividya-vṛddhebhyaḥ pratyavahṛtya niṣṭhāṃ gamayet"—"vicārakānām-anyonya-vipratipattau traividya-vṛddhebhyaḥ samadhigata-caturdaśa-vidyā-sthānebhyaḥ nyāyam pratyavahṛtyāvagamya vyavahāraṃ niṣṭhāṃ samāptiṃ nirṇayaṃ gamayet (p. 599).

It is interesting to point out that the above survey of different smṛti works shows that the sphere of the king's justice was gradually enlarged. The topics of litigation, treated in Gautama's chapter on Vyavahāra are limited because he deals with only those cases which came to the king's court as litigation. Many other disputes in his time were settled by the popular tribunals. In course of time, the king gained more power and prestige and people welcomed him as a better judge. So the various topics of law were gradually absorbed under Vyavahāra in later law books. The king who was first concerned with only serious crimes by reason of his duty to maintain law and order in the society, had subsequently to settle all sorts of disputes and he became practically the fountain of all justice in India. The king's justice in India may be compared to the Practor's justice in Rome and the king's courts in England which gradually absorbed the functions of the Pontiffs, the Curiae, the Hundred and the Baronial courts until the latter were entirely replaced.

Śukranīti[35] preaches the idea of the *Mahābhārata*[36] in which the dictum 'Rājā kālasya kāraṇam' occurs. It speaks of the king as "Yuga-pravartako rājā dharmādharma-praśikṣaṇāt". To rule in strict accord with the śāstras was in India a personal responsibility of the king. The *Rāmāyaṇa*[37] gives us the picture of the Golden age when the world becomes free from robbers (nirdasyu-r-abhavad loko') as the result of the good administration of Rāma.

That the king was the fountain of justice is evidenced by the following historical evidences as to the title '*Dharmamahārāja*'. The Pallava king Śivaskandavarman was styled so. (Hirahadagalli grant, *E.I.* 1, 5 and VI, 88). Sinhavarman II had the same title.[38] Mahendravarman (600-630 A.D.) bears almost the same title—"*Mahābhūta-Sadharmā*", referred to in the "Mattavilāsaprahasana" and his office as "Dharma-rāja' is indicated by the very name 'Dharma-rāja-ratha', attributed to the rockcut temple at Mahābalipuram, constructed during his rule. Mṛgeśvara-varmā, the Kadamba king also is styled as 'Dharma-mahārāja'. The same title is also borne by the Gaṅgas, as for example, Mādhava Koṅgaṇi-varmā (430 A.D.) as 'Dharma-Mahādhirāja' and Mārasiṃha (690-970 A.D.) as 'Dharmāvatāra'.[39]

Now the question may arise how far the king was a real source of justice. Dr. Kane shows that the king was the real head of the judicial system of the country but the reverse cases were not wanting when the king worked in defiance of the existing law of the land . The case of the tanner, as described in the Kashmir Chronicle[40] may be cited here as an example. The tanner went against the king Candrāpīḍa when the latter wanted to build a temple in the place of the house of the tanner. Nārada[41] enjoins that the king should not interfere with the land occupied for habitation of the people. But Candrāpīḍa, proud of his strength, confiscated the property of the tanner in defiance of the Smṛti text of Nārada, ignoring the sentimental appeal to the effect that the house where the tanner was born and bred up was loved by him more than his mother. This story indicates that the king did sometimes render injustice and there was no higher court of justice where people could have appealed against the wrong of the king. Merutuṅgācārya[42] mentions a similar case of the king's injustice when king Yogirāja of Gujarāta failed to punish his sons for their act of robbery, committed with violence. These references show how the king exercised partiality to his own near and dear ones, to the utter distress of the people.

The Jaina texts, too, refer to some kings who exercised absolute power and whose orders must have been carried out. Some persons violating the king's orders are told to have been thrown into salt (*kharantaka*) and reduced to skeletons.[43] People creating suspicion in the minds of the kings were punished severely and often deprived of their life. The stories of Kappaya, minister of Nanda being cast into a well with his whole family by the capricious order of Nanda,[44] of Śālivāhana of Paiṭṭhāna passing order for the execution of his minister who was somehow saved[45] and also of king Saṅkha of Vārāṇasī at some slight fault of his minister ordered his execution secretly[46] show nothing but rule of autocracy defying all sense of justice.

Besides, instances of judgement as a mere farce of it are numerous in Jaina texts like Bhāṣya and Chūrṇi. To quote a few, may be mentioned the stories of a simple villager's case concerning a bullock-cart[47] and of Kappaka murdering a washerman.[48]

However, theoretically at least the law of ancient India tried to secure the life and property of the people from the arbitrary exercise of royal power, as evidenced by Manu,[49] Viṣṇu,[50] Yāj.[51] *Matsya Purāṇa*,[52] *Mbh.*[53] and Kauṭ.,[54] each of whom insists that the king must not punish the innocent. The Dharma-dhvaja Jāt.,[55] the Mahābodhi Jāt.,[56] and the Mahāpadma Jāt.[57] also confirm the same idea that the king must not punish an innocent man. Nor did the king in ancient India, as a general rule, enjoy the prerogative of pardon, though, of course, cases of pardon in special cases are heard of, as evidenced by the *Mbh.*[58] in which king Sudumna says: "If you consider that sin is wiped out by being punished by the king, then you must know that if he forgives the offender, his guilt is removed;" by Kauṭilya,[59] Aśokan Edict (P.E.V) and the *Mṛcchakaṭikam*[60] in which the executioner speaks of the possibility of prisoners being set free.

REFERENCES

1. II. 2. 19-21.
2. II. 4. 26-27.
3. J.IV. p. 192-GG. 61-67; cf. Aśoka's Separate Kaliṅga Edict I.
4. J. I, p. 176; cf. Aśoka's P. E: IV.—"Vivohalasamatā and Daṇḍa-samatā".
5. Hopkins, *J.A.O.S.*, XIII, p. 132.
6. J., II, p. 2.
7. V, p. 228.
8. J., V, p. 125.
9. J., III, p. 292.
10. J., II, p. 186.
11. J., I, p. 384.
12. I. 19.
13. XXVII, pp. 70-71.
14. Uttara, 53, 18, 19 & 25.
15. Anuśāsana, 6.38 and Chap. 70.
16. VII. 53-54.
17. *Kṛṣṇa-yajurveda*, 2.2.1 and 2.3.1; *A. V.*, 76.117-119; and *Yāj. Saṁ.*, 30.5.
18. AŚ, III. 1.17.
19. AŚ, II. 9.11.
20. *I.A.*, 1877, pp. 131-32.
21. Cf. K.V.R. Aiyangar: "Some Aspects of Ancient Indian Polity", p. 44.
22. *Early History of Bengal*, p. 110.
23. II. 25.24 and II. 82.1.

24. Sabhā, 7.10 & 11.
25. VIII. 1 & 2.
26 II. 1-2.
27. VIII. 1-3.
28. On Yāj. II, 1.
29. VIII. 9-10.
30. VIII. 11.
31. VIII. 20.
32. II. 2.
33. I. 312
34. 12.2.22
35. IV. i, 11.90-125.
36. Śānti, ch. 69, vv - 74-105.
37. VI, 131, 97-104.
38. Māṇgaḍūr Grant, *Ind. Ant.* V, p. 155.
39. Cf. Fleet, 'Dynasties of the Kanarese Districts', in the *Bombay Gazetteer*, I, i, p. 305.
40. *Rājataraṅginī*, IV. V. 66-67.
41. xi, 142.
42. *Prabandha-cintāmaṇi* p. 14.
43. *Ācārachurṇi*, Jinadasagani, Rutlam, 1941, p. 38.
44. *Avaśyaka Chūrṇi*, Jinadasagani, Rutlam, 1928, II, p. 182.
45. *Bṛhatkalpa Bhāṣya*, Saṅghadasagaṇi, 6, 6244-6249.
46. Uttarā,'ṭikā, 13, p. 185 a.
47. *Dasaveyāliya Churṇi*, Jinadasagaṇi, Rutlam, 1933, p. 58 and *Āvaśyaka Chūrṇi*, Jinadasagani, Rutlam, 1928, p. 119.
48. *Āvaśyaka Chūrṇi*, II, p. 181f.
49. VIII. 128.
50. XIX. 43.
51. I. 356 & II. 307.
52. Ch. CCXXV, 2-6.
53. Śānti p., ch. 85.
54. IV. ch. XIII. 235.
55. Ed. Ghosh, Pt. II, No. 220, p. 118.
56. *Ibid.*, pt. V, No. 527, p. 140.
57. *Ibid.*, pt. IV, No. 492, p. 134.
58. Śānti p., ch. XXIII.
59. II, ch. 36, 44-47.
60. Act. X

CHAPTER III

Judges and Judgement

The sovereignty of law (dharma) and the king's function as 'Dharma-pravartaka' are already referred to. The king as fountain of justice was gradually firmly established on the soil of India, as discussed before. In this connection we have noticed the different hands as assessors of adjudication, viz., the brahmin priest, Prāḍvivāka and the jurors. Now let us enquire into the character of judges and of their judgments.

The king was the highest judge in his realm but it was not possible for him to have always dispensed justice personally. In a vast empire like that of the Mauryas the king had to appoint judges in important centres throughout the length and breadth of the country. For the administration of justice properly-constituted courts were established in important centres like Saṃgrahaṇas, Droṇamukhas, Sthānīyas and in junctions of provinces.[1] The *AŚ.* shows how the laws of Kaṇṭaka-śodhana were administered by both Amātyas and Commissioners (Pradeṣṭāraḥ), who exercised the authority and jurisdiction of police-officials and criminal investigators to prevent crimes and save the country from violators of peace or law. The Jātakas also mention the appointment of royal amātyas, Chodakas and Viniśchaya-mahāmātyas with judicial powers, who tried all cases according to customary laws and awarded punishment in the shape of fines etc., even up to capital punishment.

Tradition tells us how criminal law was administered in the Republic of the Vajjians by the series of regularly appointed officials. Judges, lawyers and rehearsers of the law-maxims, the council of representatives, the general, the Vice-President and the President could acquit the accused. The president awarded punishments according to the book of precedents. During the Buddhist period criminal justice was administered by experts through the President and the Elder of the Kula-courts. The *Mahāparinibbāna Sutta* mentions two judges known as Aṭṭhakulaka and Suttadhāra among the Licchavis. The administration of justice in Veśāli was a complicated affair, one of the courts being that of the Aṭṭhakulakas, i.e., of eight heads of families.[2]

From the inscriptions of Aśoka we learn that the Mahāmattas exercised judicial power in cities (nagala-viyohalaka). The First Separate Rock Edict, addressed to such Mahāmattas lays stress on just behaviour and impartial judgments. Aśoka cautions against weaknesses, such as, anger, laziness, fatigue, want of patience any of which may prejudice a judgment. For the precaution against injustice the king decided to send a Mahāmatta every five years to supervise the judiciary in cities. This edict shows Aśoka's solicitude for proper justice so that "there occurs no restraint or torture to the townsmen without any cause".[3] These Mahāmattas were also concerned with problems arising from the administration of cities and connected with artisans, merchants and others.[4] Justice in rural areas was dispensed by Rājukas who acted as assessment officers as well. An entire Pillar Edict[5] is devoted to their juridical function. The English rendering of some of relevant lines of this edict is quoted here—"I have granted to them (Rajjukas) full freedom in the matter of bringing an accusation or plaint or punishing (offenders), ... in the matter of arrest and punishment, ... That there should be uniformity in judicial procedure and also uniformity in the criminal punishment. With regard to men who are confined to prison and later sentenced to death, after their punishment has been adjudicated, a grace of three days is granted by me. Their relatives (during this reprieve) will make some (of the Rajjukas) to ponder (as a revision or review case) over the question of saving their life (i.e., by submission of an appeal for life concession). If there does not occur any such person for making them reconsider (the matter), they (condemned persons) may (by themselves) give alms or gifts or will observe fasts (for benefits in the other world)".[6] From this record we learn that a criminal case consists of four stages, (i) accused stage, (ii) trial-decision stage, (iii) execution stage, and (iv) review-concession stage. The term 'padesike' of R.E. III is, according to Prof. Basak, be equated with Pradeṣṭṛ-s of Kauṭilya in the sense of magistrates who tried and determined criminal cases like thefts etc. It is very likely that previous to Aśoka's arrangement by R.E. IV, justice in villages was in the hands of higher officials who were not accessible to the entire population. This new policy of Aśoka gave Rājukas greater power. With regard to death-sentence an appeal could be made to them.

The *Mṛcchakaṭikam* says: "Reproach indeed is easy, discrimination but of rare occurrence and the quality of a judge is readily the subject of censure. A judge should be learned, sagacious, eloquent, dispassionate, impartial; he should pronounce judgment only after due deliberation and enquiry, he should be a guardian to the weak, a terror to the wicked, his heart should covet nothing, his mind be intent on nothing but equity and truth and he should keep aloof from the anger of the king".[7] The judges were commonly called Dharmādhikārin, the Pradeṣṭṛ or the Paṇḍita.[8]

Now about the village headman: The Grāmaṇī, corresponding to modern village-Patel is referred to as early as the *Taittirīya Brāhmaṇa*, as belonging to the Vaiśya caste. He was the main channel of royal authority and was entrusted with local administration. Petty offences in the village seem to have been left to the "Grāmyavādin" or "village-judge" for disposal, as evidenced by the *Śatapatha Brāhmaṇa*.[9] The Grāmaṇī seems to have been in this period more often a nominee of the king rather than a popularly elected officer and sometimes this post was hereditary. Another official named in the *Śrauta-Sūtras* of Kātyāyana[10] and Āpastamba[11] is the "Sthapati" in the sense of "Governor". Some passages of the same works point to the "Chief Judge". Thus in this stage like the "Grāmaṇī", the "Sthapati" also held both executive and judicial powers. In

Āpastamba's time village officers were appointed by the king to protect the country from thieves to the distance of one krośa from each village; and they must be made to repay what is stolen within their boundaries.[12]

A village headman (gāmabhojaka) was allowed to exercise judicial powers even to the extent of criminal cases. One issued prohibitions against the killing of animals[13] and another stopped the sale of wine (*Ibid.*). Elsewhere he fined a fisherman's wife for stirring up a quarrel and she was tied up and beaten to make her pay the fine. From the *Kharassara Jātaka*[14] we learn that it was the duty of Gāmabhojaka to secure the village against the inroads of robbers with the help of the local people. His judicial powers were limited because the final authority rested with the king or his court.[15] The administration of justice was one of the essential links that bound the villages to the Central government. From Kauṭ.,[16] we know that the village headman (grāmika) had exercised some executive power to drive out of the village a thief or an adulterer and elsewhere[17] Kaut. says that the village headman (grāmakūṭa) could try some offences and sometimes was exiled if he unduly extorted money from anybody. He was assisted "by a number of officials, (probably?) elected by the people, who were probably maintained by grants of land".[18] Nīlakaṇṭha, while commenting on Sabhā parvan, Ch. V mentions the names of these officials forming a group of five, "Pañca" - Samāhartā, Saṃvidhātā, Gaṇaka, Lekhaka and Sākṣī. There was little scope for the highhandedness by the village-headman, as he had to abide by the advice of the village-elders ('grāma-vṛddha') who sometimes rectified the errors of the headman.

Viṣṇu[19] refers to his judicial authority when he says, "If any offence has been committed in a village, let the Lord of that village suppress the evil and give redress to those that have been wronged". According to Viṣṇu[20] the village headman, if unable to control the criminals in the village, should apply to the chief of the district and the governor and it may be assumed that such defiance took place very frequently. Manu also[21] speaks of a hierarchy of officers beginning with the Lord of one village up to that of one thousand villages, each entrusted with the duty of administration and judiciary. The village-headman had to inform his next higher officer, the Lord of the villages of the crimes in his village, that is, those offences which he could not deal, according to Kullūka and Medhātithi. Thus the lowest unit of the local government was the village under its head "Grāmika" and other elders (Mahattaras).[22] Bṛhaspati also speaks of the appointment of Mahattamas for the guidance of villagers. These Mahattaras or Mahattamas of villages are frequently met with in the inscriptions. Jolly cites the example of the judge Asajjatimisra of the farce Dhūrtasamāgama, who as an arbitrator (madhyastha) keeps for himself the Hetaera Anaṅgasenā.[23]

Bṛhaspati's Pratiṣṭhita is the name of the court of justice in a village[24] and he brings out the relation of the village with the king. "Whatever is decreed by them (the village elders) in accordance with the laws and customs, be it favourable or otherwise, to the people, must be approved by the king as well.[25] The king interfered and imposed his own judgment only when the members of the village council were at variance with one another. That means people could appeal to the king. From the inscription[26] we learn that the village had to pay 'daśāparādha' (fines from ten offences) and this fact indicates the village wielded the power of punishing offences.

That the village headman (grāma-mahattara or grāmakūṭa) was in charge of administration to help the higher officers like Rāṣṭrapati or Viṣayapati is evidenced by the Kavi grant of Jayabhaṭa of the year 486[27] and by the Samangad grant of Dantidurga of Śaka era 675 (= 753-54 A.D.).[28] The Bhumara Stone Pillar ins. of the Mahārājas, Hastin and Sarvanātha mentions Vasu as the village-headman.[29] According to Śukra[30] the headman of the village was positively a member of the Brāhmaṇa class, thus confirming the evidence of the Gāthā Saptaśatī (vi. 100). Śukra[31] mentions the traditional territorial division of the rural area, the grāma and 10, 100, 1000 and 10,000 grāmas, showing thereby the existence of an organised local administration. Each official in-charge of these divisions was appointed by the Samāhartā (i, 201). These officers were graded in power and were responsible to the immediate superiors.[32]

The village Sabhā-s are heard of in South Indian Inscriptions. The sabhā had for its members the village elders, the Bhaṭṭas (learned men), the viśiṣṭa-s (distinguished and moral men) and prominent priests of the temple and sometimes included representatives of the merchant class (nagarattār), of the common folk (urār) and of the district. The Ukkal and other inscriptions[33] show how the Sabhā worked efficiently in the period of the 10th and 11th centuries. Besides other duties, the sabhā had the right to punish the internal enemies of the village.[34] The Mahāsabhā is heard of as deciding "about the payment of fines imposed on several castes and communities of the place either in the king's courts or otherwise".[35]

Now about the caste of the judges. No such caste-rule existed under the Mauryas who appointed ministers on merits, nor is such a caste-rule found in Āpas. Dh.S.[36] As Manu amalgamated Dharma and Vyavahāra into one, he insisted on the condition that the judge should be a brahmin. It may be historically justified by the revival of brahmanism under the Śuṅgas. The judicial functions of the king, the Chief Judge and the Jurors are already noted before and the caste-question of those judges has been discussed. One thing should be borne in mind that Manu described Śūdras as atheists[37] and his target of attack is the later Mauryan system of administration. Buddhism recognised no caste-distinction. The Buddhist bias of the later Mauryas opened the Jury to learned Śūdras and Buddhists. That is why Manu forecasts the divine punishment like famines and diseases, if the country be 'Śūdra-bhūyiṣṭha', that is, if the jury be dominated by Śūdras either by birth or by religion.[38] Medhātithi comments on this text—"Yantra Śūdrā bhūyāṃso vivādanirṇayakārā-s-tad-rāṣṭram-āśu vinaśyati". It may be pointed out that in Mauryan times there had been prolonged famines. Manu[39] prefers even an unlettered brahmin to a Śūdra. The author of the *Mānasollāsa*[40] follows Manu in this respect.

About judgment the ancient jurists insisted on impartiality. Kauṭ.[41] warns the judges to be very careful and impartial and prescribes fines or dismissal or even corporal punishment for judges for their wrong decision or for corruption. Aśoka exerted his best to bring uniformity in judicial procedure and in aware of punishment in criminal procedure.[42] Yāj.[43] says that if the 'Sabhyas' decide against the rules of Smṛti, usage etc., being actuated by attachment, greed or fear, each of them would be liable to be fined twice the amount of fine to be paid by the defeated party. He enjoins elsewhere[44] that the king should review the cases, not rightly decided ("Durdṛṣṭam"). This principle is confirmed by Somadeva Sūri who says that the king is the highest court of appeal against the decisions of lower courts in villages and towns and his decision is final. It is curious to note that the *Agni-Purāṇa* differs from Yāj. because it recognises no other court lower than the king-in-council.

Kātyāyana, quoted by Aparārka (p. 604) states that the Chief Judge and the jurors should not talk in private with any one of the suitors while the court is going on with the case, or they would be fined. This rule is definitely meant for the antidote against corruption of judges. Kātyāyana (81) warns that the loss caused to the party by the fault of the jurors must be made good by them but the decision they verdict must stand.[45]

Bribes of judges are heard of as early as the Jātakas, if not earlier. Kauṭ.[46] prescribes the employment of spies in various disguises to test the honesty of judges and banishment for those who take to bribes. Manu[47] says: "Where justice is destroyed by injustice, while the judges look on, there they shall also be destroyed". "One quarter of (the guilt) of an unjust (decision) falls on him who committed the crime, one quarter on the (false) witness, one quarter on all judges and one quarter on the king; but where he who is worthy of condemnation is condemned, the king is free from guilt and the judges are saved (from sin)".[48] In the *Daśakumāracaritam*[49] the cynical jester Vihārabhadra reports to the king that the judges decide cases according to their will by taking bribes and the king incurs thereby sin and infamy. ("Tatrāpi Prāḍvivākādayaḥ svecchayā jaya-parājayaṃ vidadhānāḥ pāpenākīrtyā ca bhartāram-ātmānaṃ cārthai-r-yojayanti"). The *Mattavilāsa-prahasana*[50] also refers to the giving of bribes to the presiding officers of courts ("adhikaraṇa-karaṇikānām"). The *Mānasollāsa*[51] enjoins strictly that the king must not accept any bribe from the suitors ("nādadīta tathotkocham"). That the Indian jurists took so much pains to safeguard the life, liberty and property of the people from the transgressions of the court at so early an age, is itself a great tribute to the sense of justice of the ancient Indians. Though every ancient state prescribed penalties for corrupt judges, India, I think, stands first to enunciate in clear-cut terms the faults of the presiding judges of the courts and to prescribe punishments for the same. The laws of other states of antiquity may be mentioned here for comparative study: In Babylonian law judges were dismissed for wrong judgment and they had to pay a penalty of twelve times that had been awarded.[52] In Athens a man bribing a judge or a juror or a judge or juror taking the bribe with a view to give corrupt judgment was equally punishable with death or a fine of eight times the amount of the bribe or with a further penalty at the discretion of the jury.[53] The "Twelve Tables" prescribe a death-penalty for a corrupt judge. [T.T., 93 (Nas)]. In medieval France and in England (18th Cent. A.D.) the corrupt judges were dismissed or fined. It may be noted that in ancient India jurors were punished for wrong verdict, whether or not they were influenced by bribes. Not only the judges or jurors but also even the clerks or other officers of the court were equally subject to punishment for intentionally perverting the course of justice, as evident from Kauṭ. (ed. Gaṇapati Śāstri, p. 161).

The judge (Adhikaraṇika) is said to have the following qualities, mentioned in the *Mṛcchakaṭikam*[54]: He must be learned in the śāstras, expert in finding out deceits of both parties, plaintiffs and defendants, a good speaker, not susceptible to anger and impartial to friends, foes and relations. He must answer or give verdict on seeing the conducts of people, he must protect the weaker, chastise the cheats and respect the pious and he must be meditative to come to decision on the basis of evidences and must avoid the anger of the king by passing right judgment. ("Śāstrajñāḥ .... kopāpahāḥ"). The *Mānasollāsa,*[55] repeats the same rule. It is in favour of a brahmin judge who would, on behalf of the king, decide cases. ("Ātmanaḥ pratirūpam tu kuryādekam mahīpatiḥ"). It states that the Prāḍvivāka would try suits when the king would not be available either for his engagement in royal affairs or for his indisposition. The Chief Judge is noted here as 'Prāḍvivāka' because he asks questions to the suitors and speaks out the truth. (*Mānasollāsa,* II. 20. 1257). It is interesting to note that the term "Praśnavivāka" occurs in *Vāj. Śaṃ.*[56] and *Taitt. Brāhmaṇa*[57] and so we may presume that such an officer as the head of the judicial system was appointed as early as the period of the Brāhmaṇas. Gautama also mentions the Prāḍvivāka but only as an assistant of the king. It seems that at that time he acted practically as a chief of the assessors, who used to ask questions to witnesses and give his own opinion. Some scholar thinks that the Prāḍvivāka was the judicial head, while the Praśnavivāka was the executive head in the pre-Christian era.[58] However, in later texts the position of the Prāḍvivāka was highly elevated. He became the chief officer in-charge of criminal courts. He had to work under the king but was free to act as justice demanded, not always subservient to the will of the king. So his social position was so high as to rival even that of the king. In the subsequent period the brahmin, learned in the laws (vidhi) alone was held fit for the post of 'Nyāyādhīśa'. Nārada[59] says that the king is directed to act "according to the opinion of Prāḍvivāka" ("Prāḍvivāka-mate sthitaḥ").

The post of 'Nyāyādhīśa' is heard of in the *Rāmāyaṇa* as protector of 'Dharma' whose duty was to control the king from any partial treatment in justice. During the absence of the king this Purohita presided over the court. The court had seats arranged for the king known as 'Dharmāsana' and for the jurors who were held in high esteem, as evidenced by the form of addresses to them like "bhavantaḥ" by Daśaratha (II. 2.25) and "bhavadbhiḥ" by Rāvaṇa (VI. 12.24).

From the *Mṛcchakaṭikam* we may glean the following facts of the judicial procedure. The court was called 'adhikaraṇa' and the chief judge was termed 'adhikaraṇika' and he was assisted by a rich merchant and a scribe ("Śreṣṭhi-kāyasthau"). These three were addressed as "adhialaṇabhoiā" (Sans. 'adhikaraṇabhojakāḥ') and they were appointed ("adhikṛta" or 'niyukta') by the king. They could be summarily dismissed by the despot king at his sweet will, as hinted in Śakāra's threatening the Chief Judge when the latter tried to delay the hearing of the case. The court had a servant named 'Śodhaka' who would sweep the court-house, arrange its seats, enquire about the suitors and summoned the mother of Vasantasenā and Cārudatta. The Śreṣṭhi and Kāyastha noted down the statement of the complainant. Anyone might lodge a case of an alleged murder. An elderly person like the mother of Vasantasenā or Cārudatta was allowed to sit, while called to the court but Cārudatta had to stand, when he had to face the charge against himself.

The ministers, spies, envoys, a horse and an elephant were always present in the court and their services could be easily utilised to make judgment as prompt as possible. The town-police was asked to go riding a horse to the public garden and to report whether the corpse of any woman was lying there. Cārudatta was asked by the judge and his assistants to tell the truth ("Satyam-abhidhīyatām"). He was asked to confess by the Śreṣṭhī and Kāyastha, when he was taken to be guilty by the circumstantial evidence. He was taught the utility of truth in the act of judgment where no trick should be allowed to pass, just in the same style as Yājñavalkya who teaches "Chalaṃ nirasya bhūtena vyavahārān nayen-nṛpaḥ".[60] Cārudatta was warned of whipping in case of any suppression of fact.

It is interesting to note here that the trial scene ends with the remark of the Chief Judge ("Nirṇaye vayaṃ pramāṇam śeṣe tu rājā") which means that the judge is to come to a decision on the basis of the religious texts, the evidences and reasoning ("Dvividho vyavahāraḥ vākyānusāreṇa arthānusāreṇa ca") and pronounce it but the king is the highest authority to award the actual punishment. The Chief Judge reminded the king Pālaka here of Manu's text by which Cārudatta, being a brahmin should be banished along with all his property, kept intact. But the king issued order for the execution of the culprit. Ordeals of fire, water, poison and balance ("Viṣa-salila-tulāgni-prārtithe me vicāre") were known and Cārudatta prayed for such trial by ordeals but he was rejected by the Chief Judge who decided on witness and circumstantial evidence.

This play shows a sense of justice even in the executioners. One of them delayed the time of the execution which alone saved Cārudatta. One of the executioners stated it as the advice of his late father to make reasonable delay which might give the culprit a chance of escape like a ransom by some munificent gentleman or release owing to the birth of the king's son etc.[61] Thus the play indicates that even in autocratic states the administration of justice was carried on such healthy lines that open trial by the jury was the consequence. We hear of such a trial in Kālidāsa's *Śākuntalam* presided over by Piśuna, evidently the Chief Judge.

The Chief Judge, the jurors and learned brāhmaṇas were most probably all elderly people, as reflected in Nārada[62] who says that it is not a real court where there are no elderly men. ("Na sā sabhā yatra na santi vṛddhāḥ" Cf. Udyogaparvan, 35.58). The *Agni Purāṇa* states that the judicial bench is to be assisted by respectable persons, an accountant and scribe. It adds that the brāhmaṇas constituting the court should be learned and free from anger and the assessors should be knowers of the Vedic literature and free from attachments, prejudices, fear and greed. It does not fix any number of jurors or of assessors as is done by Manu and others. According to

Kauṭilya and Manu, the number of jurors must be uneven, three, five or seven, for the sake of getting a quick decision in case of difference of opinion, as pointed out by Mitramiśra: "Saṃkhyā-vaiṣamyaṃ tu bhūyo alpa-virodhe bhūyasāṃ syāt iti" (*Vīramitrodaya*, p. 35). Jayaswal writes "They (the judges) made up the Sabhā and were, to quote a modern word, the jury of the court".[63] P.N. Banerjee also accepts the prevalence of the jury system.[64] S.K. Aiyangar thinks that influential and qualified persons often formed the jury of the court and these were chosen then and there .... and that the jury was not a permanent institution while the judges held permanent offices".[65] The *Agni P.* makes no consideration of caste distinction in the appointment of judges or jurors, as is done by Yāj. and Kātyāyana (Mitā on II. 3), the *Nītiprakāśa* (8.16), the *Abhilasitārtha-cintāmaṇi* (1.2. 1261-63) and the *Mānasollāsa* (II. 1261) who exclude the Śūdras from such posts. Thus the Agni P. is liberal to Śūdras, as evidenced by its recommendation for the appointment of Śūdras as ministers or executive officers of the state (218-220). It may be noted that in later years not only caste-restriction of judges was softened but also judgment was advised to be based on the application of reason in interpreting the customary laws of the land, as evidenced by Bṛhaspati (*Supra*. pp. 8-9). King Someśvara of the 12th century, following Bṛhaspati is found to have enjoined the magistrate to award sentences, not merely depending on Smṛti-texts but also by the exercise of his own reason: "Pramāṇe niśchitairvāpi divyai-r-vāpi vichārite/yuktyā daṇḍaṃ nṛpaḥ kuryāt yathā doṣānusārataḥ//"[66]

REFERENCES

1. AŚ., III. 1.1
2. Cf. Fick., pp. 107, 111-112; Jayaswal's *Hindu Polity*, II, pp. 156-157 and Beal, Vol. I, pp. 84-85 and also the commentary on the *Digha.* II, p. 519 (ed. Rhys Davids J. Carpenter P.T.S.), London, 1889-1911.
3. *Select Ins.* (ed.) D.C. Sircar, p. 42.
4. AŚ., Bk. IV.

5. P.E. IV.
6. *Aśokan Inscriptions*, ed. by R.G. Basak, p. 95.
7. Trans. by Wilson, Act. IX.
8. AŚ, iv. 9 and Śukra, ii, 99, 100.
9. V. 4
10. 1.1.12.
11. IX. 14.12.
12. S.B.E., vol. II, p. 162.
13. Jāt, IV. p. 115.
14. No. 79, 1. 354.
15. Cf. Gāmaṇichanda Jāt., J. II, p. 301.
16. III. 10
17. IV. 4.9.
18. 'Kauṭilya' by N.C. Banerji, p. 257.
19. S.B.E., vol. VII, p. 15.
20. III. 12 ff.
21. VII. 115 ff.
22. *C.I.I.*, III, Nos. 24, 38 and 46.
23. *Hindu Law and Custom*, p. 295.
24. 1. 2-3.
25. *S.B.E.*, vol. 33, *Bṛhaspati*, xvii, 18.
26. *C.I.I.*, vol. III, No. 38.
27. *E.I.*, V, p. 114.
28. *E.I.*, XI, p. 112
29. *C.I.I.*, III, p. 112.
30. ii, 121-2.
31. i, 190-192.
32. Cf. AŚ, II. 1 and also Viṣṇu, VII. 114-115.
33. *S.I.I.*, vol. iii, part ii.
34. "grāmadrohin-s", cf. Ep. Report, 1910-11, p. 72.
35. Cf. The Ins. during Rājarāja I, Year 9, day 158, at Uttaramērūr, Chingleput dist., "The Cholas", p. 485.
36. II. 11.29.5.
37. VIII. 22.
38. VIII. 22.
39. VIII. 20.
40. II. 1258-61.
41. IV. 9.18-19.
42. *P.E.* IV.
43. II. 4.
44. II. 305.

45. "Sabhya-doṣāt tu yan-naṣṭam deyaṃ sabhyena tad tadā, kāryaṃ tu kāryinam-eva niśchitaṃ na vichālayet".
46. IV. 4.
47. VIII. 14 and 18-19.
48. Cf. *Baudh. D.S.*, I, 10.30-31 and Nār. III. 12-13.
49. VIII. p. 131.
50. pp. 23-24.
51. II. 1274.
52. *Ham.*, 5.
53. *Demon.* III, App. VIII, p. 343.
54. IX. 5.
55. II. 93-94.
56. 30.10.
57. III. 5.6.
58. "Prāchīn Bhārat me Rājya aur Nyāyapālikā", by H.N. Tripathi, p. 140.
59. Intro. I, 35, *S.B.E.*, vol. 33, p. 14.
60. II. 19.
61. Act. X.
62. III. 19.
63. *Hindu Polity*, pt. II, p. 154.
64. *Public Administration*, p. 143.
65. *Hindu Administrative Institutions*, 1929, p. 246.
66. *Mānasollāsa*, V. 1286.

CHAPTER IV
Subsidiary Courts

The court of the king and of the Chief Judge, assisted by Brāhmaṇas and 'Sabhyas', already referred to was the highest court. But there were others, lower in order which served as tribunals, as mentioned in Smṛtis and digests. Yāj.[1] states clearly that other courts were appointed by the king to decide disputes, such as, Pūga, Śreṇī, and Kula. Vijñāneśvara comments on 'Pūga' as villages and towns where people of various castes and occupations live, on 'Śreṇī' (Cf. *Vyavahāra-mayūkha*, "nānājātīnām-ekajātīyaṃ karma kurvatāṃ samūhāḥ śreṇayaḥ".) as the corporation of persons of varied castes but of one avocation, e.g. that of horsedealers, betel-leaf-sellers, weavers etc., and on 'Kula' as the assembly of relations, associates and friends. Yāj. prefers the preceding one to the succeeding in the matter of settling disputes. ("Nṛpeṇādhikṛtāḥ pugā śreṇayo'tha kulāni cha / pūrvaṃ pūrvaṃ guru jñeyaṃ vyavahāra-vidhau nṛṇām//"). Thereby he means to say that the king's court is the appellate court of the highest grade and the party, defeated in the lower court may appeal to the higher one but not *vice versa.* Hence he mentions, next to the king and the king's court, the tribunals of Pūgas, Śreṇīs and Kulas in order of importance.

Nārada[2] again states that cases may be decided by Kulas, Śreṇīs, Gaṇas (like Pūga-s of Yāj.), the judges appointed by the king (adhikṛtāḥ) and the king himself, each succeeding one being superior to the preceding one. ("Kulāni śreṇaya-ś-caiva, gaṇā-ś-cā' dhikṛtā nṛpaḥ/pratiṣṭhā vyavahārāṇām gurveṣām-uttarottaram". Vijñān's note on the above terms is given above. Medhātithi on Manu, VIII.2 explains: "Kulāni" means a group of relatives, as Vijñān. thinks, or according to some, impartial persons ("madhyasthapuruṣah); Gaṇa means builders of houses and mansions or brahmins residing in maṭhas; Śreṇī as stated in the *Mitākṣarā*. Kulāni means 'the agnates of the parties' according to *Smṛticandrikā*. P.V. Kane suggests that Kulāni' means officers who presided over a group of 8 or 10 villages and who were granted the produce of one kula of land as their salary.[3]

The Damodarpur C.P. inscription[4] (*E.I.*, XV, p. 130) records that the head of the district (viṣayapati) was assisted by the Nagara-śreṣṭhin, the merchant, Prathama-kulika, and Prathama-kāyastha. ("Puṇḍra-vardhana-bhuktād uparika-cirātadatena-anuvalavāmāka-koṭivarṣa-viṣaye ca tan-niyuktaka-kumāramātya-vetravarmaṇyadhiṣṭhānādhikaraṇaṃ ca Nagara-śreṣṭhi-Dhṛtipāla-Sārthavāha-Bandhumitra-Prathamakulika-Dhṛtimitra—Prathamakāyastha-Sāṃbapālapuroge-saṃvyava-harati"). Here is a reference to a Panchayat Board of four members to assist the governor in the administration of justice. Vetravarman, the prince-viceroy is noted as the judge. Elsewhere[5] we hear of the same local court ("grāmāṣṭakulā-dhikaraṇam". Cf. Dhanaidaha C.P. ins. of Kumāragupta I, G.E. 113=432 A.D.). R.D. Banerjee explains it as "a local officer who exercised authority over eight villages". R.G. Basak,[6] however, says that "he was rather an officer in the village having super-vising authority over eight Kulas", each Kula being the extent of land, as explained by Kullūka. Kātyāyana defines 'gaṇa' as 'an assembly of families' and 'pūgas' as assemblies of traders and the like. According to *Vyavahāraprakāśa* 'pūga' and 'Kula' are synonyms. The Sanchi Stone ins.[7] of the period of Chandragupta II refers to "Pañcamaṇḍalī", ("Pañca-maṇḍalyāṃ praṇipatya"—*C.I.I.*, vol. III, p. 32; Cf. "Pañcaka" of a Nepalese ins. *C.I.I.*, III, Intro., p. 133), an assembly of five persons, evidently like the Panchayat of the present day, "the village jury of five or more persons, convened to settle a dispute by arbitration, to witness and sanction any act of importance. The term 'rājakulam' of this inscription means, according to D.C. Sircar, "the king's court or court of justice and hence a member of that court". Three such members, Maja, Sārabhaṅga and Āmrarāta are mentioned here.

The Maliya C.P. Ins. of the Mahārāja Dhruvasena II of Valabhi, dated c. 571-72 A.D. mentions some officers like Āyuktakas, Viniyuktas, Drāṅgikas, Mahattaras, Dhruvādhikaraṇikas, Daṇḍapāśikas Rāja-sthānīyas, Kumārāmātyas and others. The Allahahad Pillar Ins. of Samudragupta also refers to 'Āyuktapuruṣa'. Drāṇgika means the head of a town or a city, according to Bühler and Monier Williams. Mahattara (Mahattama in some inscriptions) means, according to M. Williams, the head or the oldest man of the village. "Dhruvādhikaraṇika" means one who has the superintendence of Dhruvas. Bühler explains 'Dhruva' as a person who, on the part of the Rājā, superintends the collection of the royal share of the produce in grain which is made by farmers as revenue". "Daṇḍapāśika" means, according to M. Williams, one who holds the fetters or noose of punishment, i.e., a policeman. The inscriptions on clay-seals of Basārh mention three officers, either judicial or executive in charge of the police department, (i) Daṇḍapāśādhikaraṇa—office of 'Daṇḍapāśa', Chief of the Police, (ii) Mahādaṇḍanāyaka—Chief Justice and (iii) 'Vinaya-sthiti-sthāpaka'—officer-in-charge of law and order (Cf. R.K. Mukherjee, *The Gupta Empire*, p. 50 and *ASIR*, 1930-34, pp. 107f). Thus the above survey shows how different officers were in charge of administration in villages and towns and we may easily presume that some of them checked the malpractices and crimes of the society and performed the duties of the modern police. (*India in Ins. of the Gupta period* by H.P. Chakraborti, pp. 205f).

Bhṛgu[8] speaks of 10 tribunals, the village people, the assembly of the citizens of the capital, gaṇa, śreṇī, men learned in four Vedas, the vargins, kulas, kulikas, judges, appointed and the king himself. The term 'Kulika' means the elderly people of the family of the complainant, according to *Sm. Ch* ('Kulikāḥ kecanārthigotrā vṛddhāḥ'). It means 'the best of the family' ('Kula-śreṣṭha') according to *Vyav. Prakāśā*, (p. 9). The term 'Sārtha-mukhyāḥ' means the heads of villages and others, according to Parā, Mā, III, p. 25. Here Kulika and Kula are noted as two separate tribunals. Kātyāyana[9] defines Vargins as the groups of different types, viz., gaṇas, pāṣaṇḍas, pūgas, Vrātas, Śreṇī-s and other corporate bodies. The Saṅghas of Buddhists and Jainas who disbelieved in the authority of the Vedas are known as pāṣaṇḍas. The above list of Bhṛgu shows how disputes of the particular people were settled by men of the same categories, as for example, foresters' disputes should be decided by foresters, members of caravans should seek the help of other members of the party, soldiers should get their disputes settled by other soldiers and villagers by other co-villagers. Vyāsa[10] and Bṛhaspati[11] opine that the disputes of traders, artisans, cultivators, actors and of such other groups should be settled by members of the same groups who know their conventions and usages. Thus people liked to have their disputes settled by their peers or at least by a jury. This system of trial by the jury may be traced from Gautama,[12] noted before where the king is asked to decide in collaboration with heads of husbandmen, merchants, cattle-rearers, money-lenders and artisans whose opinions were valued in their respective groups. Pitāmaha mentions 18 low castes, viz., washermen, shoe-maker, dancer, bamboo-worker, fishermen, Mleccha, Bhilla, Ābhira, Mātaṅga and others as 'Prakṛti'-s and Hārīta[13] says that the king should consider the usages of these prakṛti-s, while deciding disputes.

Bṛhaspati mentions courts of four types, one established in a town, one not fixed in any place but moving from place to place as on a circuit, mudritā, i.e., the court of a judge appointed by the king, who is empowered to use the seal of the king and 'śāsitā'[14] (or 'śāstritā' according to Parā, Mā, III, p.24) the court in which the king himself presides. He mentions also ten limbs of the court, the king, the Chief Judge appointed by the king, the sabhyas, Smṛti, gaṇaka (accountant) and lekhaka (scribe), gold, fire, water and sva-puruṣa (a bailiff). The Chief Judge declares the law, the king awards punishment, the sabhyas examine the dispute, Smṛti lays down the rule of decision, the success (of one of the parties) and punishment. Gold and fire are required for taking oaths, water for the thirsty, gaṇaka for counting money or subject-matter of dispute, the scribe writes down the pleadings, depositions and decisions, the Puruṣa (as Śodhanaka in *Mṛcchakaṭikam*) summons the sabhya-s, the defendant and witnesses and guards the plaintiff and the defendant when they have not given any surety for appearance in the court. (q. by Aparārka, p. 600, Sm. ch. II, p. 20 and Parā, Ma, III, p. 31). Bṛhaspati says that the decision of cases depended on the judges or jurors while the king carried out the sentence. The number of jurors, according to Bṛhaspati (1.1.63) should be seven, five or three. Elsewhere he mentions the amātyas (ministers, as in Kauṭilya) and the Purohita as members of the court without giving any information of their duties (1.1.22).

The court of justice presided over by the king was called 'Dharmāsana' (Manu, VIII. 23, Śak. V and *Uttararāmacaritam*, I) 'Dharma-sthāna' (Saṃkha-Likhita) and 'Dharmādhikaraṇa' in Kātyāyana, *Mṛcchakaṭikam* IX and *Kādambarī*, para 85. Bāṇa describes 'the Rājakulam' as a court of king's justice in which "high personages administering justice, dressed respectfully and occupying high cane-seats looked as if they were 'Dharma' (Law) himself in that form. (Kādambarī, ed. Kale, p. 121 "Adhikaraṇa-maṇḍapa-gatai-ś-cāryaveśai-r-attucca-vetrāsanopa-viṣṭai-r-dharmamayai-riva Dharmādhikārikai-r-mahāpuruṣai-r-adhiṣṭhitam .... rājakulam"). The fables of the *Pañcatantra* (1.21; Katha-s 4 & 19 etc.) also describe the 'rājakulam' (royal court) where the disputing parties are heard by the judges ("dharmādhikārinaḥ" and "sabhyas"). The police too are mentioned in the fables. It is interesting to note that the royal court and particularly the king's voice came to be regarded as the highest authority to which appeals could be lodged against the decisions of the other courts. The Gāthā is quoted by Asahāya—"Rājñā dṛṣṭah kudṛṣto vā nāsti paunarbhavo vidhiḥ" to explain Nārada. It means that "what has been decided in a village, goes into the town and what has been decided in the town goes before the king but what has been decided by the king, though wrongly decided, cannot be tried anew". This shows definitely the rise of power and popularity of the king in the age concerned. Bṛhaspati[15] also speaks of successive appeals from the lower local courts to the higher ones and ultimately to the king's judge and also to the king in person. Kalhaṇa also says that the king was the highest court of appeal. King Yaśaskara is heard of in the *Rājataraṅgiṇī* (6.14-41) as ḥearing the case of an appeal of a person who had sold his house without the well but on returning after a long absence he found his well usurped by the purchaser and who became defeated in a lower court because the scribe was bribed to write "Kūpasahitā" (with the well) instead of "Kūparahitā" (without the well). The king, however, came to realise this cheating conduct of the purchaser, applying a trick. The *Rājataraṅgiṇī* (4.82-108) shows also that a brahmin wife appealed to the king of Kashmir to find out the culprit who had murdered her husband in his sleep and the king won success in holding a sorcerer as the real culprit.

The *Vyavahāra-mayūkha* (p. 3) on the authority of Bṛhaspati and Vyāsa mentions another court-official, 'Sādhyapāla', whose duty was to bring a conclusion matter at issue ('sādhyasya sādhakaḥ') by inviting and protecting the witnesses and both the parties of litigation. Wilson[16] explains this term as the bailiff or officer appointed to enforce the decree. He must be honest, truthful and in the confidence of judicial officers. It deserves mention that he belonged to the Sūdra class ("Akaraṇe rakṣaṇe ca sākṣyarthi-pratīpādīnāṃ/sabhyādhīnaḥ satyavādī kartavyastu svapuruṣaḥ//Sādhyapāla-s-tu kartavyo rājñā sādhyasya sādhakaḥ/Kramāyāto dṛḍha-śūdro sabhyānāṃ ca matesthitaḥ//". This is an evidence of the rise of the Śūdras in the society from among whom the choicest man was picked for this post.

Thus the above account shows how the judges had to shoulder heavy responsibility, the tenure of their office depended on their capacity in deciding cases. Side by side with their responsibility their independence was unquestioned.

Jayaswal rightly remarks: 'the administration of justice under Hindu monarchy remained always separate from the executive and generally dependent in form and ever independent in spirit.[17]

REFERENCES

1. II. 30.
2. 1.7.
3. *H.D.S.*, III, p. 280.
4. *G.E.* 124.
5. *E.I.* XVII, pp. 345 and 348.
6. *E.I.*, XVII, p. 348.
7. *G.E.* 93.
8. q. in *Sm. Ch.* II. p. 18 and *Parā Mā.*, III, p. 24.
9. q. in *Sm. Ch.* II, p. 18.
10. q. in *Parā. Mā.*, III, p. 42.
11. q. in *Vyav. Pra.*, p. 23.
12. XI. 21-22.
13. q. in *Parā. Mā.*, III, p. 46.
14. q. by Aparārka, p. 600. "Pratiṣṭhitā pure grāme nāgrāme' pratiṣṭhitā/mudritādhyakṣa-saṃyuktā rāja-yuktā cha śāsitā//".
15. 1. 29. 32.
16. *Glossary of Judicial and Revenue Terms*, p. 449.
17. *Hindu Polity*, pt. II, p. 152.

CHAPTER V

Crime and Punishment

A crime may be defined as a breach of law of a particular society, which should be prevented for the maintenance of peace and order by a particular process of public punishment. A breach may be held as a crime in a particular society at one time but the same may not be held so at another time or in another country. As for example, adultery is a crime under the Indian Penal Code (Sec. 497) but it is not so in England where it is regarded as a civil wrong. In the Vedic period theft was considered to be a great sin and crime but in the Sūtra period the thief was taken to the king and particularly during the period of Bṛhaspati theft was of the same category as defamation and assault. Up to the age of the Sūtras neglect to read the Veda was taken as a sin and a crime as well but in the later Smṛti period it was only a matter of sin but it could not be the cause of punishment or atonement. In the period of the Saṃhitās and Brāhmaṇas physical assault or marriage of a younger brother before that of his elder one was punished with death-sentence but in the Smṛti-period it was otherwise.

Viṣṇu[1] gives us a long list of sins, though not an exhaustive one, of which the gravest are 'ati-pātaka', i.e., sexual intercourse with mother, daughter or daughter-in-law, punishable with death-sentence; 'mahāpātaka' viz., murder of a brāhmaṇa, indulgence in wine etc., 'anupātaka' or sins equal to great sins and upapātaka or lesser crimes and others. The deadly sins and the minor sins are also mentioned in the *Mahābhārata*[2] and in the inscriptions.[3] The Buddhist lists of sins agree largely with the Smṛtis.[4]

The theory of penances was enunciated in India as old as the lists of sins. Dr. J. Jolly[5] thinks that "it is not improbable that the principle of spiritual punishment goes back even to the Indo-Germanic epoch". In India the Sāmavidhāna-brāhmaṇa contains the oldest detailed exposition of the penances. The association of penances with punishment for crimes shows how the distinction between the compensation aspect and the reformation aspect was recognised in ancient India and how one had developed an idea of one's moral duty. 'Prāyaścitta' and 'Daṇḍa' are distinctly mentioned as the two modes of purification in Kātyāyana Smṛti (472). Expiation is an invariable necessity for one's making up the loss in one's spiritual life, which one incurs as the result of one's deviation from the path of dharma because the deviation from one's own duty (sva-dharma) was regarded as harmful to the society and individual as well and this made him unfit for social communion and for spiritual acts. Hence penance, expiation and post-mortuary punishments were also logical limbs of a system, religious or philosophical in character, sincerely accepted in the life of ancient India, as proved by the report of Yuan Chwang—"They dread the retribution of another state of existence".[6] Robson's remark shows the same state of things prevailing in Europe in the medieval period: "The Church required penance for homicide, wounding, way longing, treason against the Lord, perjury, incest: for some offences penance formed the only penalty and sometimes it was reinforced by secular punishments. Those who refused to undergo penance were liable to be sentenced by the secular authority to fine or imprisonment or to be outlawed, ... it suited both state and Church in those days to identify crime with sin and hold that the secular law had a religious purpose as well as a punitive function".[7] The theory of expiation served the very purpose of modern penology because it involves two things, contrition (anutāpa) and abstenance from wrongs. The political theory of ancient India involves the enforcement by the king of both types of punishment, worldly and spiritual. Gautama and Āpastamba show how the offender sometimes surrenders himself voluntarily for punishment for atonement of the sin and for fear of punishment in the next life. The penances, prescribed by Gautama (XVI), Manu (IX. 236 & 240) and Yāj.

(III) are meant for whitewashing of one's own self and getting rid of all sins, committed. Paiṭhīnasi[8] says: "Akārya-kāriṇāṃ-eṣāṃ prāyaścittaṃ tu kalpayet/yathā-śaktyanurūpaṃ ca daṇḍaṃ caiṣāṃ prakalpayet//"—the wrong-doer should commit expiations and undergo punishment according to one's capacity. According to Viṣṇu,[9] the penance for killing a cow is the 'Govrata', the sinner should accompany the cows to the meadow and serve them in all respects. Even Kālidāsa describes the service of the cow (Nandinī) as the penance for a minor crime, committed by king Dilīpa. The various penances are prescribed in the Smṛti-s, sometimes by prayers, by presents to brahmins and by visiting holy places and even by suicides. These penances were strictly observed for fear of excommunication out of the caste.[10]

Thus the ancient India witnessed the application of both spiritual and worldly punishments. The question may naturally rise regarding the inter-relation of these two. Dr. Jolly weighs the theories of Burnell and of Weber, Barth and Konow and supports the view that "the two systems of punishment had developed independently of each other".[11] Sometimes the criminals preferred both types of punishment, as evidenced by the Smṛtis like Manu, IX. 240 and VIII. 318. That is why the thief surrenders to the king with a club, confesses his crime and wishes to be beaten to the ground only for self-purification. Originally the Mahāpātakin belonged only to the spiritual law. The blood-money, on the other hand, has gone over to spiritual law from secular law. The rules of Gaut.[12] for punishing the woman for adultery by tearing to pieces by a dog and the man by roasting on a bed of glowing iron are obviously criminal laws. Thus both types of punishments were interrelated and both these systems recognised the caste distinction and the privileges of brāhmaṇas. Bodhāyana (I.19, 4) prescribes both at the same time when a man killing a bull is asked to pay the fine and perform the *Cāndrāyaṇa*. Even Nārada, a later jurist (12.77) enjoins that in cases of grave sexual crimes the king should decree a punishment and at the same time the sinner must undergo a penance. Even as late as the period of Rājendra I was in practice the system of offering lands and money for the burning of a perpetual lamp in a temple as an atonement for homicide.[13] Alberuni[14] also refers to the application of both the penance and punishments for punishing an act of murder: only penance in the shape of fasts, prayers and alms-giving in case of murder of men of lower castes by a brahmin and punishment in the shape of confiscation and banishment for murdering brahmins and Kṣatriyas and other grave crimes.

It is interesting to note the character of law in ancient India and mark its difference from that of ancient Greece or Rome. While law in ancient Greece or Rome may be called technically the law of torts by which the person wronged proceeds against the wrong-doer and realises compensation in the shape of money, law in ancient India prescribes, in addition to such monetary compensation, corporal punishment and demands that the king should, though not reported by the party, take immediate action against criminal cases like theft, assault, rape etc., after getting reports of these by his own effort.[15] Manu[16] says that "if a blow is struck against men or animals in order to give them pain, the judge shall inflict a fine in proportion to the amount of pain (caused). If a limb is injured, a wound (is caused), or blood (flows, the assailant) shall be made to pay (to the sufferer) expenses of the cure or the whole (both the usual amercement and the expenses of the cure as a) fine to the king". Yāj.[17] also says the same thing. ("Duḥkhamutpādayet yastu sa samutthānajaṃ vyayaṃ dāpyo daṇḍaṃ ca".). Kātyāyana[18] prescribes that the assailant is made to pay the expenses of curing the injury and some solatium to the injured. The main object of the law of torts is to give compensation to the injured and the state does not get any profit nor does it take any direct interest in the matter. But the above references and the minute scrutiny of the criminal laws of ancient India show that sometimes the penalty imposed on the wrong-doer is not pecuniary at all and even when a money penalty is inflicted, it is in the shape of a fine and not of compensation because it goes to the royal treasury and not to the pocket of the injured except in cases of payment for medical treatment.

The term 'daṇḍa' is found in the Vedas but its use as the means of judicial administration is distinctly mentioned in the *Śata. Brāh.*[19] and particularly in the *Dh. Sūtras*. Gaut. and Baud. think that it should be applied in accordance with place, time, age and learning. The *Mahābhārāta*[20] mentions its utility for the administration and protection of the people. It wakes when the world sleeps, so the learned regard it 'dharma'. 'It leads to 'tri-varga', three ends of human life'. In the age of the Brāhmaṇas man was considered as pure as God[21] but in the period of *Mbh.* the concept changed itself and Arjuna expresses his view that man obeys laws for fear of punishment.[22] This punishment was, as already noted, both secular and spiritual. The king himself is believed to be controlled by 'Daṇḍa'.[23] Kṛṣṇa equates himself with 'Daṇḍa' ("Daṇḍo damayatām-asmi"—*Gītā*, X. 38). Kauṭilya[24] speaks of its utility in the maintenance of law and order in the society and quotes the view of his teacher that "never can there be a better instrument than the sceptre to bring people under control". The author of the *Mānasollāsa*[25] also eulogises the utility of Daṇḍa (II. 1294 ff). He follows the policy of milder punishment like Kauṭilya because severer punishment torments the people. According to him the king should apply 'reasoning' ('yuktya') in II. 1286 and also follow the principles of punishment, as laid down in the scriptures "Yathokta-daṇḍa-vinyāsād" (in II. 1298). Like Śukra he also holds that punishment leads to the eradication of bad practices in the society and to the furtherance of religion and fame of the king, the stability of the state and its treasury.[26]

Now let us examine the motives or purposes of punishment with which it was applied in ancient Indian society. Modern thinkers speak of four purposes of punishment—(i) retributive, (ii) deterrent, (iii) preventive and (iv) reformative. Harry

Elmer Barnes opines in his "The study of punishment" (1930, New York) that treatment of criminals in ancient India was more humane than that of the Western countries. The retributive aspect of punishment is much heard of as applied in the Vedic society as in earlier societies of the Western countries. The law of retaliation, viz., an eye for an eye and a tooth for a tooth prevailed here as elsewhere, as evidenced by the ancient Hebrew code, the code of Hammurabi in Babylon and the Law of the Twelve Tables in Rome. Hence any wrong done to an individual was revenged not only by himself but also by his relations, the village and different corporate institutions. This was known as 'Vairadeya'. The *Ṛgveda*[27] shows the spirit of revenge in the punishment for theft. Johnes proves this spirit even in the texts of Manu.[28] The Vedic seers thought of divine anger and death as the result of violation of the dictates of *Ṛta* or divine will.[29] The crime of an individual was believed to have resulted in the penalisation of the entire society. Thus the system of 'divine ordeals' came to be introduced. God was regarded as the protector of laws and nobody had power to suppress any crime. The divine ordeals were accepted in the later Smṛti-s as the method of proof.

In the Smṛti-period, however, the society grew up with a more developed shape. The individual could not take law into his own hands and the state came forward to the rescue, as it satisfied the individual's urge for revenge or retaliation by the adequate measures of punishing the wrong-doer. Yāj.[30] and Nār.[31] warn that the person who wants to get what is denied by his opponent without complaining to the king, becomes liable to punishment.

Next on the deterrent purpose. Daṇḍa should be an exemplary one which serves as a warning to all others who might be tempted to commit such a crime. The Śānti-parvan[32] states that people abstain from committing crimes for fear of punishment. This idea has been emphasised in the *Mahābhārata* also. Arjuna says: "Your Majesty, it is the rod of punishment which governs and protects the people; and it is awake even when they are asleep; so the wise call it "dharma". ..... Laws of punishment have been established for the preservation of the wealth and security of the people. In the state where the king deals even-handed justice, and where the blue-coloured and red-eyed punishment is present, the subjects are never sinful".[33] So also Bhīṣma says: "If there had been no punishment in this world, men would oppress each other. Well, Yudhiṣṭhira, it is from fear of punishment that men do not strike each other".[34] The *Gāthā*[35] shows that a criminal, sentenced to death by the court was taken to the place of execution while his crime was proclaimed to the public by the beat of drum. The defect in one's moral character was also similarly announced, as reflected in the *Gāthā* (VII. 85). This aspect is well illustrated by the *Mṛcchakaṭikam*[36] ("Śṛṇuta Ārya śṛṇuta ...... yadyapara idṛśam-ubhayaloka-viruddhaṃ-akāryaṃ karoti tam-api rājā Pālaka evam-eva śāsti") (Cf. *Mudrārakṣasaṃ*), when the sentence on Cārudatta for the alleged murder of Vasantasenā is proclaimed to the citizens by the executioners. Manu-(8.334)'s injunction that "with whatever limb a thief in any way commits an offence against men, even of that (the king) shall deprive him in order to prevent (a repetition of the crime, "pratyādeśāya")", confirms the above purpose of punishment. Bṛhaspati (22.27-28) supports even the death sentence for the prevention of the crime. The rules of punishment like the selection of an open place, visible to all, maiming the limbs, capital punishment etc. show the same purpose. The jurists were, however, careful to see that by punishment no one would be losing his means of livelihood. ("Nānupakaraṇān kuryāt tan-mūlā hi vṛtti-r-bhavati", Śaṃkha q. in *Vivāda-ratnākara*, p. 656). Śukra[37] was against confinement in jail. Kauṭilya prescribes for confinement in lock-up and prison[38] in separate places for men and women. Manu[39] ordains that all prisons must be made near a highroad where the suffering or disfigured offenders can be seen. The system of lifelong imprisonment was introduced with the same deterrent motive.[40]

The third purpose is preventive, i.e., a criminal should be imprisoned only to prevent him from repeating the crime. The method of sentencing one to death or transportation for life is also of similar nature. Here stress is laid more on the prevention of the crime than on the criminal. Śukra[41] insists on the clearance of the road and service in public places by the criminals for the same purpose. He enjoins also rigorous imprisonment for the same.[42] He says emphatically, "The punishment of the wicked means prevention of wicked action by them".[43]

Punishment is also inflicted with the purpose of reform or redemption of the criminal. It aims at the moral regeneration of the wrong-doer so that he may be restored to the right path and his unsocial tendencies are brought to the end. This sort of punishment is compared to the act of surgery which is meant for curing an injury and not for killing the patient.[44] The *Mahābhārata*[45] recommends that the king should reform or correct miscreants by punishment. According to Yāj.[46] the king should punish with proper consideration of offence, the families, castes, guilds, the gaṇas and the people of the janapada-s who have deviated from their own duties and place them in the right path. ("sva-dharmāccalitān rājā vinīya sthāpayet pathi",). Śukra[47] describes 'daṇḍa' as the means of making an end of all evil tendencies. He admits the utility of lighter punishment (4.49) and according to him, the king is responsible for the removal of crimes and neither time nor the people are to blame. ("Yugānāṃ na prajānāṃ na doṣaḥ kintu nṛpasya hi", 4.56). Kauṭ. emphasises this process when he enjoins the right punishment, neither lighter nor heavier than what is due. What he wants is to reform the mind of the criminal and thereby to erase crimes from the society. According to Śukra, punishment is the mere means to the end, the reformation of the wrong-doer, and he believes that not only men but even animals are controlled by reformative punishments.[48] Śukra[49] says that even a good man does wrong, when associated with bad men but he should be restored to right path by punishment, inflicted by the king. ("Evaṃ-vidhān-asādhūṃśca saṃsargena ca duṣitān / daṇḍayitvā ca san-mārgaṃ sikṣayet tān sadā nṛpaḥ//"). That is why Manu[50] says that punishment makes a criminal pure ("nirmalaḥ"). Kāmandaka (p. 64) also admits that punishment helps the regeneration of an individual, his character, morality and humane qualities. The same idea is conveyed by the *Mahābhārata* when king Sudumna tells the great sage Likhita: "If you think that punished by the king an offender is cleansed of his sin, in that case he becomes equally sinless if he be pardoned by the king".[51]

Now let us discuss the different ways of punishment. The Jātakas refer to fines, imprisonment, mutilation, banishment and death-penalty.[52] The Pillar Edict IV refers to the system of confinement of the suspect criminal ("niludhasi pikālasi"). Aśoka intends that there occurs no restraint or torture to the townsmen without any cause.[53] The P.E. V refers to jail-deliveries as well ("bandhanamokhāni kaṭāni"). Kauṭ.[54] speaks of "Sarvabandhanamokṣaṇam" and in II. 36 enjoins such release of prisoners in cases of new conquests, coronation of the prince and the birth of a son.[55] The Jāt.[56] states that of four robbers brought before the king, one is sentenced to receive a thousand strokes from whip barbed with thorns, another to be imprisoned in chains, a third to be smitten with a spear and the fourth to be impaled. Confiscation of property was not uncommon (J.V., p. 357). Trampling the criminals to death under the feet of elephants was also in practice[57] —(*Daśakumāracharitam*, 4th Ucchāsa) and (*Mṛccha.* 146). This system was in vogue for instance in Golconda in the 17th century and as late as the 18th century when two out of seven dacoits of the Berad caste were ordered to be trampled to death by the feet of an elephant.[58] But such harsh methods were resorted to in the case of tried thieves and robbers. Some offenders were sometimes banished from their country in great humiliation with all their property confiscated to the State or were ordered to live in a Cāṇḍāla settlement.[59] Shaving the heads of criminals was regarded as a great punishment (J., VI, p. 135, G. 588). Megasthenes[60] mentions cropping of the hair as a punishment. (cf. also *JBORS*, XX, pp. 80-86). It may be noted that the shaving of the head on certain occasions is noted as an Iranian form of punishment.[61] Both the *AŚ.* (IV.9) and the *Mahāvaṃsa*, VI, 42 list it as a punishment. Thus it was an earlier custom among the Indo-Iranian people to employ it as a form of punishment and this has been practised even now. A thief was first belaboured by the people and then dragged before the king for punishment. Sometimes thorough investigation was made to find out the criminal, such as shutting all city-gates and searching all suspected places.[62] Fetters for a thief were current.[63] Impaling a criminal on a wooden stroke[64] (vide also *Gāthā Saptaśatī*, VI. 63) and the execution by axe[65] are also heard of. The entire system of execution and the function of an executioner seem to present a realistic picture.[66] Impaling was in practice in the ancient world. Impaling the criminal upon a sharp stick was a common custom in Assyria and Persia. Darius is said to have impaled 3000 Babylonians. It was also used among the Romans. It may be noted that banishment was a common punishment in the ancient world, practised specially in ancient Greece and Rome. This system had its origin in outlawry and ex-communication. Transportation as a modern method of punishment, however, had its origin in England. The discoveries of new lands furnished good facilities for this form of banishment, because colonies planted there greatly demanded labour. The first Indian penal settlement was located at Bancoolen in Sumatra in 1787. It was shifted to Penang in 1823 when Bancoolen was occupied by the Dutch. Next in 1865 it was removed to the Andaman Islands. But in ancient India, unlike in modern times there used to be no particular place of exile and the Hindu law did not provide for surveillance by state officials. The state was least interested in where the exile would go or how he would live. It was to see that the exile did not return.

Branding was often used as a supplementary punishment to exile and it was meant for bringing infamy on the culprit.

Particular signs were imprinted for particular offence, as for example, for drinking, a wine bowl was branded on the forehead, for murder in case of a brāhmaṇa, the figure of a headless body and for adultery that of a female organ and so on.

We learn of jail administration in the period of Jātakas.[67] Learned and trusted ministers were once thrown into prison for plotting against the life of an innocent man.[68] The life of prisoners, bound in chains was very hard. The sad plight of a released prisoner is often counted as a standard of comparison (nikkamanakālo viya) for one who has not bathed for days together, nor rinsed his mouth nor performed any bodily ablutions.[69] During the time of Kauṭilya, jail administration was nicely organised. Kauṭ. speaks of two types of jails, 'bandhanāgāra' and 'charaka' (lock-up). The Jail Superintendent was known as 'bandhanāgārādhyakṣa'. The prisoners were provided with food, clothes, and other amenities of life. If a jailor was found guilty of mal-treatment to or of acceptance of bribes from the prisoners, he was penalised. The prisoners were given all opportunities to reform their character so that they might come out as citizens helpful to the society. Imprisonment was made not only in jails but in mines and this signified hard labour (AŚ). On the other hand, the prisoners were sometimes at the mercy of the king because once a king is heard of as promising to send one prisoner daily as the food of a Yakkha, only to save himself from the latter.[70] The Jaina texts also refer to the existence of regular prisons. The general conditions of the prison were not good. Prisoners were severely tortured very often to death. The Vivagasūya tells us of a prison in Sihapura, well-equipped with all sorts of instruments of torture.[71] The prisoners were sometimes after death in prison thrown away into ditches where they were devoured by birds and beasts.[72] The *Jayadhammakahā*[73] refers to a prison where the merchant Dhanna of Rayagiha was put along with the robber Vijaya who had already killed the daughter of Dhanna. It describes also the troubles they were to face. We are told of king Seniya being imprisoned and of the sufferings he had to meet.[74]

Both Fa-hien[75] and Yuan Chwang[76] refer to the "Earth-prison" or "Hell" of Aśoka at Pāṭaliputra made for the purpose of torturing living creatures.[77] Yuan Chwang claims to have actually seen the pillar marking the site of Aśoka's "Hell"[78] and if this story of "Hell" be accepted as a fact, this hell might have been used as a prison for the criminals where they were tortured with all sorts of instruments like vast furnaces of molten metal, sharp scythes etc.[79] Yuan Chwang refers to another hell of punishment, made by Aśoka at Ujjayini.[80]

Roughly speaking, the attitude of earlier jurists on criminal offences was more severe than that of the latter ones. Kauṭilya rejects the stiff attitude of the ancient teachers who prescribe that "the king should ever hold the Rod lifted up (to strike), for there is no such means for the subjugation of being as the Rod" —and suggests instead that the king, "just with the Rod is honoured, because he thinks that the king, severe with the Rod, becomes a source of terror to beings".[81] Kauṭilya's view on punishment is that it should be mainly reformative in character. He treats crime as contaminating disease and provides measures to do away with it. He says: "When the guilt is got rid of, there will be no guilty persons, but when a guilty man is got rid of, the guilt will contaminate others". He sees seeds of discipline in punishment and so he like Aristotle accepts punishment as educational discipline of the people.

Manu[82] and other jurists[83] were in favour of the gradation of punishments. Manu says that the king should "punish first by gentle admonition, afterwards by (harsh) reproof, thirdly by a fine and after that by corporal chastisement". These punishments may be inflicted separately or jointly according to the nature of the crime.[84] Bṛhaspati prescribes that preceptors, priests and sons should be punished by wordy admonition (vākdaṇḍenaiva), other disputants by reproof or fines (dhig-dhanābhyām) and the doers of graver crimes (mahāpātaka-yuktān) with corporal punishment (q. by *Sm. ch.*

II, p.126). This shows that the jurist was aware of the fact that persons like preceptors and others of the higher grade were sensitive enough to be restrained simply by wordy admonition. Bṛh.[85] says that the first two punishments could be inflicted by the Brāhmaṇa, appointed as the Chief Judge but the king alone, on the suggestion of the Chief Judge could inflict the last two punishments, as confirmed by the *Mṛcchakaṭikam* (X). But Yāj.'s attitude was lighter than that of earlier jurists. He was in favour of mild punishment because he believed in the theory of 'Karma-vipāka'. He says that a man committing grave crimes is born in the next life, being afflicted with diseases or deformity of the body or as a low or filthy beast or bird.[86] Yāj. and his successors like Nārada and Bṛhaspati often soften punishment to mere fines instead of severer ones like corporal punishment. Fa-hien also confirms this attitude of the Gupta age: "The king of Madhyadeśa governs without decapitation or other corporal punishments. Criminals are simply fined, lightly or heavily according to circumstance. Even in circumstances of repeated attempts at wicked rebellion they only have their right hands cut off".[87]

It deserves mention that the jurists who prescribed that factors like time, place etc. of the acts of crimes should be carefully considered before inflicting any punishment, belonged to that school of criminology who holds that an act of crime is due to biological, physiological, pathological, psychological or sociological grounds or the particular environment of the criminal. Mere severe punishment is not enough to prevent capital offences, as evidenced by Stephen's remark on the state of things in England: "There can be no doubt that the legislation of the 18th century in criminal matters was severe to the highest degree and destitute of any sort of principle or system".[88] Dr. Hart[89] observes that England at the beginning of the 19th century witnessed more than a hundred offences which were punished by death. In 1832 a child was convicted at Ludgate Hill for stealing a box of paints worthy only two pence, was tried at the Old Bailey and hanged".[90]

Now about fines, Indian jurists differ in the amount of fine, though they generally prescribe in terms of the first, middling and the highest amercement. Saṃkha-Likhita says, as quoted by *Vivāda-Ratnākara* that the first amercement is the fine from 24 paṇas to 91, the middling from 200 to 500 paṇas and the highest one is from 600 to 1000 in proportion to the value of the thing of dispute or the injury made. Manu[91] says that 250, 500 and 1000 paṇas are fixed for the first, middling and the highest fines respectively. Yāj.[92] prescribes 270, 540 and 1080 in order instead of the amount of Manu and Vijñān. comments that Manu's lesser figures are meant for crimes done without a previous plan ("tat pakṣāntaram-amati-pūrvāparādha-viṣayam"). Nārada[93] lays down the lowest limits of these amercements as 100, 500 and 1000 paṇas. Nārada, q. in the *Smṛti-saṃdarbha,* vol. I means by the highest amercement sometimes capital punishment, forfeiture of all property, banishment, branding and excision of limbs.[94] The Agaram (South Arcot) inscription of the period of Rājarāja I (year 21) records that an officer Parāntaka-cola Muvendavetan sent an order to the assembly that the property of those who ran away without paying the fines imposed on them was to be sold for any price it could fetch and the money credited to the talam (treasury) at Kaccipedu and a receipt be obtained. It should be borne in mind that the fines were not of the nature of damages or compensation for injuries caused to the aggrieved party. They were essentially of penal character and they were not meant for compensation because these fines were to be deposited with the State treasury and not to be paid to the injured person.

Scholars differ as to the valuation of a paṇa. Manu[95] and Yāj.[96] take 'paṇa' in the sense of a copper coin, specially in cases of fines to be paid. ("Sahasraṃ Brāhmaṇo daṇḍyaḥ" in Manu, 8.378 without mentioning any metal of the paṇa). The *Sarasvatīvilāsa* opines that local usage should be followed. Vijñān. on Yāj. 1.365 comments that Karṣa is a quarter of a pala. A copper coin of one Karṣa in weight is called Karṣika or

Kārṣāpaṇa, according to Manu. The *Vyav. Mayūkha* (p. 255) states that in all texts on fines where no metal is mentioned, the paṇa should be taken as this Kārṣāpaṇa. Bṛh. (q. in *Sm. ch.*, II, p. 99) says that Manu's[97] rules on fines are to be followed in ordeals and fines. Nār. as noted above, (Sāhasa, 7-8) follows Manu, differing slightly only in mentioning 100 paṇas as the first amercement and including in the Uttamasāhasam even death-penalty. Kātyāyana,[98] q. by *Sm. ch.*, II, p. 127 prescribes that fines are to be paid to the king in paṇas of copper or their equivalent. The fine of a quarter or a half of a māṣa should be taken in the sense of that portion of a golden māṣa ("Sauvarṇam māṣakam talva kalpayet")—and when the fine is announced in māṣa, it should be taken as a silver māṣa and when the fine is declared in Kṛṣṇalas, the same is to be taken and a masa is 1/20th of a Kārṣāpaṇa. ("māṣo viṃśati-bhāga-s-tu jñeyaḥ kārṣapaṇasya tu"). It should be pointed out that the name 'paṇa' was also sometimes applied to coins of gold and silver. The Rājanīti-prakāśa (part of Mitramiśra's *Vīramitrodaya*) refers to the gold paṇa which is also mentioned by Bhāruci, as referred to by Kane.[99] That paṇas of gold and silver coins were used in ancient India is corroborated by the use of the word in South India. (Paṇam in Tamil and Malayalam means 'money' and also a coin of silver or gold). The Ratnagiri Plates[100] of Somavamsi Karṇa mention officials like '*sannidhātṛ*' (receiver of stolen articles or an officer who introduces people of court, 'daṇḍapāśika' (Police officer) and 'piśuna vetrika' (one who canes the wicked). That the fines were realised sometimes in terms of 'paṇa's and gadyāṇā's is supported by an inscription of Calukya Vikramāditya V[101] (dated Śaka 934) from Gadag. Kauṭilya generally prescribes 12 paṇas for abusing and for assault with or without the infliction of wounds 48 and 24 paṇas respectively.[102] After a learned discussion Dr.D.C. Sircar shows that "the fines, sometimes given specifically in paṇas and often mentioned without such specification were usually regarded as payable in copper coins, but there was no absolute unanimity amongst the authorities on the subject".[103]

Last about capital punishment. Almost all the religious codes approved of this form of punishment. The *Bible* may be quoted. "Whoso sheddeth man's blood, by man shall his blood be shed .... All things are cleansed by blood and apart from the shedding of blood there is no remission". Islam also retained its practice because of its deterrent value. Viṣṇu ordains, "Great criminals should be put to death". Plato, Galen and Seneca opined in favour of the death penalty. But it is worthnoting that Jesus Christ repudiated all sense of vengeance. He would have all sinners including criminals reformed rather than killed. Some think that ancient India was not in favour of capital punishment. Jayaswal says that the softening of punishment was due to the spread of Buddhism.[104] But we hear of the horrible account of various methods of cruel punishment in the Buddhist Jātakas. Buddha is said to have given the description of 12 processes of such punishment in the Mahādukkha-Khandha: "Śaṅkha-muṇḍika, Rāhumukha, Hastaprajyotikā, Eraka-vartikā, chīraka-vāsikā, eynelyaka, Baḍi saṃamāsika kārṣāpaṇaka, paridhi-parivartikā and .....[105] So it is hard to agree with Jayaswal. Rather the above account leads us to assume the practice of cruel punishments as deterrent factors.

It is interesting to note the discussion of the *Mahābhārata*[106] on this issue. The Pūrvapakṣa argues that if capital punishment was abolished, the distinction between virtue and vice would disappear, the proprietory rights like "this is mine, and that is his" and other rights and obligations of the society would come to an end. But this argument is fallacious because other modes of punishment would serve these purposes no less than the capital punishment. Hence the conclusion is in favour of the abolition of capital punishment on the ground of four reasons: (i) Capital punishment hits hard the innocent dependents of the offender because he, being killed, the whole family gets ruined (verse 10); (ii) the offender may be corrected, sometimes a wicked man is found to follow a good mode of life (V.11); (iii) it is also found that good persons come out of wicked ones (V.11) and so if all wicked ones are killed, the society loses the chance of rise of some good citizens; and (iv) the offender should not be uprooted because it goes against the traditional law (V.16) which aims at mental purification. Hence other methods of punishment like mental pain, imprisonment, disfiguring and confiscation are advised but this theory of the *Mahābhārata* was not accepted by any jurist of the land. However it might have influenced some kings, if the evidence of Fahien who mentions capital punishment conspicuously absent in actual administration is believed to have carried some weight.

Some scholars like Lüders, R.K. Mukherjee and Dikshitar believe that there was no practice of death-sentence in the time of Aśoka. Aśoka's inscriptions speak of imprisonment and torture. But R.K. Mukherjee explains 'bandhanaṃtika' of Separate R.E. of Dhauli as "execution". All jurists beginning with Gautama mention the practice of this punishment.[107] *Viṣṇu Dh. Sūtra*[108] enjoins this penalty on all guilty of 'mahāpātaka' except on Brāhmaṇa. Kauṭilya[109] prescribes death-sentence for murdering with a sharp weapon. But Kāmandaka[110] and Śukra[111] reject this mode of punishment even in the gravest offence except for the offence of subverting the state. ("mahatsvaparādheṣu daṇḍaṃ prāṇāntikaṃ tyajet/ ṛte rājyāpahārāt tu yukta-daṇḍah praśasyate//"). According to *Daṇḍa-viveka* (p.20) capital punishment is of two kinds, Śuddha and Miśra. 'Śuddha', i.e., the simple one is again of two types, 'avicitra' when the culprit is beheaded with a sword and 'Citra' or 'Vicitra' when he is impaled or burnt; whereas in the Miśra process his hands or feet or other limbs are cut off and then he is killed. The *Mānasollāsa*[112] speaks of different ways of death sentence: "Viṣekṣu (?)—danti-bhujaga-śastrānala-jalādibhiḥ/pāpānāṃ prāṇa-haraṇaṃ vadha-daṇḍaḥ prakīrtitaḥ//" i.e., by poison, an elephant, a snake, weapons, fire, and water etc. Corporal punishment in the shape of mutilation of limbs like hairs, ears, eyes, noses, tongue, hands, feet etc. and also imprisonment, beating and rude rebuke are known as 'Kleśa-daṇḍah' in *Mānasollāsa.*[113]

Punishment is, according to Nārada[114] of two kinds, corporal and monetary ("Śārira-ś-cārtha-daṇḍa-ś-ca") of which the former begins with that which causes pain to the body and ends in death and the latter begins with a fine of Kākini and ends with the loss of properties ("Sarvasvāntaḥ"). The term 'daśadhā' means, according to Mādhava, various ways (of corporal punishment) without any limitation of number, as for example, binding, stamping, reduction to servitude, imprisonment and beating etc. Others like shaving the head, banishment from the country (city, according to Nārada), a mark branded on the forehead indicative of the offence and one's being paraded on an ass are also heard of in Nārada[115] and the term indicating two types is merely illustrative and not exhaustive. While Manu[116] mentions ten places on which the corporal punishment may be applied in cases of three lower castes, the brahmin being exempted, Bṛhas. (27.4-12) mentions 14 instead of 10 traditional places for the infliction of such punishments, in which extra places like neck, one half of the feet, the thumb and index etc. are included. He recommends the combination of different kinds of punishments in cases of grave crimes. Yuan Chwang mentions the frequent use of the following punishment in India—life-long imprisonment, particularly in cases of rebels, mutilation of nose, ears etc., banishment and ransom. It may be noted that even now death-sentence is inflicted here on criminals for five principal offences, viz., : (i) Treason, (ii) Perjury and Murder, (iii) Abetment of suicide of minor or insane person, (iv) attempted murder by a transported convict and (v) dacoity with murder.[117]

It is difficult to accept the view of Jolly in connection with Hindu criminal law when he says: "Capital punishment in various aggravated forms, such as impaling on a stake, trampling to death by an elephant .... are also frequently inflicted even for comparatively light offences".[118] It is true that capital punishments in various shapes were in practice in ancient India, as evidenced by Manu and others, though of course, less numerous than in medieval England or Europe, yet with the growth of civilisation in India an attempt to humanise the criminal law is distinctly traceable in Hindu law. However, Jolly's remark is nothing but an exaggeration of fact because capital punishments and mutilation, as prescribed in Hindu law are meant only for heinous crimes. Jolly alleges again that "Jus talionis" which is not universally represented in archaic legislations becomes specially conspicuous in these punishments". (*Ibid, E.R.E.*). Thus a criminal is condemned to lose whatever limb he has used in insulting or attacking another. It is true that sometimes in cases of assault the offender is condemned to lose the offending limb but that is not the general punishment for assault and sometimes mutilation of parts other than the offending limbs is also enjoined and the motive for such punishment was not to satisfy the vindictiveness of the injured party but only to deter people from the commission of such crimes. Hence Jolly's allegation is baseless.

REFERENCES

1. 33-42.
2. XII, 165, 34ff.
3. *E.I.*, I, 366, 69.
4. Kern, *Der Buddismus,* 2.100-138.
5. *Hindu Law and Custom,* 1928, p. 255.
6. Beal, II, p. 83
7. "Civilisation and the growth of Law", pp. 78-79 and 93.
8. Q. by *Daṇḍaviveka,* p. 76.
9. 50, 24 etc.
10. Manu, XI, 183 ff.
11. H.L. & C., p. 263.
12. III. 5.-14.
13. Ins. at Mellappaluvier (Trichinopoly), 372 of 1924.
14. 2, 162f.
15. Cf. Maine, *Ancient Law* ch. X, and P.N. Sen, "Hindu Jurisprudence", 1918, Tagore Law Lectures, No. XII.
16. VIII. 286-287.
17. II. 222.
18. Q. in *Sm. Ch.*, II, p. 329 and Parā Mā., III, pp. 419-20.
19. 5.4.4.7.

20. *Śānti*, 15.2.5, 12.
21. *Śat. Brah.*, 5.4.4.7.
22. Cf. Manu, VII, 15.
23. Śānti, 56. 6-7.
24. 1.4.
25. II. 1294 ff.
26. II. 1296 & 1298.
27. 5.61.8 and 7.86.5.
28. *Institute of Hindu Law*, p. 192.
29. "Ṛtasya panthāṃ na taranti duṣkṛtaḥ" *ṚV*, 9.73.6.
30. II. 16.
31. 1.46.
32. 15.5.6.
33. Śānti-parvan, ch. XV.
34. Śānti-parvan, ch. 121.
35. *Gāthā-saptaśatī* 1.29: "vajjha-paḍaho va".
36. Act X.
37. IV. 73.
38. IV. 9.
39. IX. 288.
40. Viṣṇu, 5.71 and Śukra, 4.1.82, 92 and 108-9.
41. 4.81-82.
42. 4.83.
43. Ch. IV. Sec. 6.
44. Cf. Manu, VIII. 12.
45. Śānti, ch. 121.
46. I. 361.
47. 4.40.
48. Tr. by Benoy K. Sarkar, pp. 130-31 & 136.
49. 4.1.110.
50. VIII. 318.
51. Śānti-parvan, ch. 23.
52. "Vadha-vandhana-chejjabhejja", J.V. p. 245-46 and 444; cf. *AŚ.* IV. 2; R.E. V and P.E.IV.
53. Cf. First Sep. Kaliṅga R.E.
54. XIII. 5.
55. Cf. also Nāyā I, p. 20.
56. VI., p. 3.
57. Dasā, ucc. IV.
58. "Selections from Peshwa's Dafter" ed. by Mr. G.S. Sardesai, Vol. 43, No. 143. p. 114, dated 7.9.1775 A.D.
59. J., VI, p. 156.

60. Frag. XXVII.
61. Kingsmill, Athenaeum, 1902; Smith, *EHI*, p. 137, n. 2.
62. J., II, pp. 122-23 and III, p. 436 and p. 461.
63. J., I., pp. 370 and 500.
64. J., III, p. 34.
65. J., II, p. 124.
66. J., III, p. 41 and IV, p. 447 and also *Mṛccha, X.*
67. "Vandhanāgārāni" in J. I, . 385; III, pp. 326 and 392; V, p. 459 and VI, pp. 3, 387-88 and 427.
68. J., VI, p. 387-88.
69. J., VI, p. 8.
70. J., II, p. 326.
71. 6, pp 36 ff.
72. Panha—Pannavana, com. Malayagiri, Bombay, 1910-19, Guj. trans. Bhagavandas Ahmedabad, V.S., 1991, 3, p. 54.
73. 2, p. 54 ff.
74. *Āvaśyakachūrṇi*, II., p. 171.
75. Giles, Travels of Fa-hien, p. 56.
76. Beal, II, pp 86 ff.
77. Cf. also 'Divyāvadāna', ed. Cowell and Neil, Cambridge, 1886. XXVI, pp. 374-382.
78. Cf. Watters, II, p. 89.
79. Cf. Beal, II, p. 86.
80. Cf. Beal, II, p. 271.
81. "Su-vijñāta-praṇīto hi Daṇḍaḥ prajā dharmārtha-kāmai-r-yojayat". *AŚ*, I. 4.6.7.
82. VIII. 129.
83. Yāj. I. 367 and Bṛh. *SBE*, 33, p. 387, verse 6.
84. Cf. *Daṇḍa-viveka*, published in Gaikwad Oriental Series, 1931, p. 20.
85. *Ibid.*, p. 388.
86. "Karma-kṣayāt prajāyante mahāpātakina-s-tviha", III. 206.
87. Legge, 1886, p. 43. 88. *History of Criminal Law*, vol. I, p. 47.
88. *History of English Criminal Law*, vol. I, p. 471.
89. *Way to Justice*, p. 94.
90. "In the Service of Youth" by Dr. J.M. Brew, 1943, ch. XV, p. 208.
91. VIII, 138.
92. 1.366.
93. Sāhasa, vv. 7-8.
94. Sāhasa, vv. 6-7.
95. VII. 136.
96. 1. 365.

97. VII. 132.36.
98. 490-93.
99. H.D.S., III, p. 393.
100. *E.I.*, 33, pp. 263f.
101. Cf. also *E.I.*, XX, pp. 64-66.
102. *AŚ*, 3.19.12.
103. *S.I. Coins*, p. 87.
104. Manu & Yāj. p. 172.
105. Mahādukkha Khandha-suttaṃ 13.1.5.
106. XII, ch. 267, 10-16.
107. Gaut., II. 3.41, *AŚ* Manu (IX. 279). Yāj. II. 278 and 279, *Matsya-Purāṇa*, 227. 200 and Nārada (Pāruṣya, verse 31).
108. V.I.
109. IV. II
110. XIV. 16.
111. IV. 1.93.
112. II. 20. 1287, p. 144.
113. II. 20. 1289-90.
114. q. by Parā. Mā., p. 155.
115. Sāhasa, 9-10.
116. VIII. 124. ff.
117. Cf. I.P.C., Section 121, 194, 305, 302 and 396 respectively.
118. *Encyclopedia of Religion and Ethics*, (Hastings), vol. IV, "Crimes and Punishment", (Hindu) by Jolly.

CHAPTER VI

Principles of Decision

Manu[1] says that decision in courts must be made according to the principles derived from local usages and from the institutes of the sacred law. ("Deśa-dṛṣṭai-ś-ca śāstra-dṛṣṭai-ś-ca hetubhiḥ"). Yāj.[2] also lays emphasis on "dharma-śāstras" and elsewhere says that in cases of conflict the principles of Dharma-school should be preferred to those of the Artha-school.[3] The guiding principles in awarding punishment are also prescribed in Manu, VIII. 126: "Anuvandhaṃ parijñāya deśa-kālau ca tattvataḥ/sārāparādhau cālokya daṇḍaṃ daṇḍyeṣu pātayet//". Here 'anuvandha' means motive. Medhātithi explains it as repetition of the offence or the cause of the act. ("pravṛttiḥ kāraṇam vā anuvadhyate prayujyate yena"). The second meaning is proved by Aśoka's inscription.[4] In view of the first meaning the punishment would be invariably severer, while in that of the latter it may be lighter. Aśoka uses 'anuvandha' in connection with remission of punishment. His officers were to examine and reduce punishment awarded to prisoners on the consideration of 'anuvandha', children of the prisoner, absence of free agency and old age. Besides 'anuvandha' in the sense of motive, Manu wishes knowledge also to be considered. Gaut.[5] advises thorough ascertainment about the doer (puruṣa), the capacity of the culprit, the crime itself and the motive. Kauṭilya prescribes the searching enquiry into the doer (puruṣa), the offence (aparādham), the cause or agency (kāraṇam), the motive (anuvandham), the time of the offence (tadātvam) and place and time (deśa-kālam). Āpas.[6] speaks of shares in an offence among the employer, advisor and doer ("prayojayitā mantā karteti svarga-naraka-phaleṣu bhāginaḥ). Thus the above survey shows that the legislators stressed on four main points: (i) motive, (ii) magnitude of crime, (iii) capacity of the culprit whether or not to do the entire crime and to bear the punishment, and (iv) the circumstances. Yāj.[7] omits 'anuvandha' and the act itself was perhaps the evidence of motive. He opines that repeated offences are to be dealt with severely. Āpastamba[8] also says that the punishment should be doubled in case of repetition. The earlier jurists took into consideration before punishing the factors of motive and intention behind the crime. Manu enjoins that "men of other castes who have unintentionally committed such crimes ought to be deprived of their whole property and if they committed them intentionally, they shall be banished."[9] (Cf. Viṣṇu, 5.104). The abettors were equally punishable like the criminals.[10] Kullūka, while commenting on this verse (IX. 271) of Manu, speaks of the responsibility of the abettor towards the crime, "Cauraṃ jñātvā", i.e. knowing fully well any body to be a thief. Kauṭilya and Yāj. think that the amount of punishment should be fixed in varying degrees on the basis of the intentional or unintentional character of the crime committed.

It is interesting to note that both Dharma and Arthaśāstras prescribe differential punishments, mostly on the basis of castes. This might have been due to various reasons. When the Vedic Āryans mixed with the un-Āryan population, the former wanted to absorb the latter as the members of the lowest class or the Śūdras. The non-Vedic sects like the Buddhists, Jainas and Cārvākas raised their heads in the teeth of the opposition of the Brahmanical school. Besides, India became prey to foreign inroads and the Brahmanical society had to develop itself and adjust in new circumstances when the Greeks, the Sakas-Parthians, the Yuetchi-s, the Pulindas, Khaśas and Huṇas infiltrated in Indian society. Hence it is quite natural that the rules of punishment were framed by the Smṛtis with an eye to groups or castes of the society. The caste-institutions made their influence felt even on the judicial system, as evidenced by the rules regarding the appointment of the Chief Justice (Nyāyādhīśa), the laws of evidence and also punishment.

In the P.E. IV Aśoka enjoins the Rājuka-s to introduce uniformity in judicial procedure and punishment. ("icchitaviye hi esa kiṃti viyohāla-samatā ca siya daṇḍa-samatā"). A question may be raised how far Aśoka broke the tradition of grading punishment according to caste. The term 'samatā' suggests that the judge should be impartial to all. It contradicts the legal procedure as prescribed in Dharma and Arthaśāstras. An ideal ruler as he was, Aśoka wished to do away with all legal discriminations based on caste. Possibly in the face of the long-standing prejudices of the society dominated by the Brahmanical ideas, such wishes of the ruler had little effect on the mind of the people. Besides, Aśoka issued this decree at the fag-end of his rule in 238 B.C.[11] and hence he had little time at his disposal for its proper execution. The term 'samatā' has been translated as 'uniformity' (Bloch, p. 165) i.e., a uniform penal code must be followed throughout the Mauryan empire. Bloch, however, suggests that by the addition of an 'anusvāra' to 'samatā' (saṃhatā), it would read 'sammatā' (Sk. Saṁyaktā) meaning 'correctness' instead of 'uniformity'.[12] This explanation may be accepted but the difficulty is that the 'anusvāra' does not occur in any other version.

It deserves mention that decision on punishment was made after cool calculation of many factors, viz., caste, sex, circumstances etc. But that does not preclude the idea that the judges acted uniformly under similar sets of circumstances.

Women were treated with more liberal attitude. Kauṭilya says that "a woman twelve years of age attains majority, whereas a man when sixteen years; if after this there is a failure to carry out marital duties, there shall be a fine of 12 paṇas for the women, twice that for a man". He adds that if a man and a woman, with sexual intercourse in view, indulge in gestures with limbs or indecent conversation in secret, 24 paṇas is the fine for a woman, double that for a man".[13] Similar was the ratio of fines imposed on man and woman for any forbidden transactions.[14] Aṅgiras[15] says that an old man of 80 years, a boy of less than 16 years, women and diseased persons deserve only half expiation ("Aśīti-r-yasya varṣāṇi vālo vāpyūna-ṣodaṣaḥ/ prāyaścittā-r-dham-arhati striyo roginaḥ eva ca//"). And

Sumantu and Viṣṇu also, quoted therein, prescribe half expiation for such people. It is interesting to note that Śaṅkha, quoted also here, says that a child less than five, committing a crime or a sinful act is free from royal punishment and he is not to undergo any expiation. The I.P.C., sec. 82 also regards nothing as "an offence which is done by a child under seven years of age". Kauṭilya is emphatic on this point. He exempts the infant altogether: "If the driver of a carriage causing hurt is a minor, the master inside it shall be punished".[16] Lastly, according to the *Mbh.*[17] a boy below 14 is not a sinner, even if he commits a sin, as per the rule prescribed by Aṇī-Māṇḍavya, and so he must not be punished. Gaut.[18] shows how one's caste determined the punishment for the same offence. The Śūdra is made to pay eight times the value of the thing he has stolen ("aṣṭāpādyaṃ steya-kilviṣaṃ śūdrasya"), each of the other castes, Vaiśyas, Kṣatriyas and Brāhmaṇas to pay twice the amount of the preceding one in order ("dviguṇottarānītareṣāṃ prativarṇam"). Gauṭ.[19] argues that a man of the higher caste is expected to be more learned and so he must pay more for violating the prescription ("Viduṣo' tikrame daṇḍabhūyastvam"). Manu[20] also prescribes almost the same thing (VIII. 338), adding the higher amount, i.e. a hundredfold or even twice four-and sixty fold for the Brāhmaṇas who is a knower of the nature of the offence.[21] Elsewhere[22] Manu says that a Kṣatriya, a Vaiśya and a Śūdra, having defamed a brāhmaṇa shall pay the fine of 100, 150 or 200 and undergo corporal punishment respectively and likewise a brāhmaṇa shall be fined 50 paṇas for defaming a Kṣatriya, 25 paṇas in case of a Vaiśya and 12 only in case of a Śūdra.[23] Yāj.[24] also follows the same principle of punishment on the basis of varṇas and castes ("daṇḍa-praṇayaṇaṃ kāryaṃ varṇa-jātyuttarādharaiḥ") like his predecessors, put above. Kauṭ.[25] and Nār.[26] also prescribe the rise and fall in punishment on the basis of the superiority or inferiority in rank of persons abused or defamed. The castewise distinction of punishment was also maintained in cases of rape and adultery. Yāj.[27] prescribes the highest punishment for adultery with a woman of the same caste (sajātāvuttamo daṇḍaḥ), the middling in case of a woman of a lower caste (ānulomye tu madhyamaḥ) but the man of the lower caste, if found to have offended a woman of a higher caste is to be sentenced to death and the woman concerned must have her ears etc. cut off. ("prātilomye vadhaḥ puṃso nāryāḥ karṇādikartanam").

It should be borne in mind that impartiality in rendering justice was the goal of ancient jurists. Nārada enjoins upon Yudhiṣṭhira not to make any discrimination between the rich and the poor in adjudicating cases.[28] But a question may arise how a poor man could pay a heavy fine if it were imposed on him. The *Mahābhārata* prescribes the following principle of discrimination for fairness of justice: the rich are to be heavily fined, the poor put in chains and the wicked to be subjected to blows.[29] ("Viyojayed-dhanai-r-ṛddhān-adhamān-atha bandhanaiḥ / vinayacchāpi durvṛttān prahārai-r-api Pārthivaḥ //").

Our Smṛtis prescribe the rule that local affairs ought to be settled by local courts and not by the central court and this indicates the operations of the principle of neighbourhood as the most important factor. We have the inscriptional evidence in favour of this principle.[30] The Chola inscriptions contain passages testifying to the criminal jurisdiction exercised by the local courts.

The Hindu jurists were aware of what is indicated in the legal maxim, "Actus non facit reum, nisi mens sit rea", i.e, the act alone does not amount to guilt, it must be accompanied by guilty mind". The guilty mind is expressed by the mental attitudes like intention and negligence, as indicated in Salmond's Jurisprudence.[31] According to modern jurists a man is liable to punishment only when he does any offence either intentionally or out of criminal negligence. The ancient jurists like Gautama, Kauṭilya, Manu, Viṣṇu, Yāj., Bṛhaspati and others lay emphasis on these issues of intention and negligence.[32] According to modern jurisprudence ignorance of law is no excuse. But in criminal cases ignorance of fact is generally a good defence.[33] It is difficult to determine how far ignorance was acknowledged as a good excuse in ancient India, Manu,[34] however, opines that punishment should be awarded in consideration of the time and place of the offence and the strength and knowledge (vidyām) of the offender. Some jurists do not count ignorance as a factor for excuse but it deserves mention that in such cases punishments are lighter. Kauṭilya says that when a person supplies murderers or thieves food, dress etc. under ignorance, he shall be censured.[35]

In modern jurisprudence offences made by lunatics or insane persons are not generally punishable. The ancient Indian jurists also considered these factors, though, of course, they did not wholly let them go without punishment. Manu[36] recommends whipping for women, infants and insane persons etc. Yāj.[37] enjoins no punishment for offences committed by insane persons or persons under the influence of intoxication ("moha-madādibhiradaṇḍanam").

"Negligence", says Salmond, "is rightly treated as a form of "mens rea", standing side by side with wrongful intention as a formal ground of responsibility".[38] So a man doing offence negligently is liable to punishment under modern criminal law. The ancient Indian jurists also enjoin punishment in such cases, of course, lighter.

REFERENCES

1. VIII. 3.
2. II. 1.
3. II. 21, see *Mitā.* on it.
4. P.E. IV.
5. XII. 51.
6. II. 11.29.1.
7. I. 366 – 368
8. II. 11.29.2.
9. IX. 242.
10. Cf. Manu, IX. 271 "bhakta-dāyakāḥ".
11. *C.I.I.*, Intro, p. XXXVI.
12. Le Ins. L' Aśoka, p. 164, n. 10.

13. 3.3.25.
14. 3.3.30-31.
15. q. in *Mitākṣarā* on Yāj., III. 243.
16. IV. ch. 13, 332.
17. Ādi-p., ch. 107 and 108.
18. II. 3.12.14.
19. *Ibid.*, 14.
20. VIII. 338.
21. "tad-doṣa-guṇa-viddhi saḥ"; cf. Kātyā, q. by *Sm. Ch.*, II, 127 and Parā. Mā. III. 211.
22. VIII. 267-69.
23. Cf. Gaut., II. 3.8.10.
24. II. 205-207.
25. 3.18.
26. 15.
27. II. 286.
28. Sabhāparvan, V. 92.
29. Śānti Parvan, LXXXV. 20-21.
30. Valhudalampattu ins. of Devaraya II. cf. *Madras Ep. Rep*, 1915, pp. 106-8.
31. Ch. XVI, Sec. 12, p. 378.
32. Cf. G. XII. 1 & 4; Manu, IX. 242; VIII. 290-296; Viṣṇu V. 104: K., IV. XIII. 232 and K. IV. ch. XIII, 233; Yāj. II. 298-99 and 162; Bṛh. XIX, 27 & 28.
33. Cf. Salmond, ch. XIX, 177, pp. 375 & 376.
34. VII. 16.
35. IV. ch. XI.
36. IX. 230.
37. II. 214.
38. Salmond, *Jurisprudence*, ch. XVIII, Sec. 140, p. 357.

CHAPTER VII

Exemption from Punishment

Now let us trace the method of exemption from punishment from the pre-Mauryan days. Gaut.[1] prescribes that a brāhmaṇa of wide vedic learning (Vahuśruta) is exempted from being sentenced to death, confinement by fetters, from seizure of all wealth, from banishment, from condemnation and social boycott. ("Avadhya-ś-cāvandhya-ś-cādaṇḍyaś-cāvahiṣkāryaścāp/ rivādyaś-cāparihāryaśceti".). Haradatta comments that this exemption is allowed only in cases of offences, done without any foresight ("a-vuddhi-pūrvāparādhe"). Śaṅkha's law of exemption, mentioned above means exemption from corporal or monetary punishment but not from an ordinary one.[2] Gautama mentions that only a brāhmaṇa of wide Vedic learning, purified by 44 sacraments (1.8.8) enjoys this exemption. Vijñān.[3] makes it clearer when he says that these immunities are meant for a brahmin of wide learning and not for an ordinary one ("pratipādita-vahuśruta-viṣayaṃ na brāhmaṇa-mātra-viṣayam"—*Mitā.* on Yāj., II, 4).

Manu[4] says, "Akṣato brāhmaṇo vrajet" and "na jātu brāhmaṇaṃ hanyāt sarva-pāpeṣvavasthitam" / rāṣṭrād-enam vahiṣkuryāt samagra-dhanam-akṣatam //"[5] i.e., the brahmin even when indulging in all sorts of crimes should under no circumstances be sentenced to death; he should be banished from the country with all his wealth and uninjured. Thus Manu follows Gaut. who prescribes no corporal penalty for brahmins (na śārīro brāhmaṇa-daṇḍaḥ). Gaut.[6], however, is in favour of punishing a brahmin otherwise, as for example, preventing him from repeating the same offence (karma-viyoga) by depriving him of all his wealth and taking sureties from him etc., proclaiming him as a thief in towns and villages etc., banishment and branding him with a mark. Medhātithi on Manu (VIII. 125) explains more distinctly that a brahmin is exempted from a fine only when he is the first offender, who commits a crime without the previous plan, who is born of a good family and who is gifted with learning and good character. Āpas.[7] says that a brahmin, guilty of murder, theft, forcible seizure of another's land etc. should be punished with the covering of his eyes with cloth for the rest of his life, while others are punishable by death for these crimes ("puruṣa-vadhe steya bhūmyādāna iti svānyādāya vadhyaḥ cakṣu-r-nirodha-s-tveteṣu brāhmaṇasya").

Vṛddha-Hārīta[8] also like Gautama and Manu prescribes the same penalty on brahmin offenders. It is noteworthy that the jurists are unanimous on the point of inviolability of the brāhmaṇa's body, which was regarded as sacred. That is why Pārāśara comments on Gaut.[9] that the brāhmaṇa should not be subjected to any mutilation of limbs ("tad-aṅga-bhaṅga-rūpa-daṇḍa-niṣedhārtham"—*Pārā. Mād.*, III, p. 158), as confirmed by Hārīta ("na tvaṅga-bhedaṃ viprasya pravadanti manīṣiṇaḥ"). Śaṅkha prescribes "Vivāsana-dhik-karaṇaṃ brāhmaṇasya", i.e., banishment and admonition in cases of poor brahmins. Manu teaches that tonsure (of the head) is ordained for a brāhmaṇa instead of capital punishment, while others shall suffer capital punishment. He[10] says elsewhere that one should have a headless corpse stamped on the forehead for murdering a brahmin, which he mentions as one of the moral sins.[11]

Vijñān. on Yāj. II, 21 opines that the term 'vā' in Manu's 'brāhmaṇaṃ vā vahuśrutam' (VIII. 350) suggests that the preceptors and others including the learned brāhmaṇa should not be sentenced to death ("na gurvādīnāṃ vadhyatva-pratītiḥ"), as confirmed by Sumantu's statement which he quotes "nātatāyi-vadhe doṣo'nyatra go-brāhmaṇa-vadhāt".[12]

Though the brāhmaṇa is exempted from capital punishment, he must not be left scot-free. Manu[13] and Yāj.[14] unanimously declare almost in the same language that nobody is exempt from punishment in the eye of the law whether the person be the king's parents or his teacher or friend or a priest or any relation of his. Śaṅkha-Likhita and Kātyā. (481), however prescribe no penalty in such cases. But, the *Sm. Ch.*[15] explains that the real meaning is that the king should not inflict corporal punishment on such persons but he must punish them by other means. Manu says emphatically that "this expiation has been prescribed for unintentionally killing a brāhmaṇa but for intentionally killing a brahmin no atonement is ordained".[16] Vijñān. also justifies the inviolability of the brahmins, as mentioned above, and argues that the injunction "guruṃ vā vāla-vṛddhau vā brāhmaṇam vā vahuśrutam" is nothing but a mere laudatory statement (arthavāda), made to strengthen the cause of killing an assailant. Thus the above analysis suffices to show that the brāhmaṇas were not entitled to escape from penalisation, though they were not to be punished by any corporal punishment. In the eye of the law of the land they were not given any special privilege of being tried in any special method like the Europeans or Americans in British India who were allowed in I.P.C. to be tried by the Jury, composed mainly of their countrymen or in a special court like the English Peers who were tried by the House of Lords alone. It is worthmentioning that the clergymen and other religious persons of England and other Western countries enjoyed similar privileges like brahmins of ancient India.[17] Even in the matter of death-sentence on the brahmins we find the opposite theory, preached in the epic, the Dharmaśāstras and Arthaśāstra and other works of Kāvya. Let us examine these sources.

Kauṭ.[18] prescribes that if a brahmin aims at the kingdom, forces entrance into the king's harem, instigates wild tribes or enemies (against the king) or creates disaffection in forts, countryparts or in the army, he shall be drowned ("brāhmaṇaṃ tam-apaḥ praveśayet"). R.P. Kangle reads the passage as 'tamaḥ praveśayet', and says that the brahmin shall be made to enter darkness. To Meyer this passage means "the brahmin should be made blind". In the actual administration of law under the Mauryas the exception was unknown. A brahmin culprit, convicted of treason to the state was to be drowned. In some cases he was subjected to severer punishments than men of other castes, as he stood on the highest rung of the social and intellectual ladder, punishment varying in inverse ratio to social order.[19]

Manu places a brahmin above criminal penalty in felony.[20] He suffered only what Hobbes called a "change of air" after having committed the most heinous crimes, acts of treason, murder etc. This claim was probably due to the fact that the king in that period was a brāhmaṇa. But the *Mṛcch.* (IX) shows how even a good brahmin like Cārudatta was not allowed to enjoy this special privilege. Yāj. places no one above law. It may be pointed out that neither Āpas. nor Vaśiṣṭha had any such claim. At an earlier period when offence was sought to be proved by circumstantial evidence and no direct evidence was available, and any person was suspected to be of foul character, he was brought to trial before a criminal court. He had to clear his character. Sometimes the prisoner was subjected to torture for confession. This was abolished by the Mauryas because the prisoners sometimes admitted guilt to avoid pain; hence conclusive evidence must be put forward, torture or hard labour was allowed only when one was proved guilty (āptadoṣam karma kārayet). When spies proved the guilt at the trial, the prisoner could be subjected to whipping etc. A brahmin was subjected to either the same amount of pain as a healthy woman or he was only to be subjected to the torture of cross-examination. The learned and the ascetics were not to be subjected to any pain and their offence had to be proved by the evidence of detectives. In after-trial punishments a brahmin was not to be subjected to any torture but a degrading symbol of his guilt was stamped on his forehead as a deterrent. Sometimes he was declared "countryless" after a public proclamation, just in keeping with the Hindu principle of the object of punishment. Originally punishments were devised to be prāyaścitta-s, i.e., mental chastisement and to be deterrent. The brahmin culprit was to face severe ignominy, over and above his punishment. Owing to learning and birth he was only spared physical tortures. Branding was a severer penalty inflicted on him and he received a social boycott and was denied all legal rights.[21] Āpas. seems to be harsher on the brahmins. He[22] prescribes penances for homicide, theft and misappropriation of land viz., a brahmin was subjected to blinding until he agreed to undergo the required penance, whereas members of other castes were given solitary confinement. Solitary confinement was awarded to a brahmin for lighter offences. Capital punishment on a brahmin is not prohibited in Āpastamba. Kaut. expressly lays down severer punishment for the brahmins.

It may not be unlikely, as Jayaswal would have us believe, that under the Śuṅgas when the Brahmin became the ruling caste, he made the claims of no branding, no capital punishment, no torture and no confiscation in cases of adultery, rape, theft, and murder. Compared with Gautama, Āpas. and Kaut., Manu is lenient to the brahmin. Manu[23] enjoins that the killing of a brahmin is a heinous crime ("Brāhmahācha, etc.").

These immunities of the brāhmaṇa are open to strong criticism. Maine comments that the brahmins claimed "to be free of the criminal law which they themselves prescribed".[24] K.P. Jayaswal condemns Manu for "placing the brahmin above the law". He says that the earlier law was strict to the brahmin. Manu became lenient but Yāj. took a rational attitude, set aside their special claims and brought them under the king's law. He also points out how the brahmin was not exempt from capital punishment, as evidenced by the *Mṛcchakaṭikam.* But these criticisms should be judged from the proper historical perspective. What S. Varadachariar says in this connection deserves mention: "The apparent partiality of the law to this community will cease to loom so large, if it is remembered that the Hindu Criminal Law prescribed two kinds of punishments, secular and spiritual, that in the case of the brahmin the spiritual penalty .... was more severe than in the case of other castes ..... and the fear of such punishment was even greater than that of secular punishment".

Gaut.[25] prescribes that the offender, if he is a learned man or a member of the higher castes, should be liable to severer punishment. Thus he stood above the principle of caste-distinction. Haradatta comments on it; "The offence is greater when it is done by one who knows that the act is prohibited". ("Niṣedhadoṣaṃ jñātvāpi pravartamānasya doṣādhikyaṃ bhavati"). Manu also accepts the same principle, as distinctly mentioned in VIII. 338 ("Tad-doṣa-guṇa-vat hi saḥ"). But at the same time a severer penalty on the offender is prescribed in the smrtis when a member of the lower order of the society offends one of the higher rank. This was nothing peculiar to the brahmins because the same differential treatment is allowed even now among the white races when one of them gets offended by any coloured person. As regards capital punishment it may be argued that the notion of a brāhmaṇa's life and body seems to have come down from the Vedic period and it is nothing new in the age of the jurists. Both Gautama and Bodhāyana preach exemption of brahmins from capital punishment. The particle "vái" in "Avadhyo vai brāhmaṇaḥ sarvāparādheṣu" means, according to some commentator that what is enunciated here is well-known and it suggests only the Vedic origin of such exemption.

Some allege that the brahmins were most advantageously situated, while the lot of the Śūdras was sometimes very hard. We cannot deny that it is partially true. As regards the hard lot of the Śūdras it is sufficient to mention that the Śūdras were originally the non-Āryans, conquered by the Āryans, and they were quite distinct from the Āryans in respect of colour and culture. R.P. Dasgupta's remark deserves mention here: "It speaks volumes in favour of the Indo-Āryans that they did not make a short work of the dark-skinned vanquished foes or convert them into slaves. They admitted them into the fold of Hindu society, though at the same time they were careful to maintain the purity of their stock".[26] Dr. Priyanath Sen's explanation for the discrimination in punishment may also be quoted here: "..... a person belonging to a lower caste abusing or assaulting a person belonging to higher caste was subjected to a heavier punishment than a person belonging to a higher caste found guilty of a similar offence in relation to a person belonging to a lower caste." This may to some extent be accounted for on the ground that in cases where insult or injury was a constituent element of the offence, the punishment was to be severe when the delinquent belonged to a lower caste in relation to the complainant, for the outrage proceeding from the former against the latter made the insult more keenly felt and consequently deserved to be put down with a heavier punishment.[27]

In spite of the partiality of the ancient Indian jurists towards persons of higher castes, particularly the brāhmaṇas, it should be admitted that no one, however high his position, was entirely free from punishment for crimes. Even a brāhmaṇa, vastly learned was subject to punishment other than the corporal one. Even the king himself was liable to punishment, for Manu[28] says: "where an ordinary man would be fined one Kārshāpaṇa, the king shall be fined one thousand". Of course, very few kings would abide by this recommendation; but there is no denying the fact that in ancient India, everyone was at least theoretically under law and punishable for any offence done by him.

REFERENCES

1. 1.8.13, p. 53.
2. "tacchārīrārtha-daṇḍayor-niṣedhārthaṃ na punar-daṇḍamātrasya" Cf. *Sm. Ch.*, II, p. 126.
3. "pratipādita-vahuśruta-viṣayaṃ na brāhmaṇa-mātra-viṣayam", *Mitā.* on Yāj. II, 4.
4. VIII. 125.
5. VIII. 380.
6. 2.4.44.
7. II. 10.27. 16-27.
8. VII. 209-210.
9. 2.3.43.
10. IX. 237.

11. IX. 235.
12. Cf. also Manu, VIII. 351.
13. VIII. 355.
14. 1. 358.
15. II, p. 126.
16. XI. 90.
17. Cf. Pollock and Maitland, vol. I, pp. 424-440 and Holdsworth, *Hist. of English Law*, vol. I, pp. 615-616 and vol. III, pp. 294-302.
18. IV. 11.
19. Ch. 83, p. 218, "Vaiśyam dviguṇaḥ, Kṣatriyaṃ triguṇaḥ brāhmaṇam caturguṇaḥ".
20. VIII. 378-81.
21. Manu. IX, 238-39.
22. II. 10.27.
23. IX. 235.
24. *Early Law and Customs*, p. 47.
25. II. 3.14.
26. C & P. in *A.I.*, p. 36.
27. *Hindu Jurisprudence*, Lect. XIII.
28. VIII. 336.

CHAPTER VIII

State and Crimes

The sovereign authority of the state is best exhibited in the administration of criminal justice because the state asserts its power in declaring some acts as unlawful and in fixing punishment for doers of such acts and in convicting and punishing them.

The Dharmaśāstras prescribe punishments for particular offences. Some allege that a regular system of criminal law is not available in them but such observation is not correct. Sir H. Holdsworth remarks on the state of things in England in the 14th century: "Even the statutes of Edward III's reign show that the boundary line between the criminal and the civil liability was as yet uncertain. Many offences the commission of which would in our time be represented by a criminal prosecution were then remedied either by civil or criminal proceedings and sometimes only by civil proceedings. There was as yet no organised police-force, nor were there armies of inspectors of different kinds. Except in the central courts, the administration of justice was in the hands of amateurs whose purity and impartiality were in many cases open to suspicion. It was necessary to enlist the injured man in the cause of law and order by holding out the prospect of obtaining heavy damages or of using the speedy process available in the action of trespass".[1] Even today it is hard to demarcate the civil from criminal wrongs. The Dharmaśāstras are eloquent on the role of a king in the matter of maintaining law and order which ultimately depends on the proper dispensation of justice, i.e. proper punishment of the wrong-doers. The survey of penal science in ancient India shows that the ancient law-makers made a clear distinction between a civil wrong and a crime, the main feature of which is its quality of causing alarm to the people ("lokodvejakatvam"). The king must punish the wrong-doer for maintaining social order and the Dharmaśāstras take into account not only the objective circumstances of the offence but also the subjective limitations of the offender.[2] The ancient jurists were aware of the fact that cruel penalties like mutilation of limbs, whatever their value may be as deterrents, are largely retributive and they cannot reform the offenders who are thereby simply disabled. It may be noted here that the English criminal law of even the 18th century was defective in the sense that it was built "on an indiscriminate application of the death-penalty and on purely external tests of responsibility".[3]

It is better to consult the *Daṇḍaviveka* of Vardhamāna (published in Gaekwad's Oriental Series) for a better view of the Hindu Criminal Law. The conception of "breach of the king's peace" is not only basis for criminal law, it is expressed in the language of a particular order. Nor is it proper to test the criterion of the criminal case as that it is to be initiated by a public officer and not always by the injured individual, as is usually done in civil disputes. Of course, in certain criminal wrongs the king can start the case in his own initiative even without the complaint from the injured party for the maintenance of peace and order in the realm. The modern law of our land, however, insists in some cases on private complaints. Criminal law is primarily based on our natural desire to avenge a wrong. Hence for the proper justice the law demands that the injured person should be given a chance to lodge his case for the proper redress of the wrong done to him. Specially when the police-force was not so thoroughly organised, it was a crying need of the land. It is interesting to note Medhātithi's comment: "In disputes relating to debt, gift etc., the parties may come to some settlement, the king has no right to interfere with their doing so; .... but an offender has to be punished by the king even though the other party may like to come to some agreement with him". (Ṛṇādiṣu itaretare saṃdadhate na tatra rājño hasta-prakṣepaḥ .... sāhasakārī tu rājñā avaśyaṃ nigrahitavyaḥ itareṇa saṃdhīyamāno'pi".[4] We should note also the remarks of *Daṇḍaviveka*[5] in connection with the passage of Bṛhaspati which refers to titles of law (vivādapadas) as initiated by a plaintiff (vādikṛta) as opposed to the Prakīrṇakas, some miscellaneous offences as depending on the king (nṛpāśraya): "Though questions like murder are also matters to be dealt with by the king, an enquiry is in such cases made of witnesses respectively produced by the one party or the other and the king pronounces judgment against one side; in the case of prakīrṇakas, however, the king holds an enquiry even when there is no complaint by a particular party, action being taken on reports received from spies etc., as regards wrongs done by subjects and on such enquiry the king punishes them appropriately and restores them to the right path". ("Yadyapi manuṣya-maraṇādi-vyavahāra api nṛpāśrita eva tathāpi teṣu vādi-prativādibhyāṃ sva-sva-pakṣeṣu darśiteṣu vicārya tayo-r-ekatarasyāparādhinaḥ rājñānuśāsanam. Prakīrṇate tu śirovīdinaṃ vināpi carādimukhād varṇāśraminām doṣam śrutvā vicārya teṣam yathāvihitaṃ daṇḍaṃ vidhāya dharmye pathi sthāpanam-ityevāsya tebhyo bhedaḥ"). The author of *Daṇḍaviveka* makes the same observation on Nārada's laws making distinction between civil and criminal cases. He insists on the king's initiative on the report of his spies in criminal cases and his power to arrest the criminal by his officers. Kautilya refers to two sets of tribunals, Dharmasthīya (civil) and Kaṇṭakaśodhana (criminal). The South Indian inscriptions also refer to such separate courts, though not corresponding to the modern ones. Some think that the Vedic age witnessed the practice of Vaira-yātana, corresponding to payment of wergild, as suggested by the *Vedic Index*. The spirit of private vengeance vanished or at least was softened by the time of the Dharma-sūtras, as evidenced by Āpas. and Bodhā. Āpas.[6] prescribes the gift of cows by a murderer by way of wergild, though silent as to whom the gift is to be made. Some think that as this gift is meant for expiation of sin, the cows are to be given to a brahmin. Others opine that as the Vaira-yātana is meant for removal of enmity, the gift is to be made to the relations of the murdered. Bodhāyana,[7] however, enjoins that the cows are to be given to the king and one bull to a brahmin for expiation of sin. This punishment served as deterrent, as evidenced by the term 'pratyādeśāya' of Manu, VIII. 334 explained by the commentator "anyasyāpi niṣedhāya". Sāyaṇa explains 'Śatadāya' of the *ṚV*, II, 32.4. as "one possessed of plentiful heritage or wealth". Kane's suggestion that Keith's interpretation of this term as "a hero whose wergild is a hundred" is incorrect is preferable in the light of the Vedic society in which a son was always regarded as a wealth, irrespective of his quality and it is strange to conceive that one would pray to Rākā (the full moon) for the boon of a son and at the same time think of the compensation of the son, if murdered in terms of money. However, that the Dharma-sūtras 'tried to regulate crimes by expiation and also by the king's intervention admits of no doubt'. It is interesting to note in this connection Dr. Sen's remark on the authority of Pitāmaha: "Whether it was generally directed that neither a king nor his officers should create or foster litigation of their own accord but should ordinarily refuse to take cognizance of a cause of action without a complaint from the person aggrieved, yet cases of frauds and the various other forms of crimes furnished exceptions to the general rule, for there it was directed that the king should take cognizance of them even without a complaint",[8] showing thereby that the state considered itself injured by individual acts of crimes. It is worthmentioning that in graver crimes like murder it was not only the right of the relations of the murdered to prosecute the murderer but any member of the society had the right to demand justice, as evidenced by the *Mṛcchakatikam* in which Saṃsthānaka, the brother-in-law of the king who was not at all related to Vasantasenā accused Cārudatta of the murder of Vasantasenā in spite of the fact that Vasantasenā's mother was still alive and present in the town. "Obviously Saṃsthānaka demanded justice against Cārudatta because as a member of the state he considered himself injured by the heinous crime".[9] The state was here represented by a citizen and it would not let go the culprit even if the relatives of the victim would forgive him. Vasantasenā's mother took pity on Cārudatta and wanted to withdraw the case, but Saṃsthānaka insisted on the trial and the judge took up the case in the interests of the state. Thus though in criminal cases the state was not generally a party, it was adequately interested. It is not unlikely that sometimes the injured party might come to an amicable settlement with the culprit and drop the prosecution and in such cases the state became helpless because the state would have to depend on the injured party for the successful conduct of the case and there was every possibility that the culprit would evade punishment. The state had generally to depend on the injured party for the first information of the crime, though, of course, anyone of the public had the equal right and duty of informing the matter to the police. It may be pointed out that the law did not permit anyone to come to a private settlement with the culprit, as evidenced by Yāj.[10] who enjoins that if a person called the paramour of his female relative a thief so as to hide his shame, he must be penalised with a fine of 50 paṇas and if he did not arrest the person and bring him to justice on receiving some gratification, he should be punished with a fine of 8 times the hushmoney.

POLICE

The Police-system is as old as the Vedic works, as evidenced by the terms 'jivagṛḥ'[11] and 'Ugra'.[12] Jivagṛḥ means 'a police-official', according to Roth (St. Petersberg Dictionary) and 'Ugra', used in the sense of a 'mighty man' in the *ṚV*, noted above means 'a man in authority' and a 'police-man', according to Max Müller.

The pre-Mauryan age was conspicuous by the absence of any strong central power in India but it witnessed the benefits of democratic government because the local administrative units were governed by the Chief, elected by the people and every citizen was entrusted with the duty of defending the state and was equally protected by the latter. The state was based on the love and goodwill of the people and hence there was little need of organising a separate police-force in the country. But the Mauryan age saw the rise of a strong central power in India and the vastness of the empire required the efficient organisation of the army which enabled the Mauryan king "to overrun and subdue all India" (Plutarch) and also the smooth working of the government machinery binding together the central and the local units, which required the aid of the five institutes of espionage. This system of espionage represents the activity of the police-organisation to a large extent.

The Jātakas mention the functions of a village headman, the Chodakas, and Viniścaya-mahāmātyas with their criminal jurisdiction, who maintained peace and order in the country, specially in small tribal states. But Kauṭilya speaks of the police-measures which were imperatively necessary for the maintenance of peace in the vast Mauryan empire. The frontiers of the state were to be fortified and protected by officials appointed for the purpose. ("Janapada-dvārāṇī-antapālādhiṣṭhitāni sthāpayet, Anteṣvantapāla-durgāṇi"). Kauṭilya advises the establishment of police-headquarters within the kingdom in various principal centres like a Saṁgrahaṇa in the midst of 10 villages, a Khārvaṭa in the midst of 200 villages, a Droṇamukha in 400 villages and a Sthānīya (mod. 'Thana') in 800 villages,[13] each of these being the place of law-courts and well-protected by troops under officers of different grades. These troops were also to assist the officers-in-charge of peace of both villages and towns. The duty of maintaining peace was entrusted to the Samāhartā who with officers like Sthānikas and others and with local officers and with an elaborate system of espionage carried on the administration. The Nāgaraka and the Grāmika were in charge of the police in towns and villages respectively; and their functions are already noted. The Vivītādhyakṣa was in charge of the lonely intervening areas with adequate criminal and police powers. Cāṇḍālas, Śavaras, Pulindas and forest-dwellers were engaged for police duties in the intervening regions.[14] The Vivītādhyakṣa and Nāvādhyakṣa and other officers employed at the gates of villages and towns examined the passports only to check the movement of undesirable persons; and those who could not show such permits were fined ("dvādaśapaṇam janapado'mudro dadyāt"). Different spies called the Kāpaṭikas, Udāsthitas Vaidehakas,

Gṛhapatikas and Tāpasa-vyañjakas and also Satrinaḥ Tikṣṇas and the Bhikṣukī were employed to facilitate police-duties. The special officer called Cora-rajjuka was employed for detecting thieves. The king could charge the loss due to theft from his officers and the guards of thieves (Cauragrāha, Cauroddhatṛ and Cauroddharaṇikas of the inscriptions) in whose jurisdiction theft or robbery took place. (Yāj. and Nārada). Kauṭilya[15] speaks of cases like protection of artisans, merchants etc., suppression of the undesirable, detecting criminals by means of spies, arresting the suspicious or real culprits, post-mortem examinations and discipline in various state departments as police-duties, the ultimate control of which rested with the Pradeṣṭṛ-s of criminal courts. The police helped the magistrates of criminal justice, as evidenced by AŚ.[16] because they were the agents for bringing to book lawbreakers. Their functions like the investigation of criminals find a parallel in the present system of the secret police organisation.[17] The police checked the indiscriminate trading in arms or their carrying by subjects. Private citizens trading in weapons, armours etc., were also regulated with the punishment of the loss of goods by the Collector of Customs and Tolls.

We are told that when a robber named Vijaya carried off the daughter of a merchant Dhanna, the latter approached the City police (Nagaraguttiya) and the police-officers, clad in mail-coats, duly armed with bow, arms and weapons, started in search of the robber, got him arrested and punished[18] in various ways and ultimately the robber died.

Kālidāsa's *Śakuntalā* refers to the police administration. When the fisherman unknowingly took the signet ring into the country for sale, he was arrested by two spies, one of whom was addressed as Śyāla (guardsman of the low caste) and the other as Sūcaka (spy). Wilson explains Sūcaka as "an informer, a spy and in law 'a person appointed to detect culprits' and also one who volunteers to get evidence in a court of law".[19]

Manu[20] recommends that "assembly-houses, houses where water is distributed or cakes are sold, brothels, taverns and victualler's shops, cross-roads, well-known trees, festive assemblies and playhouses and concert-rooms, old-gardens, forests, the shops of artisans, empty dwellings, natural and artificial groves—these and the like places the king shall cause to be guarded by companies of soldiers, both stationary and patrolling and by spies in order to keep away thieves" showing thereby the efficient police arrangement of the then state. Not only should the king prevent the thieves from carrying on their nefarious business but should also detect and punish them with the help of old and reformed thieves.[21]

The terms like "Mahādaṇḍanāyaka" and "Daṇḍapāśadhikaraṇa", found in Allahabad pillar inscription of Samudragupta and in the epigraphs on Basārh seals[22] suffice to show the police and judicial administration during the Gupta age.

Śukra speaks of rest houses (śālās) between villages, each under an official śālādhipa whose duty was to protect travellers at night and who was responsible for any loss to them. This policing ensured the safety to the travellers, and facilitated the method of detecting the suspicious, criminals etc. Sentinels were stationed at each dvāra or outpost and nightwatchmen were engaged in each village like modern chowkidars whose charges were met with taxes, imposed on villages for the purpose.[23]

The sense of responsibility of villagers for protection of the country was also very keen in South India, as evidenced by the inscription of Tanjore (Tirumagaḷpōla) of the 29th year of the rule of Rājarāja I, which refers to a "list of villagers in the Cola country who had to supply watchmen in accordance with the king's command".[24]

REFERENCES

1. *History of the English Law,* vol. II, p. 453.
2. H.D.S. (P.V. Kane, III, pp. 408-410).
3. Sir P. Vinogradoff, *Historical Jurisprudence,* I, p. 30.
4. *Dharmakoṣa,* I, p.160.
5. pp. 259-260.
6. *S.B.E.,* II, p. 78-79.

7. *S.B.E.*, XIV, p. 201.
8. Hindu Jurisprudence, Lect. XII, p. 336.
9. *Crime and Punishment in Ancient India* by R.P. Dasgupta, 1930, p. 10.
10. II. 301 "Jāraṃ Cauretyabhivadan-dāpyaḥ pañcaśataṃ damaṃ/ upajīvya dhanaṃ muñchaṃ-stadevāṣṭa-guṇīkṛtam//").
11. *RV,* X.11.
12. *RV,* VII. 38.6 and *Bṛh. Upa.*, vi. 3.37-38.
13. AŚ. II.1.
14. AŚ. II. 1.6.
15. IV.
16. IV. 10-13.
17. Cf. also Manu, IX. 261.
18. *Nāyādhammakahā,* ed. by N.V. Vaidya, Poona, 2, pp. 53f.
19. *Glossary of Judicial and Revenue Terms,* p. 491.
20. IX. 264-266.
21. *Ibid.*, IX, 267.
22. Basārh excavation by Bloch, *ASIR,* 1930-34, pp. 107f. of *E.I.*, vol. 38, pp. 263f.
23. Śukra i., 405f.
24. 58 of 1893, *S.I.I.*, II, 70.

CHAPTER IX
Criminal Suits

It is interesting to note that in ancient India no one had to pay any court-fee in connection with criminal suits unlike modern India. The person found guilty had to pay to the king the fine prescribed in the smṛtis or decided by the Court.[1] Kauṭilya deals with criminal suits in the *AŚ.* IV, entitled 'Kaṇṭaka-śodhana' for the suppression of criminals who are thorns of the society. These criminals include thieves, robbers, murderers etc. as well as artisans, craftsmen, traders and others who cheat. Kauṭilya's laws may be comparable with the Indian Penal Code of modern times. He deals with some offences in the Dharmasthīya section and with others in the Kaṇṭaka-śodhana one. Probably those cases which are lodged in the court and fought out by the parties themselves were treated in the Dharmasthīya section, though some of them, verbal and physical injuries, gambling and betting were nothing but criminal offences. The offences of the Kaṇṭaka-śodhana were such as not to be excused as mere private matters but they were taken up by the king or his officers for trial in the court because of their gravity which the state could not neglect for the maintenance of law and order. Kane's comment[2] deserves mention: "Kauṭilya represents a much earlier stage of judicial administration than Nārada or Bṛhaspati", because in *AŚ.* IV. 1. Kauṭilya says that if the death of a patient is due to carelessness in the treatment, the physician shall be punished with the middlemost amercement and the growth of a disease due to indifference of a physician shall be regarded as assault (daṇḍa-pāruṣyam) and it should be noted that 'daṇḍapāruṣyam' has been treated by him in the Dharmasthīya section. Only Manu[3] discusses such criminal offences which he enjoins that the king should regulate. ("Kaṇṭakānāṃ ca śodhanāt"). Yāj. gives many of these rules under steya, sāhasa or saṃgrahaṇa. Nārada or Bṛhaspati mentions under Prakīrṇaka all offences which the king took up for trial in the interest of the entire state. The *Agni Purāṇa* declares such suits as bereft of shelter. ("Prakirṇakaḥ punarjñeyo vyavahāro nṛpāśrayaḥ"). But as the king is expected to help those who require it, it implies that the king should initiate such cases. Thus the *Agni Purāṇa* favours the institution of law suits by private parties but it does not exclude the possibility of the king's initiative at least in cases of violation of the king's orders. Cases concerned with violation of royal orders are covered by the term 'nirāśraya' (without shelter) and not by the term 'nṛpāśraya' (resting on the king) as in *Nārada-Smṛti.* According to *Agni Purāṇa,* cases of theft, violence etc. are criminal acts which require immediate judicial probing ("vichārayet sadya eva") just like cases of the session courts of the modern times.[4]

A scholar known as Nibandhanakāra[5] makes a nice-distinction between civil and criminal cases: "Ṛṇādānādi-dāya-vibhāgāntānāṃ deya-nivandhanatvaṃ sāhasādi-pañcakasya daṇḍa-nivandhanatvamiti dvi-r-utthānatā ityarthah".—i.e., in civil cases the claim stands for something to be given by one party to the other, whereas in criminal cases the relief claimed for is in the shape of punishment. Bṛhaspati[6] says that lawsuits are of two kinds, either originating in wealth or in injuries. (Dvipado vyavahāraḥ syāt dhana-hiṃsāsamudbhavaḥ). Lawsuits, originating in injuries are again of four types, vāk-pāruṣya (defamation and abuse), daṇḍāpāruṣya (assault), sāhasa (murder and robbery) and saṃgrahaṇa (adultery). Yāj.[7] speaks of civil suits as 'artha-vivādeṣu' thus differentiating them from criminal ones. Kātyāyana[8] also follows Bṛhaspati. The *Sm. Ch.*[9] and *Parā. Mā.*[10] show the opinion of Pitāmaha that the king should take the initiative in some criminal cases like 'aparādhas', 'padas' and 'chalas' ("Chalāni cāparādhāṃśca padāni nṛpatestathā/svayam-etāni gṛhṇiyān-nṛpa-s-tvāvedakair-vinā //"). Nārada,[11] mentions the 'aparadha'-s as the following "Ājñalaṅghana-kartāraḥ stri-vadho varṇa-saṃkaraḥ/para-strīgamanaṃ cauryaṃ garbhaśchaiva patiṃ vinā//vāk-pāruṣyaṃ avācyaṃ yad-daṇḍa-pāruṣyameva ca/garbhasya pātanaṃ caivetyaparādhā daśaiva tu//" i.e.; disobedience of the king's order, murder of a woman, confusion of varṇas, adultery, theft, pregnancy by one other than the husband, abuse and defamation, obscenity, assault and abortion. The king could investigate these cases of aparādha-s either of his own accord or being reported by others. Kātyāyaṇa[12] says that he who with the sole intention of earning money and without being prompted by the king informs the king first of the action (of the wrong-doer), condemned by the sacred texts is called a Stobhaka and he, who being appointed by the king to find out the wrongs of others and learning them, reports to the king, is called a Sūcaka. All these cases of wrongs were met with a fine as suggested by the expressions like "sa-daśāparādhaḥ" in Valabhi grant of Dhruvasena III, 653-54 A.D.[13] and in the Gupta inscription.[14] The Monghyr C.P. inscription[15] of Devapāladeva mentions the 'daśāparādhika' (a high official in charge of detection of 10 crimes, trial of criminals and collection of fines from them, evidently a member of the revenue department). The ten crimes are theft, murder, adultery, using harsh words, falsehood, defamation, talking non-sense, avarice, bad thought and attachment for untruth. Some think that the term 'sa-daśāparādha' means that the donee enjoyed the right of exemption from guilt, caused by some offences he had done or he was given the power of deciding the cases of 'aparādha'-s, committed by evil-doers and enjoyed the fines imposed upon them.[16] But Kane's suggestion seems to be preferable. It is less likely that the king granted any donee crimes like the aforesaid 'aparādha'-s or that the king authorised any private person to decide such grave crimes specially when even a guild was not allowed to deal with acts of robbery. Hence it is safer to assume that the king allowed the donee to enjoy the fine, levied by himself as a part of the gift, when realised from the criminals of the villages, already donated by the king.

Next to these 'aparādha'-s we hear of 22 pada-s from Pitāmaha who states : "Utkartī sasyaghātī chāpyagnidaśca tathavia ca / vidhvaṃsakaḥ kumāryāśca nidhānasyopagopakaḥ // setu-kaṇṭaka-bhettāca-kṣetra-sañcāraka-s-tathā /

ārāma-chedakaiścaiva garadaśca tathaiva ca // rājño droha-prakartā ca tan-mudrā-bhedakas-tathā / tan-mantrasya prabhethā ca vaddhasyaiva ca mocakaḥ // bhoga-daṇḍau ca gṛhṇāti dānam-utsekam-eva ca / paṭāghoṣaṇāchhādī dravyam-asvāmikaṃ ca yat // rājāvalīḍhaṃ dravyaṃ yad-yacchaivāṅga-vināśanam / dvāviśṁśatim / padānyāhu-r-nṛpajñeyāni paṇḍitāḥ//[17]—these are piercing upon the body of an animal (with a sharp weapon), destruction of growing crops, incendiarism, rape of a maiden, concealment of a treasure-house, making a breach in an embankment or thorny hedge, grazing cattle in another's field, ruining a public garden, poisoning, high treason, unauthorised breaking of a royal seal, divulging the secret policy of the king, releasing a prisoner from a jail, approbation of the taxes or fines levied by the king, appropriating gifts made by the king or the Utseka (Utsarga) gift to the public one who prevents the announcement of royal order from being heard by beat of drums, to receive things from one who is not the real owner, enjoying things of the king (without his permission) and destruction of the limbs of the state.

Pitāmaha speaks of 50 chalas : "pathi-bhangī", breaking the road, 'Karākṣepī'—raising the hand with threatening attitude, 'prākāroparilaṅghaka'—leaping over the wall of the fort without permission or reason, 'nipānasya vinaśī ca'—destroyer of a cistern, 'tathā cāyatanasya ca'—destroyer of a temple, 'parikhā-pūrakaścaiva'—the filler of a ditch (dug round a fort for protection), 'rāja-chhirda-prakāśakaḥ"—one who divulges the weak points of the king, "antaḥpuram vāsagṛhaṃ bhāṇḍāgāraṃ māhanasam praviśtāniyukto"— unauthorised entrance into the harem of royal palace or the treasury or the royai kitchen, "Yo bhojanam ca nirīkṣate"—one who peeps into the meals of the king, "Viṇmūtra-śleṣṃa-vātānāṃ kṣeptu-kāmo ṇrpāgrataḥ"—voiding ordure or passing urine or throwing coughs or passing wind in the presence of the king, "paryañkāsana-vandhī chāpyagra-sthāna-nirodhakaḥ"—to sit before the king on the bed-seats, to occupy the foremost place before the king, "rājñotirikta-vesa-ś-ca vidhṛtaḥ praviśet tu yaḥ"—one who puts on a more gorgeous dress than the king's or who enters before the king, being supported by another, "yaśchāpad-dvāreṇa viśed-velāyāṃ tathaiva ca"—one who comes in being in company with a wrong-doer or in improper time, "śayyāsane pādukayoḥ śayanāsana-rohanam"—to lie on the bed or seat of the king or to put on his shoes, "rājanyāsanna-śayane ya-s-tiṣṭhati samīpataḥ"—to go near the king (without permission) when the latter takes rest on his bed, "rājño vidviṣṭa-sevī chāpyadatta-vihitāsanaḥ"—to serve the enemies of the king and occupy a seat that is not offered, "vastrābharaṇayoś-caiva suvarṇa-paridhāyakaḥ"—to put on clothes or ornaments, set with gold, "Svayaṃgrāheṇa tāmbulaṃ gṛhītvā bhakṣayet tu yah"—to take betel (from the king's betel box) and chew it, "aniyukta-prabhāṣī ca nṛpākrośaka eva ca"—to speak without being asked by the king and to go against the king, "eka-vāśa-s-tathābhyakto mukta-keśo'vagunṭhitaḥ"—to wear only one garment, to appear before the king with oil and with hair thrown open and covering his face, "vicitritāṅgaḥ sragvī ca paridhāna-vidhūnakaḥ"—to get one's limbs painted with figures, to wear a garland and to shake one's garments, "śiraḥ praccādanaścaiva chhidrānveṣaṇa-tatparaḥ"—to cover the head and to be seriously searching for the loopholes of the king, "āsaṅgī mukta-keśaśca yaśca karṇākṣikarṣakaḥ"—to be thick with bad persons, to get hairs dishavelled and to point out the ears and eye, "dantollekhanakaścaiva karṇa-nāsa-viśodhakaḥ"—to pick the teeth, to cleanse the ear or nose, "chhālanyetāni pañcāsad-bhavanti nṛpa-sannidhau"—these are fifty 'chala'-offences committed in the presence of the king.

MEASURES AGAINST CALAMITIES

It is interesting to note that Kauṭilya prescribes remedial measures of the state against eight great calamities, which are like thieves and robbers, sources of untold troubles to the people. He wants that the state should keep vigilant watch over these different thorns of the society like fire, flood, disease, famine, rats, wild animals, serpents and evil spirits. People must be saved from fire by the collection of ten fire-fighting implements ("daśa-mulīsaṃgraheṇa"). Some scholars read 'daśakūlī' to mean that groups of ten families are responsible for fire in their area. Kauṭilya prescribes a fine of 12 paṇas for those who do not go to the rescue of the man being carried away by the flood. During famine the king should help the people with food and other materials as measures of relief[18] and the actual practice of this advice is evidenced by the Mahāsthan inscription. Fines of 12 paṇas are also levied on those who catch or kill cats and ichneumons, used as remedial measures against rats. The king is advised even to impose a tax on rats. Similarly a fine of 12 paṇas is also imposed on one who does not go forth to help a man in danger from wild animals. These cases of indifference to perform civic duties were regarded as crimes, to be regulated by penal laws and brought under trial before the criminal courts of the day. Professor N.C. Bandyopadhyaya speaks of the "New Tribunals" which, like the English High Commission Court or the Court of Star Chamber of the 16th-17th century A.D. took cognizance of offences created by regal ordinances" and performed multifarious duties vested in them by the royal prerogative".[19] These courts took steps to ameliorate the condition of the people in times of perils owing to calamities, noted above.

The emergency measures are prescribed in the *Artha-śāstra* for the protection of the people from these calamities and they were entrusted to officers of criminal courts. It is curious to note that Kauṭilya believed in demons and in rites and prayers to undo their evils. Though demons or supernatural agents are no longer believed, measures against other calamities are still adopted in the modern world. The Milindapañho[20] confirms the preventive measures, taken against fire. People living on the river-side had to keep boats and rafts and they were bound to help men in danger of flood. In times of epidemic diseases the doctors were employed by the state.

Kauṭilya insists on the policy of thinning the rich by exacting excessive revenue (karṣaṇam) or causing them to vomit their accumulated wealth (vamanam). These two measures were in keeping with the tune of the Communist States of the modern world. Hoarding of foodstuffs was regarded as a national crime and that is why the rich were made to surrender them to the interests of the people. Kauṭilya enjoins upon the king the duty of protecting the people like a father ("Sarvatra co'pahatān pitevānugṛhṇīyāt") and to keep apart a stock of half the grain-collections in the royal granaries for bad days. (tato'rdhaṃ rakṣet āpadarthaṃ janapadānām). Kāmandaka[21] also holds that the king must take steps to counteract natural calamities like pestilences, famine, disease etc. and try to promote the prosperity of the people.

REFERENCES

1. Cf. H.D.S., III, p. 294.
2. H.D.S., III, p. 258
3. IX. 253-93.
4. *Agni Purāṇa,* 253, 41-42.
5. As q. in the *Sarasvatī-vilāsa,* p. 51.
6. q. in *Sm. Ch.*, II, p. 9 and *Parā. Mā.*, III, pp. 20-21.
7. II. 2.3
8. (30), q. in *Sm.Ch.*, II, p. 13.
9. II, pp. 27-28.
10. III, pp. 42-45.
11. q. in *Sm. Ch.*, II, p. 28.
12. q. in *Sm. Ch.*, III, p. 28 and *Parā Mā.*, III, p. 45.
13. *E.I.*, I, p. 85 and p. 88.
14. No. 39, p. 179 of 766-67 A.D.
15. *E.I.*, XVII, p. 310 & 321.
16. Cf. *JBORS,* 1916, p. 53 n.
17. *Sm. Ch.*, II, p. 28 and *Parā Mā,* III, p. 45 and *Sarasvatī-Vilāsa,* p. 73.
18. IV. 3.17-20.
19. "Kauṭilya", 1927, p. 226.
20. II. 2-3-15.
21. IV, 54-56.

CHAPTER X

The Right of Private Defence

Now the first question is—who is an ātatāyin ? Literally 'one who has his bow strung and is ready to shoot' is an ātatāyin. Arjuna uses this term to denote the armed foes he has to fight.[1] Strictly constructed, the ātatāyin is he who, being armed is ready to attack and kill. Now this term is used generally in the sense of a "manifest assassin". But the assault or attack with the intention of causing death or serious hurt may be open ('prakāśa) or covert ('pracchanna' or 'aprakāśa'). In ancient India people believed in the power of witchcraft or incantations or curse and so when anyone commenced the rite of witchcraft or raised the arm to sprinkle water along with the invocation of a curse, he was treated as an ātātāyin.

According to Vaśiṣṭha[2] an ātatāyin is a desperate man who is an incendiary, a poisoner, one who carries a sword in his hand, a robber, or an abductor of another's wife or the forcible trespasser into one's field. ("Agnido garadaścaiva śastrapāṇi-r-dhanāpahaḥ/kṣetra-dāra-haraścaiva ṣaḍete hyātatāyinaḥ//"). Viṣṇu[3] mentions seven kinds instead of six: "those who try to kill, with an uplifted sword or with fire or with poison, those who raise their arms for implementing a curse they utter, those who utter an incantation of the Atharva Veda to cause another's death, those who carry false news to the king or poison his ears against others, those who violate others' wives and those who try to undo the religious merit of others by destroying their public works like tanks etc. or who destroy the reputation, wealth or property of others". ("Udyatāsiviṣāgniṃ ca śāpodyatakaraṃ tathā/atharveṇa hantāraṃ piśunaṃ caiva rājaṣu // bhāryātikramiṇaṃ caiva viḍyāt saptātatāyinaḥ/ yaśo-vitta-harān-anyān-āhur-dharmārtha-hārakān//"). The *Matsyapurāṇa*[4] adds the seducer of the queen to the list. The *Smrti-Candrikā*[5] declares that the list is not exhaustive and can be added to ("ṣaḍ-grahaṇaṃ na punaḥ parisaṅkhyārthaṃ, vidhāntareṇa ātatāyināṃ loke vidyamānatvāt").

The common characteristic of all such offences is that the ātatāyin tries to kill under the influence of anger (manyuḥ) and he causes the generation of similar anger in the intended victim, as signified by the expression "manyu-s-taṃ maṇyum-ṛcchati".[6] In some cases prompt self-defence alone can prevent the accomplishment of the crime that is attempted and sometimes the resistance may end in the death of the assailant. Of course, the death of the assailant should be avoided as far as possible; and in unavoidable cases such death is treated as blameless. Now the question may arise whether the ātatāyin who accomplishes his object should be pursued and killed instead of being handed over to justice or whether the assailant should be .pursued and killed, if he flees away, being resisted and fails to commit the crime. Medhātithi thinks that in both cases the assailant may be killed. ("āyāntam-iti vacanāt āttaśastro hantum-abhidhāvan dārān vā jihīrṣan hantavyaḥ kṛte tu doṣe kimanyat karisyatīti upekṣā vruvate tadayuktaṃ yataḥ prakāśam aprakāśam vā iti vakṣyati samānau hyetau kariṣyan kṛtavāṃ-śca", on Manu, 8.350). Aparārka, however, attaches importance to the condition of the mind of the defender and opines that the ātatāyin can be killed only when he attempts to commit the crime but not subsequently. ("Atra ca vartamānāgnidānādi-vyāpāra eva ātatāyina ucyante. Tad-vyāpāra-nivāraṇaṃ ca yatra vadham antareṇa na saṃbhavati tatraiva tad-vadhānujñā). He adds that if the crime can be prevented by the application of a blow, by sticks or weapons, to kill the desperado is to blame.

Gālava enjoins that he who kills an ātatāyin who happens to be also a learned brahmin (bhrūṇa) is not guilty of killing a bhrūṇa but if he fails to kill him, he will be a bhrūṇa-slayer. ("Udyamya śastram-āyāntaṃ bhrūṇam-apyātatāyinaṃ/nihatya bhrūṇahā na syāt ahatvā bhrūṇahā bhavet//"). Devala also repeats this rule in the same words. The reason behind this dictum is that the society is to be saved from the hands of dangerous persons like ātatāyin-s. That is why like modern criminal law the ancient jurists sanctioned the right of private defence. But there are some conflicting rules in ancient Indian scriptures, which should be carefully assessed in the light of the present issue. The Veda teaches us—"na hiṃsyāt sarvā bhūtāni", i.e., one should not hurt any living being. But what should be the attitude to the ātatāyin ? The rules of Gālava and Devala show that everyone, irrespective of caste or sex is entitled to resist the desperado and kill him, if absolutely necessary. But Bodhāyana, as quoted in *Smṛti Chandrikā*[7] states that a brahmin should not use a weapon even for the protection of his wife. ("Bhāryārthamapi brāhmaṇa āyudhaṃ nādadīta"). Āpastamba also enjoins that a brahmin must not hold a weapon even for testing it. ("Parīkṣārtham-api brāhmaṇa āyudhaṃ nādadīta"). Medhātithi,[8] however, opines that these prohibitive rules are meant for raising weapons but not for carrying them. On Manu sanctioning that a brahmacārin should carry a bamboo stick ("vaiṇavīṃ-dhārayet-yaṣṭhiṃ"), Medhātithi comments that the student should not use it for other purposes than self-defence. The Veda prohibits suicide and Devala[9] repeats it. ("Ātmatyāgaḥ paratyāgāt pāpīyān pātakād-api/pātake niṣkṛtiḥ proktā katham-ātmaghna-niṣkṛtiḥ//"). The Dharmaśāstras recognise the right of private defence of one's life and property, though the king is ordained to protect the people from all dangers, internal and external.

Gautama[10] teaches relaxation of all rules for the occupation of all members of the society in cases of emergency. ("Tadapyeke prāṇa-saṃśaye"). Vyāsa confirms this principle and enjoins that one must save one's life by all means available in hours of crisis. ("Dharmārtha-kāma-mokṣānāṃ-prāṇāḥ saṃsthitihetavaḥ / tān nighnatā kim na hataṃ rakṣatā kiṃ narakṣitam//"). Gautama[11] adds that even a brahmin should use arms when his life is in danger ("prāṇa-saṃśaye brāhmaṇo'pi śastram-ādadīta"). Manu[12] also is already referred to as teaching us that the twice-born should take up arms when they are hindered in the fulfilment of their duties and destruction threatens the twice-born castes in evil times. Medhātithi holds the same view when robbers and so forth do not allow the twice-born to offer sacrifices or to fulfil other sacred duties. Bodhāyana[13] allows the brahmins and Vaiśyas to use arms in such cases. ("Gavārthe brāhmaṇārthe vā varṇānāṃ vāpi saṃkare/gṛhṇīyātāṃ vipra-viśau śastraṃ dharma-vyepekṣayā//").

Although the jurists differ as to whether the brāhmaṇa assailant (ātatāyin) should be killed, there is no difference of opinion as to the point that an assailant of any other caste must be repelled with force ending even in death. Madanaratna explains the text of Manu, VIII. 348 as follows: "Dharmastaṭākādirūpo yatra deśe kāle vā bhedana-chedanādi-noparudhyate tatra ..... tathā dakṣiṇānāṃ saṃgare go-grahaṇa-nimittake yuddhe strī-viprābhyupapattau durvala-hiṃsā-nivāraṇe dharmād-dheto-r-ghnan na duṣyati". Vijñāneśvara on Yāj., II. 286 says—"yadā tu rājño nivedanena kāla-vilambanena kāryātipātāśaṃkā tadā svayam-eva jārādīn hanyāt, "śastram dvijātibhi-r-grāhyam dharmo yatra uparudhyate iti"—Manu's rule, VIII. 348 holds good only when there is little time to report to the king or when delay in opposing violence by force means loss or ruin. Manu[14] teaches that one should not injure the teacher who had initiated him, or explained the Veda, the father, mother or guru or cows or brāhmaṇas or ascetics. But elsewhere (VIII. 350) he says that even a guru or a boy or an aged man or a learned brāhmaṇa should be killed outright without any hesitation, if he proves to be an assailant (ātatāyin). The term 'Vā' in Manu, VIII. 350, shows that a guru and others of the list should not be killed. The *Arthaśāstra* also prescribes that even a vedantist assailant should be repelled with force and if killed, one is not liable to be a brahmin-slayer. ("Ātatāyinam-āyāntam-api Vedantagaṃ raṇe/jighāṃsantaṃ jighaṃsīyān na tena Brahmahā bhavet//"). The term "api" here also affirms the sense of "vā", noted above. Manu makes it more clear when he assures that "by killing an assassin the slayer incurs no sin, whether he does it publicly or privately; in that case fury recoils upon fury". ("Nātatāyivadhe doṣo hantu-r-bhavati kaścana/prakāśaṃ vā' prakāśaṃ va manyu-s-taṃ manyum-ṛcchati//"). Thus some think that the ancient Indian jurists were not wanting in the concept of one's right of private defence, even in those cases where as a matter of general principle injury was prohibited.

Yāj. has no text dealing directly with this issue but his commentators bring up this question indirectly. According to Viśvarūpa (on Yāj. 3.222), no moral turpitude will attach if the assailant or foe, even if he be a brahmin, is killed and there will be no criminal liability in either case. Viśvarūpa takes into consideration the factor of agency in case of a murder and opines that if one is hired to murder another person, the turpitude adheres to the hirer and not to the actual assassin. ("Ya-s-tu dhanakrītaḥ para-prayukto hanyāt tasya svāmigāmivāt brahma-hatyā-janya-phala-sambhavo nāstyeva"). But Vijñāneśvara thinks that Manu's text—'nātatāyivadhe doṣo hantu-r-bhavati kaścana' should be explained as excluding the cases of brahmins and cows, as Sumantu asserts 'nātatāyivadhe doṣo 'nyatra go-brāhmana-vadhāt". Kātyāyana,[15] however, says that he who kills wicked men who are about to kill another, is not to blame but when they cease from such attempt, they should be arrested but not to be killed. ("Udyatānāṃ tu pāpānāṃ hantu-r-doṣo na vidyate / nivṛtta-s-tu yad-ārambhād grahaṇaṃ na vadhaḥ smṛtḥ//".—Kātyā. 800, q. by *Sm. Ch*., II, p. 315). Aparārka[16] says that an ātatāyin is he who is about to set fire or kill, who is engaged in the act of setting fire or killing or the like, and he should be killed only when there is no other alternative of preventing him from doing such misdeeds but when he can be prevented by being wounded with a stick and arms etc., it would be an offence to kill him. ("Atra ca vartamagnidānādi-vyāpāra evātatāyina ucyante. Tadvyāpāra-nivāraṇaṃ ca yatra vadham-antareṇa na saṃbhavati tatraiva tad-vadhānujñā. Yatra tu daṇḍa-śastrādi-prahāra-matreṇaiva śakyo nivārayituṃ tatra tu tad-vadho doṣa-nimittam-eva. Ataeva uktaṃ Bṛhaspatinā ākruṣṭastu samākrośaṃ-s-tāḍitaḥ prati-tāḍayan etc.).[17]

But Medhātithi on Manu, VIII.348 says that the ātatāyin should be killed not only when he is in the act of doing misdeed but also after he has done so. ("Āyāntam-iti-vacanād-āttaśastro hantum-abhidhāvan dārān vā jihīrṣan hantavyaḥ kṛte tu doṣe kim-anyat kariṣyati ityupekṣā iti vruvate tadayuktam yataḥ prakāśam-aprakāśaṃ ceti vakṣyā. Samānau hyetau kariṣyan kṛtavārn-ś-ca sṛṣṭa (dṛṣṭa)-ś-cediti. Tasmād-āyāntam-ityanuvādaḥ kartum-āgataṃ kṛtvā vāgatam-iti. Ātatāyitvāccāsau hanyate na ca kṛtavacana ātatāyitvam-upaiti). Vijñān. on Yāj., II, 21 remarks that one has a right to oppose and kill another in self-defence and in defence of women and others and that even if an ātatāyi of the brāhmaṇa caste is killed, while being opposed, there is no punishment at the hands of the king and the expiation for killing such brahmin is a light one. ("Ata-ś-ca brāhmaṇādaya ātatāyinaś-ca ātmādi-trāṇārthaṃ hiṃsānabhi-sandhinā nivāryamānāḥ pramādād-yadi vipadyeraṃstatra laghu-prāyaścittaṃ rāja-daṇḍā-bhāvaśceti niścayaḥ"). Kātyāyana[18] also says that one is entitled to kill with impunity animals having claws, horns or fangs or horses or elephants by which one is attacked. Aparārka seems to be more reasonable when he remarks that if one gives food (bhakta-dāyakaḥ) to a criminal conspiring somebody's murder, then the giver of food is as guilty as the actual murderer but not otherwise. It may be noted that both Manu[19] and Yāj.[20] refer to giving food, shelter and fire to thieves as themselves equal to thieves and punishable as such, thus roughly corresponding to the modern law on harbouring offenders.[21] But Aparārka holds that if one is charged with 'harbouring' simply for giving food or necessaries to a person who manifestly needs them, then, by analogy, a father is culpable for giving birth to his son who turns out a criminal. Thus he raises the point of conflict between ethics and law, which should be decided after proper enquiry as to how far the person who is helped deserves help or not. Nīlakaṇṭha, however, argues that the rules of Manu[22] refer only to one who actually attacks and should not apply to a possible killer who is asleep. ("ato jighāṃsata eva viprasya maraṇam, na suptādeḥ") and that the terms 'vā in Manu and 'api' in Kātyāyana show that the killing of brahmins in such circumstances is not acceptable. Vijñāneśvara, while commenting on Yāj. (II. 21) accepts this principle of Nīlakaṇṭha. The *Smṛti-Candrikā* (vyav.) discusses the question of ātatāyin-s and concludes that (i) all ātatāyins not excluding brahmins may be killed when they attempt assassination, (ii) with the exception of brahmins constructive ātatāyins like those who rob one of his field or outrage another's wife etc. may also be killed and the brāhmaṇa is not to be killed for the constructive offence of ātatāyin, as explained by Bhṛgu and Vaśiṣṭha (pp. 725ff). Amarasinha defines 'ātatāyin' as one who is about to murder ("ātatāyi vadhodyataḥ"), and this includes the cases of robbing others' fields and wives. Nīlakaṇṭha in his *Vyavahāra-mayūkha* follows the above principles of *Smṛti Candrikā* and concludes that "in the Kaliyuga a Brāhmaṇa ātatāyin is not to be killed even in self-defence but in other ages this was allowed".[23]

The modern law of India also permits the exercise of this right of private defence. "Nothing is an offence which is done in the exercise of the right of private defence".[24] The Law Commissioners have, however, specified the various extents to which people may exercise this right. Here the following features of this law may be pointed out: (i) Every person has a right, subject to certain restrictions, to defend his own body and the body of any other person, against any offence affecting the human body or the property, either of himself or of any other person, against any act which is an offence of the categories like theft, robbery, mischief or criminal trespass or which is an attempt to commit such offences. Self-help is the first rule of criminal law. "The right of private defence", wrote Bentham, "is absolutely necessary". It is more than a right, it is a duty which flows from human sympathy, (ii) The I.P.C. extends this right so that even a stranger can defend the person or property of another, (iii) This right extends to the voluntary causing of death or of any other harm to the assailant in certain grave offences; and (iv) This right has been restricted in a few cases. Thus there is no such right against public servants acting on their official duties; or in cases where there is "time to have recourse to the protection of the public authorities". Moreover, "nothing is an offence which is done by a Judge when acting judicially in the exercise of the power, given to him by law". About ancient Indian jurists we may say that they stood for wide safeguards against the abuse of even the duty of self-defence and demanded as a matter of virtue abstention from killing a disarmed desperado. They condemned in public interests the application of more force, even in self-defence than is absolutely necessary for safety of person or property.

REFERENCES

1. *Gītā*, 1.36.
2. III. 16.
3. V. 191-192.
4. Cited in *Daṇḍaviveka*, p. 234.
5. Vyava., p. 730, ed. Mysore.
6. Manu, 8.351.
7. *Vyav Kā.*, p. 725.
8. On Manu, 8.348.
9. Cited in *Sm. Ch.*, p. 729.
10. 1.7.23.
11. *Ibid.*, 25.
12. VIII. 348.
13. II. 2.80.
14. IV. 162.
15. Kātyā, 800, q. by *Sm. Ch.*, II, p. 315.
16. p. 1043, on Yāj. III. 227.
17. See I.P.C., Sec. 99-105.
18. 805, q. by *Sm. Ch.*, II, p. 316.
19. IX. 278.
20. II. 276.
21. Cf. I.P.C. Sec. 212.
22. VIII. 350-351.
23. Cf. Kane's notes to his edition of *Vyava. Mayūkha*, 1926, pp. 417-422.
24. I.P.C., Sec, 96.

CHAPTER XI

The Law of Evidence

Ancient Indian sources like Pāṇini, Gautama, Manu, Viṣṇu and Nārada stress on the theory that oral evidence must be direct, as opposed to mere hearsay. Medhātithi also accepts it as a matter of principle but what he means to say is that the correct mode of perception of the witness should be relied upon, no matter whether the report is based on direct perception or on inference or on any other reliable sources; and this view is confirmed by later jurists like Śukra or Govindasvāmin. Modern Law of India also insists on avoidance of hearsay evidence as far as possible. But Nārada[1] admits a second-hand statement as a matter of proof when the appointed witness dies or goes abroad and opens the matter to other men.

It is worthnoting that Kauṭilya[2] admits that in cases of the absence of direct evidence, the circumstantial evidences should be accepted as for example, the nature of hurt and other circumstances connected with the quarrel in question. This sort of evidence is unavoidable in criminal cases like sudden and suspicious death, at least for detecting the truth,[3] and specially in cases of adultery.[4] Yāj. also follows Kauṭilya on this point. This circumstantial evidence has been taken into account, besides the direct one, since the days of Āpas. at least ("Liṅga" in Āpas. II. 11.29.6). Bṛhaspati's "upadhā" ("asākṣike chirakṛte pṛcched-uttara-sākṣiṇaḥ/śapathai-r-vānuyuñjīta upadhām vā prayojayet//") is also interpreted as 'Yukti' by Vācaspati in *Vyavahāra Cintāmaṇi*. Śaṅkha-Likhita (q. in *Sm. Ch.*, p. 221) also speaks of the possession of stolen goods as proof of theft. ("Loptra-hasta-ś-cauraḥ"). It would be noted that our ancient jurists were not blind to the risk of accepting the mere circumstantial evidence as a means of proof and so Kauṭilya, Nārada and Bṛhaspati advise the need of great caution in such cases and mention as an illustration the case of Māṇḍavya, related in the *Mbh.*[5] Bṛhaspati reminds us of the fact that decision should not be passed merely by following the letter of law because if the circumstances are left out of consideration, violence of justice will be the result.[6] ("kevalaṃ śāstram āśritya na kartavyo vinirṇayaḥ/yukti-hina-vicāre tu dharma-hāniḥ prājayate//"). That is why Kauṭ.[7] speaks of the need of the study of many circumstances under which the crime is committed. Nārada also follows Kauṭilya (*SBE*, 33, p. 224). Dr. A. Thakur[8] says rightly that "the circumstantial evidence was not only criminating but exculpatory too", as evidenced by Kaut. (AŚ, IV. 8).

The next question is: the number of witnesses. Most of the ancient Indian jurists opine in favour of more than one. ("Vahavaḥ syuḥ" in Gaut., XIII. 2). Manu, Yāj., Nār. and Bṛh. think of at least three and at most nine. Almost all agree in insufficiency of a single witness to prove or disapprove a fact.[9] The High Court rejected a single witness.[10] But Yāj.[11] and Viṣṇu[12] allow the evidence of a single person if he is approved by both the parties (ubhayānumata), virtuous and competent. Vijñā. on Yāj. (II. 72) and Jīmūtavāhana[13] insist on the combination of all these factors in cases of a single witness. But the Vivādārṇava-setu[14] and Vyavahārāloka differ from them and opine that such a combination is hard to get and so the consent of both the parties will be sufficient to make the evidence valid.

Nārada[15] says : "Ubhayānumato yaḥ syāt dvayo-r-vivada mānayoḥ/a-sākṣiko 'pi sākṣitve praṣṭavyaḥ syāt sa saṃsadi//". Thus he permits the evidence of a single witness even without the combination of other qualities. The Vyavahārāloka divides the passage of Yāj., II. 72 into two parts 'ubhayānumataḥ' or "dharmavid" forming as the necessary condition of the character of the witness. The rules of Kauṭilya and Kātyāyana prove that the question of the number and quality of witness was counted only in cases of pre-appointed but not casual evidences. Jurists differ as to whether a single witness should be sanctioned in a case of 'sāhasa' (robbery, adultery etc.). While Nārada[16] rejects the evidence of a single witness because it is very risky to rely on one man whose evidence may end in serious punishment. Vyāsa[17] accepts such evidence, if available, from a reliable hand of good character or virtue. It is interesting to note that according to Bṛhaspati[18] and Vyavahārāmātṛkā[19], the king, the chief judge, each of the assessors, the court-scribe, the court-accountant, one who knows the secret of the parties and the messenger can be each a single witness.

Thus the above survey shows how the ancient jurists were very careful in the matter of judgment, they did not always reject a single witness, though they knew how it was difficult to rely on one man, nor did they forget to insist on a plurality of witnesses at least for more safety, though they were aware of the practical difficulty in the fulfilment of this condition in all cases, specially in criminal suits. It deserves mention that the Mohamedan Law insists on the evidence of at least four males to prove the adultery of a woman and the Law of Moses also requires at least two witnesses.[20] The modern law of evidence also exacts many witnesses.

Now about the competency of witnesses. Ancient Indian jurists selected such persons alone who were expected to be trustworthy witnesses and insisted on those qualities which could help in ascertaining the truth in respect of the charge made, like freedom from partiality or malice, greed etc. It is interesting to note here that the caste or class of the witness was an important factor to be considered. Manu says that under normal conditions "woman should give evidence for women and for twice-born men of the same kind (sadṛśāḥ), virtuous śudras for śudras and the men of the lowest castes for the lowest.[21] Vaśiṣṭha[22] follows Manu. Medhātithi says that "women should give evidence for women only in cases between women or in matters concerning the female sex, which they alone may be supposed to know". A woman was not allowed to be a witness in ancient Roman Law.[23] The term 'sadṛśa' of Manu means, according to Kullūka, of the same caste, (sajātīya) but according to Medhātithi, 'of the same caste, occupation, learning, character etc'. Yāj.[24] insists on the same caste or class of the witnesses. [Yathāvarṇa and Yathājāti]. Vijñān. explains 'Yathājāti' in reference to various sub-classes and 'Yathāvarṇa' to four main castes. Devanabhaṭṭa[25] explains this 'yathājāti' in the sense of 'Śreṇī', 'varga' etc. ("jātigrahaṇaṃ śreṇyāde-r-apyupalakṣaṇārthaṃ", *Sm. Ch.*, p. 176). But Vaśiṣṭha (XVI), Yāj. (II. 69) and Nār. (IV. 154) take a more liberal view: "Sarve sarveṣu vā smṛtāḥ" and "Sākṣiṇaḥ sarva eva vā" (Vaś). Vijñān.[26] thinks of this rule of relaxation only when the witnesses of the same caste or rank are not available. (*Mitā,* on Yāj., II. 69). The above survey shows that the rule of relaxation was applicable at least in criminal cases.

It may be pointed out that the various rules of exclusion regarding witnesses were mainly artificial and could hardly be applied in actual practice, at least in criminal cases, as evidenced by Manu (VIII. 72), Viṣṇu (8.7), Nār. (4. pp. 188-189) and Vivādārṇava-setu, p. 120, ("Nihṇavenaiva kriyamānatvād-daivādeva paraṃ sākṣiṇo bhavantīti kṛtvā na sākṣiṇām parīkṣa ityuktam"). Uśaṇā allows in criminal cases even a blind, a deaf, a slave, a leper, a woman, an infant or an aged man, if of course, he is not partial.[27] Medhātithi also favours the examination of any witness in cases of emergency, if he is reliable (on Manu, 8.72). It is interesting to note the spirit of modern legislation of India which allows all to make a statement as a witness, leaving its truth to be ascertained by the court.

Another problem which requires scrutiny is whether any of the parties to the suit is entitled to give evidence. The ancient legal texts are silent on this issue, though as a matter of principle it has been pointed out that witnesses should not be of interested persons. Hence as a natural corollary we may assume that the parties were debarred from the privilege of giving any evidence. Viṣṇu[28] speaks of the privileges of the prosecutor which he is entitled to get after the conviction of the accused like the expenses of cure in cases of assault and the restoration of the property stolen in cases of theft. Kauṭilya, however, prescribes the process of interrogations to which the person accused of theft was subjected. The *Mṛccha.* in its trial scene[29] shows how Cārudatta, accused of murdering Vasantasenā was asked some questions regarding the case. Ancient jurists recognised the value of this practice. But one thing should be remembered that the court assumes the guilt of the accused before proof by this practice which renders proper justice sometimes impossible.

The ancient jurists agree on the point that the witnesses should be examined in the saṃsad or sabhā, i.e., the court ("Sabhāntaḥ sākṣiṇaḥ—" in Manu, 8.79); Kāt.[30] and Nārada,[31] because they realised the utility of taking evidence in public like the modern systems of jurisprudence.[32] Manu, Yāj. and Kātyāyana insist on the taking of evidence in the presence of the plaintiff and the defendant. The thing in dispute should be exhibited in the court during the examination of witnesses. In cases of murder the dead body or at least the things connected with the crime should be produced as exhibits.[33]

Both Manu[34] and another Smṛti text quoted by the *Mitā.* on Yāj. (II. 79) insist that a witness should not be asked the same question repeatedly and what he states spontaneously ("svabhāvenaiva") should be accepted as an evidence.[35] The term 'sāntvayan' of the next verse of Manu[36] shows that a witness should be treated very politely by the judge. It is difficult to say whether the system of cross-examination of witnesses was in practice in ancient India, though of course, Kauṭilya's "vākyānuyoga"[37] has been interpreted by R. Shamasastri as cross-examination, applied in cases of women in place of torture.

Now about the weighing of evidences. Manu[38] says that "on a conflict of the witnesses the king shall accept (as true) the evidence of the majority; if (the conflicting parties are) equal in number, (that of) those distinguished by good qualities; on a difference between (equally) distinguished (witnesses, that of) the best among the twice-born". (dvijottamān"). Medhātithi, while commenting on this "dvijottamān" points out that when there is a conflict between the two equally qualified witneses, preference is to be paid to the witness belonging to the higher caste. ("Yukta-guṇa-vatāṃ sama-guṇānāṃ bhede jāti-r-ādartavyā"). Yāj.[39] follows practically Manu differing only in one point that the term 'dvijottama' is replaced by 'guṇa-vattamāḥ', i.e., the best of qualified persons. Here Yāj. is definitely more liberal and it may not be unlikely that he intends to include even the Śūdras, if they are properly qualified and the most excellent of all. Vijñān., however, an orthodox scholar explains the term "guṇa-vattama" as persons, the best of qualified witnesses who are possessed of Vedic learning, who practise vedic rituals and who have wealth and sons and so forth. That means, he understands this term in the light of Manu, confined to the twice-born class. It may be noted that Yāj. follows Kauṭ. (III. 9.16-17 and III. 11) where stress is laid on the majority, purity and respectability of witnesses without any caste-restriction. Bṛhaspati[40] uses the term 'Kriyāvantaḥ' in the same connection to mean like Manu the best of the twice-born who fulfil their sacred duties. Nārada,[41] however, follows Kauṭilya in insisting on purity of character of the witnesses and also on their power of memory. He adds that if both the parties produce witnesses equally strong in all respects, their evidence is entirely valueless.

The principle of 'Ekadeśa' proof was also recognised by ancient jurists, though the Hindu law of evidence demands that allegations must be proved *in toto* and not partially.[42] Vijñān. on Yāj. II. 20 says that this principle of partial proof is applicable in criminal cases like robbery etc. ("Sāhasādau tu sakala-sādhya-sādhanatayoddiṣṭaiḥ sākṣibhi-r-ekadeśe 'pi sādhite kṛtsna-sādhya-siddhi-r-bhavatyeva"). Kātyāyana is also quoted here as supporting this view. Yogloka also opines that this principle is to be applied in cases of theft.[43] Nāı.[44] follows Yāj. almost literally. Vācaspati explains this view of Yogloka by saying that when a part may be treated as equivalent to "Vyāpya" (the whole), that is, when the taking of a particular part implies the taking away of the whole, then and then only the partial proof may be accepted as the proof of the whole. Suppose a man is charged with stealing of a box containing gold, silver and cloth, if theft of gold is proved, conclusion may be arrived at that other things are equally stolen by the man concerned. (Cf. *Vyavahāra-cintāmaṇi* in manuscript) Kātyāyana, however, says that the proof of a part amounts to that of the whole in cases of adultery, assault and theft even when there is no denial on the part of the defendant.

("Sādhyārthāṁśe 'pi gadite sākṣibhiḥ sakalaṃ bhavet/strī-saṅge sāhase caurye yat sādhyaṃ parikalpitam//"). As for example, if it is proved that a young man passed the night at a lonely place devoid of light with a young woman, the presumption of the sexual intercourse between the two is held to be conclusive, though there is absence of (nihṇava) denial on the part of the accused. According to Devanabhaṭṭa the principle of 'ekadeśa' proof is applicable in all criminal cases,[45] as evidenced by the terms 'nihṇute' and 'apalāpinā', used by Yāj. and Nārada which imply dishonest motives. Jīmūtavāhana holds that "apahṇava", i.e., concealment of knowledge amounts to theft in cases like debts etc.

PERJURY

Perjury, according to Dharmaśāstras, leads to both secular and non-secular consequences, as evidenced by Gautama[46] and *Āpas. D.S.*[47] Manu[48] says that he who misrepresents a fact or asserts a fact of which he was not an eye-witness, resembles a blind man swallowing fish with bones. Elsewhere[49] he declares evidence given from covetousness, distraction, terror, friendship, lust, wrath, ignorance and childhood to be invalid and prescribes punishment for perjury in varying degrees on the basis of the root-cause of the crime. Kauṭilya[50] prescribes the fine of 24 paṇas for witnesses who do not testify to the truth.

Let us examine what Yāj. says on perjury. He says that "evidence being given by witnesses, if other more qualified or double in number contradict them, the first witnesses become falsified.[51] Some think that this verse of Yāj. means that when perjury is committed by witnesses produced by the plaintiff, the best way of detecting it is to see if they are contradicted by witnesses, double in number or more qualified, produced by the defendant. But Vijñān. rejects this on the ground that evidence can be produced by the plaintiff alone and not by his opponent.[52] But Kātyāyana finds no fault in this. He opines that if a certain thing is proved by witnesses, produced by the complainant, it may be falsified by a new set of witnesses more numerous or more qualified, produced by the defendant.

Aparārka also says that this rule may be applied when the subject of evidence is one and the same. Nārada also says that such a new set of witnesses is good for nothing when the case has been decided ("nirṇikte vyavahāre tu pramāṇamaphalaṃ bhavet); but this may be allowed if the court has not yet reached any decision. Manu[53] and Viṣṇu[54] enjoin that "if it is proved that a perjured witness has given false evidence in a suit, the judgment is to be reversed by the judge and what has been done must be considered as undone". Kullūka comments that in case of a perjury the proceedings of a trial must be stopped and even if the case has been finished and the decision declared, the whole case should be retried. (on Manu VIII. 117). Vijñān., however, concludes that Yāj.'s text sanctions the practice of setting one set of witnesses against the other by the same party, when one's own witnesses are found to prove hostile to him. He rejects the above argument of representation of witnesses by both parties on the ground that it has also been rejected by Ācārya who is, according to Bālambhaṭṭi and Subodhinī, Viśvarūpācārya.

Now let us discuss the punishment for perjury. Gautama[55] mentions that a false witness must be censured and punished for false statement. ("mithyāvacane yāpyo daṇḍyaśca sākṣī", Haradatta comments on 'Yāpya' as 'garhyaḥ sarvairayam-asaṃvyavahārya iti", i.e., "should be censured and boycotted by all"). Manu[56] mentions punishments of fines of varying degrees on the basis of the cause of perjury like greed, distraction, fear, friendship, ignorance or childishness. The *Mitā.* on Yāj. II. 81 states that these rules of Manu are applicable to all including the brāhmaṇas when it is known that the accused commits this perjury for the particular motive and for several times. ("lobhādi-kāraṇa-viśeṣa-parijñāne'—bhyāse ca Manunoktam"). But when the motive is not known and the crime is repeated, Manu ordains that "a just king shall fine and banish men of three (lower) castes who have given false evidence but a brāhmaṇa he shall (only) banish".

Yāj. (II. 81) prescribes that suborners and witnesses guilty of perjury should be punished separately with a fine double the amount of the suit, that is, double the amount which the defeated party is made to pay as penalty for his loss in the suit and the brāhmaṇa should be made to undergo 'vivāsana'. Vijñān. states that this rule is applicable when the crime is not a repeated one. "Vivāsana" means, according to Vijñān., denudation, destruction of the dwelling house and banishment and which of these three is to be applied should be determined according to the nature of the case.[57] The *Sm. Ch.*[58] points out that a brāhmaṇa deserves denudation, deprivation of house and banishment respectively in cases where a non-brahmin perjurer deserves a small, large and enormous fine. But Vijñān. differs from this rule and opines that the brāhmaṇa should be made to undergo a fine instead of denudation in light suits and banishment in more serious cases. In repeated crimes, however, he thinks that the brāhmaṇa must be both fined and banished. Manu's text "rāṣṭrād-enaṃ vahiṣkuryāt samagradhanam-akṣatam" shows that the brāhmaṇa offender should be banished, leaving all his property to him and his body unhurt. Vijñāneśvara thinks it to be applicable only in the first offence. Kauṭ.[59] also enjoins the punishment of banishment for perjury. It deserves mention that Vijñān. like Medhātithi means by 'pravāsa' corporal punishment as well and this corporal punishment which includes cutting off of the lips or of the tongue and deprivation of life should be awarded according to the nature of perjury. This view is again confirmed by the *Arthaśāstra.* Viṣṇu prescribes the confiscation of his entire property as the punishment for perjury and the *Sm. Ch.*, (p. 217) notes that this rule is applicable in cases of perjury connected with land or with Śūdras or such low castes.

Yāj.[60] prescribes for the witness who conceals his evidence the punishment which consists in, for non-brahmins a fine eight times the amount to be paid by the defeated party on the loss of the suit and for the brahmin 'vivāsana'. Vijñān. here says that the brahmin should be banished when he is unable to pay the fine and the non-brahmin should be made to do works according to their castes or should be chained or sent to jail, if unable to pay the fine. According to Kātyāyana also, such witnesses should be imprisoned, condemned and fined and the amount would amount to 300 coins in cases of verbal injury, fraud or quarrel.[61] Nārada also enjoins heavy punishment in such cases, because he who conceals his evidence is a greater criminal than a false witness.[62] Kātyāyana[63] prescribes for one who, out of greed engages as witness those who are known to be perjurers, the punishment of confiscation of all his property plus banishment. ("gṛhītvā tasya sarvasvaṃ kuryān-nirviṣayaṃ tataḥ"). For knowingly giving false evidence *Matsya Purāṇa*[64] prescribes a fine of 800 paṇas but the recommendation of *Agni Purāṇa*[65] is severer, because it lays down fine and banishment for brahmins and fine plus corporal punishment for others. It is interesting to point out that the section 196 of I.P.C. prescribes for the similar offence the punishment "in the same manner as if he gave or fabricated false evidence", i.e., 7 years' imprisonment plus a fine by the section 193. Thus the above survey shows how ancient jurists took perjury either by commission or by omission as a serious offence and a deadly sin too, because it stood in the way of rendering proper justice, the most essential duty of the king and the punishments, stated above, were also very heavy. Again, Manu[66] points out evil aspects of perjury to the extent how it leads to hell after death. The modern laws in India are also strict to perjurers and the offences of false evidences are regulated by punishments of various types like fine, imprisonment for both short and long terms and even death-sentence.[67] The laws of England are also still now very strict to perjurers. The Perjury Act, 1728, as amended by the Penal Servitude Acts enacts the punishment of more than seven years' penal servitude or imprisonment. "By a still unrepeated act of Elizabeth the punishment is a fine of £ 20 and in default of the payment of the fine, the pillory where the offender is directed to have both his ears nailed".

In Babylonian Law death was the punishment for false evidence in cases involving life and death but in ordinary cases double the penalty involved in the particular case was enjoined.[68] In Athenian Law[69] perjury was regarded as a civil wrong resulting sometimes in disfranchisement. In Roman

Law the "Twelve Tables" prescribed the death-penalty (throwing from the Tarpeian rock) for this offence. In medieval France this crime was punished with the pillory, a long-term imprisonment or a fine.[70] So compared with these countries, Ancient India was not at all unduly severe.

It is interesting to add that perjury which has been unanimously denounced by all India jurists is recommended at the same time by them only when one's life is endangered by true evidence.[71] Gautama, however, does not sanction it to save the life of any sinful man.[72] Manu[73] prefers falsehood to truth, if necessary for saving one's life, irrespective of any caste. ("Śūdra .... satyād viśiṣyate"). Kullūka, however, points out that perjury is not to be allowed in cases of great criminals like burglars and thieves. Medhātithi justifies this rule of Manu otherwise, the witness by his true evidence would not only be the means (hetu) but also the agent (prayojaka) of killing. Vijñān. says that Yāj. enjoins here silence or false statement on the part of the witness, which was previously prohibited and adds that in a charge based on suspicion this may be permissible to save the life of a man. Silence may be resorted to, if the king allows, for saving the life of a third party and if the king does not allow, he may make his evidence futile by contradictions. ("Bhedād-asākṣitvam kartavyam"). And when it is also not possible, truth may be spoken and in any case the sin he commits by false evidence should be expiated by the following of Sārasvata oblation.[74] *Viṣṇu Dh. S.*[75] adds that a Śūdra, guilty of perjury in such a case may for expiation of sin feed ten cows for one day. It may be pointed out that not only Dharmaśāstras but even the *Mahābhārata* refers frequently to the permission of such false statement when one's own or another's life is imperiled.[76]

REFERENCES

1. IV. 166.
2. ("asākṣika ghātaḥ kalahopaliṅganam vā", AŚ, III, 19.73.
3. AŚ, IV. 7.
4. IV. 12.
5. Ādi, ch. 116.

6. *Cintāmaṇi*, p. 59, *Bṛh.*, q. *Parā.* Māḍh - III. p. 39.
7. IV. 6-8.
8. H.L. Evidence, p. 31.
9. Cf. Manu, VIII. 66; Viṣṇu, VIII. 5; Yāj.—"nava sapta pañca vā"; Nār., IV, 179 and Śaṅkha-likhita, q. in Viram., p. 318.
10. Cf. Calcutta Weekly Notes, vol. XXIV, No. 38.
11. II. 72.
12. VIII. 9.
13. Vm., p. 319.
14. pp. 118-19.
15. IV. 192.
16. IV. 190.
17. q. in Vīram. p. 150.
18. Vīram. p. 150
19. p. 319.
20. Cf. Best on Evidence, pp. 57-58.
21. VIII. 68.
22. XVI. 30.
23. Cf. Best on Evidence, 1922, pp. 53-56.
24. II. 70.
25. "Jāti-grahaṇam śreṇyāde-r-apyupalaksaṇārtham", *Sm.Ch.*, p. 176.
26. *Mitā.*, on Yāj., II. 70.
27. *Sm. Ch.*, p. 182.
28. V. 75 and 89.
29. Act IX.
30. q. in the *Mitā.* on Yāj. II. 73.
31. Appendix, 10, *S.B.E.*, vol. 33, p. 224.
32. Cf. Best on Evidence, p. 88.
33. "Vadhe tu prāṇināṃ sākṣyaṃ vādayet sava-sannidhau tadabhave tu ciṇhasya ..... vadha-ciṇhasya". Kātyā. Vīram, p. 168.
34. 8.78.
35. Cf. Medhātithi's comm. on Manu, 8.78.
36. 8.79.
37. "Striya vākyānuyogo va", IV. 8.
38. 8.73.
39. II. 78.
40. Vm., p. 308, *SBE*, 33, p. 303.
41. IV. pp. 229-230; cf. the Comm. of Asahāya on Nār., IV. 160.
42. Cf. Nār., II. 27 and Yāj., II. 20.
43. Cf. Vm., p. 312.
44. Vm., p. 311.
45. Cf. *Sm. Ch.*, p. 209.

46. XIII. 7 and 23.
47. II. 11.28. 8-9.
48. 8.95.
49. 8.118.
50. 3.11.49.
51. "Ukte'pi sākṣibhiḥ sākṣye yadyanye guṇa-vattamāḥ/dviguṇā vānyathā vruyāḥ kuṭāḥ syuḥ pūrva-sākṣiṇaḥ//" - II. 80.
52. "Tadasat pratyarthinaḥ kriyānupapatteḥ", *Mitā.* on Yāj., II. 80.
53. VIII. 117.
54. VIII. 40.
55. XIII. 23.
56. VIII. 120 ff.
57. *Mitā.*, on Yāj., II. 81.
58. p. 215.
59. IV. 4.
60. II. 82.
61. *Sm. Ch.*, pp. 212-13.
62. IV. 197.
63. *Sm. Ch.*, p. 217.
64. ccxxvii, 199.
65. ccxxvii, 1-17.
66. VIII. 88 ff.
67. See Sec. 194 of I.P.C.
68. Ham. 3 & 4
69. *ERE*, IV, p. 278.
70. Cont. Cr. L., Pt. I, Ch. VI, 39f.
71. Gaut., XIII. 24; Vaśiṣ. XVI. 36; Manu, VIII. 104 and Yāj., II. 83.
72. XIII. 25.
73. VIII. 104.
74. Yāj., II, 83; cf. Manu, VIII. 105.
75. VIII. 17.
76. Cf. Śānti, 45.35, 109, 39.

CHAPTER XII

On Arrest and Torture

(I) CRIMINALS UNDER ARREST FOR TRIAL

In criminal cases the accused were arrested to be brought before the court for trial but measures were taken to protect them from any mal-treatment in the hands of the officer-in-charge of prisons. Against these officers-in-charge were sometimes brought the following charges—(i) the putting of undue pressure on prisoners by the process of illegal torture, (ii) creating hardships with regard to food, clothing or bed, (iii) rape on women prisoners, and (iv) transfer of prisoners from one prison to another (comparable with the Habeas Corpus Act). The officers proved guilty were punished.[1]

(II) TRIAL AND TORTURE TO ELICIT CONFESSION

Kauṭilya[2] gives us a detailed information of trial and the different processes of torture, inflicted on the accused, arrested for trial to elicit confession of the crime he is suspected to have committed (IV. 8). The accused and his witnesses should be first interrogated as to the defendant's country, caste, family, name, occupation, property, friends and residence, the nature of the work he did before the day of theft, and place of stay during the night up to the time of arrest. The accused should be acquitted if he is found innocent after careful consideration of the answers and if these answers are attested to by reliable references or witnesses. Otherwise he shall be put to torture ("anyathā karma-prāptaḥ"). Kauṭilya gives us a list of various kinds of 'karma' and specifies people who are to be subjected to them and who are to be exempted from ("na tveva striyam ...."). 'Karma' means 'kṛcchra-vyāpāra' and 'tāḍana' according to Gaṇapati Śāstri[3] and "tortures" according to Shāmasastri. That the practice was most disgraceful and cruel cannot be denied. It may be pointed out that this system was also long prevalent in the Western countries and though never legalised in England, was frequently applied there by the authority of Royal Warrant between 1557 and 1640.

Kauṭilya allows only three days' time for the arrest of any suspected person (śaṅkitaka) because after this period there is no scope for questions, unless of course, there is strong evidence to bring home the charge. Measures should be adopted for protecting the suspect against unnecessary harassment. If anybody charges an innocent man with theft, he will meet the punishment for theft. Anyone confining an innocent man (parivāsayataḥ śuddham) shall be punished with the first amercement.

To prove the guilt of the suspect the complainant must produce evidences like the instruments, used by the accused, his associates, stolen articles and agents. The validity of these evidences shall also be tested with reference to both the scene of theft and the circumstances connected with the possession and distribution of the stolen article. In the absence of such evidences and also when the accused wails much, he shall be taken as innocent. Kauṭilya reminds us of the fact that sometimes an innocent man like Māṇḍavya is taken as a thief owing to his accidental presence on the place of theft or to his accidental resemblance to the real thief in respect of his appearance, dress etc. Māṇḍavya, though innocent admitted himself to be a thief only for fear of torture. In the *Mahābhārata* (I. 101), however, there is no mention of Māṇḍavya's fear of torture, only observance of the vow of silence is held responsible for the miscarriage of justice. Kauṭilya insists on the production of conclusive evidences, before any punishment is meted out. He says distinctly that one whose guilt is believed to be true, shall be subjected to torture (Āpta-dosaṃ karma kārayet). He who causes death to anyone by torture should be punished with the first amercement.

(III) PERSONS EXEMPTED FROM TORTURE

Kauṭilya[4] advises that no torture is to be applied to a person "whose offence is trifling or who is a minor or aged or sick or intoxicated or insane or overcome by hunger, thirst or travel or who has overeaten or whose meal is indigested or who is weak". However, he enjoins the employment of spies like harlots, suppliers of water and other drinks to travellers, storytellers and hotel-keepers to watch the movements of any of the persons, mentioned above. A pregnant woman or a woman within one month of delivery should under no circumstances be put to torture. Torture of women shall be half of the prescribed standard. All women may be subjected to the trial of cross-examination. Brahmins, learned in the Vedas and ascetics were free from torture and they could be subjected to espionage. In all offences a brahmin is not to be tormented, on his forehead shall be a branded mark of the guilty to exclude him from all dealings and he should be exiled from the country or he may be settled in mines.[5] Meyer takes these lines of AŚ to be interpolations, as suggested from Manu, 9.237 where, however, branding is laid down for all varṇas and not for brahmins alone. R.P. Kangle thinks rightly that these verses "which speak of punishment for offences are not in keeping with the contents of this chapter which are concerned with the interrogation of a suspect and other means of extracting a confession from him.[6] Kauṭilya mentions four kinds of torture (karma)—(i) six strokes with a stick (ṣaṭ-daṇḍah), (ii) seven lashes with a whip (kaśa) and (iii) two suspensions from above ("upari-nivandhau"); some take it in the sense of 'tying two hands above and tying the head along with the hands". Kangle thinks that "suspension from a height by a rope twice is all that is meant", and (iv) the water-tube ("udaka-nālikā"). Some think that it means "pouring salt-water through the nose". Besides these, eighteen kinds of torture are also mentioned in the AŚ to be applied in cases of grave offences: nine kinds of blows with a cane, twelve whiplashes, two thigh encirclings, twelve beats with the naktamāla-stick, thirty-two slaps, two scorpion-bindings and two hangings up, needle in the hand, burning one joint of a finger of one who has drunk gruel, heating in the day for one day for one who has drunk fat and a bed of balbaja-points on a winter night.

From the above evidences we may conclude that in cases of theft or in certain criminal cases judicial torture was sometimes employed to elicit confession from the suspect but this was done only when the strong circumstantial evidence made the offence almost apparent. It is difficult to agree with Monahan[7] (*Early History of Bengal*, p. 119) who says, "As in ancient Europe, torture appears to have been applied to elicit a confession from an accused person whose guilt had been established by other evidence—a practice based on the view that, as the best and more conclusive evidence of guilt a confession should be obtained where that is possible, to clinch and confirm other proof." V.R.R. Dikshitar is more justified when he opines that "only avowed culprits were subjected to torture and not the 'suspected' as some scholars would have us believe".[8] Kauṭilya is always up in arms against the unjust methods of punishment and so we cannot expect him prescribing judicial torture to the suspected. As a rule no suspect could be apprehended except within three days from the date of crime. The suspect was confined in the lock-up (caraka) and on the next day he was brought up for trial. This shows how criminal cases were dealt with so speedily. In criminal cases, the presumption of law was, as is still done, to recognise the accused as free from guilt unless it was proved otherwise. No difference between castes was observed as regards punishment of crimes and even brahmin criminals were branded to a wound and after announcing their crimes in public they were either exiled or sent to the mines for life.

REFERENCES

1. AŚ., IV. 9.23ff.
2. IV. 8.
3. Aś, ed. by G. Śāstri, pp. 156-57.

4. 4.8.14-16.
5. IV. 8.27-29.
6. AŚ., ed by R.P. Kangle, p. 320.
7. *Early History of Bengal*, p. 119.
8. *Hindu Administrative Institutions*, 1929, p. 238.

BOOK II
TOPICS OF LITIGATION

CHAPTER I

Vākpāruṣya

(Abuse, Insult and Defamation)

We have already seen how offences were treated in the earliest Dharmasūtras and how the law, both civil and criminal gradually evolved itself. The chief concern of the earliest law-givers was the maintenance of the social order or Dharma and this required in course of time the king's interference. Gautama, while treating the offence by word (vāk-pāruṣya in later nomenclature) took keen interest in restraining objectionable words used by men of lower castes towards brahmins or higher castes only to check injury to social dignities. Towards the beginning all punishable offences seem to have been known as 'sāhasa' and classified with reference to their seriousness into three heads : first (prathama), middle (madhyama) and highest (uttama) sāhasa with a graduated scale of fines for each class. The term 'Sāhasa' was used often to earmark criminal disputes, as distinguished from civil ones and gradually the 'sāhasa's were classified under different heads according to the nature of the crimes and to the measures of punishment inflicted. It is interesting to note that the ancient Indian jurists denoted by Vāk-pāruṣya insult, abuse and defamation and it is wrong to translate this term simply as defamation. To quote the I.P.C. "whoever by words either spoken or intended to be read or by signs .... etc. makes or publishes any imputation concerning any person intending to harm or knowing or having reason to believe that such imputation will harm the reputation of such person, is said .... to defame that person". So when a person calls another a fool, not in the presence of a third person, it is simply an insult or abuse but not defamation. When a man calls a lame man, lame, it is not abuse but taunt. Again, when the defects of a maiden (true or false) are published to others, it is defamation and not abuse.

Gautama prescribes that the Śūdra is to undergo the punishment of the cutting of his limb with which he strikes a person of three higher castes.[1] "Abhi" indicates the preplanned cases of both sorts of injuries, according to Haradatta and so there is no question of punishment in cases of unpleasant utterances or injury, done out of fun. The Śūdra was not entitled to read the Veda, so if any śūdra heard and uttered the Vedic texts, his tongue was cut off and even his body was pierced with axes etc. If any Śūdra claimed equality with members of other castes in respect of seats, beds, speeches and ways, he was to be punished.[2] ("āsana-śayana-vāk-pathiṣu samaprepsu-r-daṇḍyaḥ"). The Kṣatriya and the Vaiśya are to pay 100 and 150 paṇas respectively for abusing a brahmin. But the brahmin is to pay 50 and 25 paṇas for abusing a Kṣatriya and Vaiśya respectively and he is exempted from punishment in case of abusing a śudra. ("na Śūdre kiñchit"). Uśanas, however, prescribes that a Kṣatriya must pay 24 paṇas and the Vaiśya 36 for abusing a Śūdra. Gautama prescribes an equal penalty in cases of abuse between a Kṣatriya and a Vaiśya as between a brahmin and a Kṣatriya. These rules of Gautama show that punishment was awarded in cases of abuses castewise and the Śūdras had been at a great disadvantage in the early pre-Mauryan society.

Āpas.[3] says that if a Śūdra abuses a law-abiding Ārya, his tongue should be perforated. Penances for the expiation of sins of abusing respectable persons and speaking minor untruths also discriminate against a Śūdra who was asked to fast for seven days in such cases (1.9.26.4). On the contrary the twice-born had only to abstain from milk, pungent condiments and salt for three days only (1.9.26.3). The Jātaka[4] also points out that slander was punished with a fine of 8 Kahāpaṇas.

Kauṭilya[5] defines 'Vāk-pāruṣya' as calumny (upavādaḥ), contemptuous talk (kutsanam) and intimidation (atibhartsanam). Calumny may be of the body, temperament, learning, occupation or nationality. In case of defamation relating to body, such as, one-eyed, lame etc. the fine is 3 paṇas, if the defect is a fact; but the fine is made double, if the defect is untrue and four times in cases of irony and likewise when a person is taunted for leprosy, lunacy, impotency and the like. Abusive expressions in general, true or untrue shall be punished with fines above 12 paṇas in the cases of persons of equal castes or rank (tulyeṣu). The fines shall be double, if abuse is towards superiors (viśiṣṭeṣu dviguṇaḥ) or a wife of another, half if towards inferiors (hīneṣu) but if abuse is due to carelessness, intoxication or loss of sense etc., the fines shall be halved ("pramāda-mada-mohādibhi-r-ardha-daṇḍaḥ"). It is interesting to note that Kauṭilya does not prescribe law with reference to any caste but to one's social rank.

In case of slander of character (prakṛtyopavāda) when between a brahmin, a kṣatriya, a vaiśya and a śūdra and the lowest, if it is by the latter of the former, the fine shall be three paṇas and upwards in the increasing order and if it is by the former of the latter, it shall be two paṇas and lower in the decreasing order. It shall be the same also in case of abuse like "a low brahmin and so on". The same rules shall apply to calumnies regarding learning, the profession of buffons, artisans or musicians and relating to nationalities like Prājjunaka, Gandhāra etc." It is noteworthy that the question of caste comes in here, because here the caste-defamation is the cause. In personal defamation, however, Kauṭilya makes no distinction of castes but of rank. Jayaswal seems to suggest rightly that a Prājjunaka or a Gandharian, mentioned here refers evidently to those nations "which were in the Maurya empire and were reproached by the Magadha people for some custom of theirs".[6] For mere threatening with words punishment prescribed by Kauṭilya was half the punishment of the commission of the injury threatened. "If a person, being unable to carry his threat into effect, pleads provocation, intoxication or loss of sense as his excuse he shall be fined 12 paṇas"; but "if a person, capable to do harm and under the influence of enmity, intimidates another he shall be compelled to give lifelong security".[7] This shows that intimidation was not always verbal but translated into execution in the period concerned. Kauṭilya advises at last that "defamation of one's own nation or village shall be punished with the first amercement, that of one's caste or assembly with the middlemost and that of gods or temples (Caityas) with the highest amercement.

The Mauryan state was secular in character but discrimination was made between Vaiśyas and Śūdras in certain matters of legal rights and punishment was meted out in order of superiority of Varṇas. Kauṭ. was lenient to Śūdras whom he accepted as Āryas but he was not free from his bias towards the higher castes and often upheld judicial iniquities to the detriment of Śūdras, because he knew that to postulate a social status for Śūdras equal to higher varṇas was to subvert the existing order of the society and that might shake the foundation of sovereignty. It is remarkable that as a result of progressive secularisation of the society owing to new changes, made by Kauṭilya's law and the administration of Chandragupta, the country became ripe for the greater and more substantial change in moral outlook, ushered in by Aśoka who tried to do away with certain legal inequalities. Aśoka's edicts testify to his attempts to set up the principles of equality of punishment and of legal justice.[8] Kauṭilya's law of punishment for defamation of objects of patriotism and reverence is a clear proof of his broad outlook to penetrate into the hearts of the people of the mighty Mauryan empire, whom he served his best.

Now let us examine Manu's Code[9] in this connection. "A Kṣatriya, having defamed a brahmin shall be fined 100 paṇas, a Vaiśya 150 or 200 and a Śūdra shall suffer corporal punishment". But a brahmin shall be fined 50 paṇas for defaming a Kṣatriya, in the case of a Vaiśya 25 paṇas and in that of a Śūdra 12.[10] These laws show that Manu was in favour of caste-distinction more strictly and was very severe to those who abused the members of the higher varṇas, specially the brahmins and at the same time he took a softer attitude to the brahmin offenders. The punishment of 100 paṇas refers to an offence from the inferior to the superior and not between equals; and here it is of a higher degree than that of Kauṭilya who prescribes only 25, as mentioned above. But if the abuser and the abused are of the same varṇa, the fine for ordinary abuse is only 12 paṇas but double of this, if the abuse is, according to Manu[11] or Nārada[12] foul (vādeṣvavacanīyeṣu) and relating to mother, sister etc. Manu has fierce laws against Śūdras whom he thinks to be of low origin.[13] He prescribes that a Śūdra, insulting a twice-born shall have his tongue cut out, that if a Śūdra abuses any twice-born, referring to his name or caste, an iron nail, ten fingers long shall be thrust red-hot into his mouth (VIII. 271) and that if a Śūdra arrogantly teaches brahmins their duty, hot oil should be poured into his mouth and ears. (*Ibid.*, 272). It is not unreasonable to assume, as Jayaswal does, that Manu is fiercer to Śūdras whom he would like to get suppressed by the king because he had in his view "the dharma-preaching learned Śūdra", i.e., the Buddhist or Buddhist Śūdra and a Śūdra who claims equality and who mentions the epithet "brahmin" itself with contempt".[14]

Manu follows closely the law of Kauṭilya, already mentioned in his code, VIII. 273-74 only changing a few terms like putting 'deśa' and 'jāti' for 'janapada', 'karma' for 'vṛtti' and 'Śarīram', for 'śarīra' and 'prakṛti' but his rate of punishment is too high, i.e., 200 paṇas. Manu, however, reduces the milder punishment to one paṇa at least in cases of slander of a person as one-eyed, lame etc., even if it is a fact. But he enjoins the higher penalty of 100 paṇas on one, defaming his mother, father, wife, son or teacher; while Kauṭilya prescribes only 25.

Nārada[15] defines 'vāk-pāruṣya' as given below: "Deśa-jāti-kulādīnam-ākrośaṃ nyaṅga-saṃyutaṃ/Yad-vacaḥ pratikūlārthaṃ vāk-pāruṣyaṃ tad-ucyate//—i.e., abusive words that loudly proclaim censure of another's country, caste, family etc. and that cause mental pain or offence to that man". Vijñāneśvara cites some examples, the Gauḍas are quarrelsome, the brāhmaṇas are very greedy, persons of Viśvāmitra gotra are of cruel conduct, these are censures of one's country, caste or family respectively. Nārada next mentions its three types: (i) reproachful (niṣṭhura) such as calling one a fool or a rogue, (ii) obscene (aślīla), and (iii) very hard (tīvra), such as charging one with the grave sins like brāhmaṇa-murder etc.

and says that each later one deserves harder punishment than each preceding one. Bṛhaspati[16] also mentions three kinds.

Yāj.'s laws of punishment show that he also had three types of abuses in view which he wanted to check. First he prescribes punishment for niṣṭhura-type of abuses, committed among the members of the same varṇas : "Satyāsatyānyathāstotrai-r-nyūnāṅgendriya-rogināṃ/kṣepaṃ karoti ced-daṇḍyaḥ paṇānardha-trayodaśān//"[17]—"He who by true or untrue or ironical (statements) attacks (or insults) persons (as) wanting in limb or faculty or as diseased shall be fined $13\frac{1}{2}$ paṇas". Thus Yāj., unlike his predecessors regards true or untrue or ironical insults as of the same category and as equally punishable. Yāj. here fixes the fine of $13\frac{1}{2}$ following Kauṭ. and Manu who prescribe 12 in such offences among equals. In cases of obscene abuses Yāj. (II. 205) is found to revive the law of Kauṭ. and prescribes the punishment of 25 paṇas, reducing the heavier one of 100 paṇas, enjoined by Manu (VIII. 275). Yāj. (205) says that "from one who abuses 'I am seducer of your sister, your mother' shall be realised by the king a fine of 25". Yāj. here follows Kauṭ. and reduces the punishment in such cases to only half, if the abuse is to an inferior and increase it to double the amount, if to a superior and thus he asserts distinctly that punishment should be inflicted in consideration of superiority and inferiority of castes.[18] Next he prescribes the fine, amounting to the double and treble of 25 in cases of slander of castes inversely ("prātilomyāpavādeṣu" in 207) and where the slander of varṇas is in the reverse order, the punishment shall decrease by half.[19] Here also Yāj. takes a softer attitude, compared with Manu (VIII. 267 ff), as analysed before. It is interesting to note that Yāj. nowhere prescribes any corporal punishment in cases of abuses, as Manu does (VIII. 267) in cases of Śūdras abusing a brahmin ("Śūdra-s-tus vadham-arhati); and thus he proves himself to be a follower of the artha laws of Kauṭ. who prescribes mere fines in such cases. Yāj. rejects and repeals the other laws of severer penalty on the Śūdras, prescribed by Manu as stated above.

Yāj.'s injunction for punishment in cases of intimidation is as follows: The verbal intimidation of causing injury to the arm, neck, eyes or thigh should be punished with a fine of 100 paṇas and half of it for the same to the foot, nose, ears, hand etc.[20] If any incapable person says so, he should be fined 10 paṇas but if he is capable, he must furnish surety for the safety of the man threatened.[21] The threat of acts of graver sins (patanīyakṛte kṣape) should be punished with the middling amercement; whereas that of acts of lighter sins (upapātakayukte tu) should be met with the first amercement. It is interesting to note that Manu is silent on this issue. Yāj. follows practically the principle of Kauṭ., though he differs a little from him. He permits the fine of 100 paṇas in place of Kauṭ.'s milder punishment[22] but in case of offences by an incapable person Yāj. prescribes the fine of 10 paṇas instead of Kauṭ.'s 12 and in cases of such by a capable person, Yāj. revives the old system of furnishing a surety, enjoined by Kauṭilya. It is more remarkable to note that Yāj.[23] agrees fully with Kauṭ. almost in the same words regarding punishment for abusing one's own nation or village, caste or assembly and one's gods or temples, differing only in one point that Yāj. includes here also the defamation of the king, which, Jayaswal[24] has rightly suggested to be of "a personal character" for treason is provided for elsewhere. ("rājño'niṣṭa-pravaktāram-etc.", Yāj. II. 302).

It is interesting to note that even the truth of imputation afforded no complete exemption. Manu[25] and Nārada[26] enjoin that he who even in accordance with the true facts contemptuously calls another man one-eyed, lame or the like, shall be fined at least one Kārṣāpaṇa. It may be noted in this context that Exception I of the Section 499 of I.P.C. provides that the mere truth of an imputation does not exonerate a man from the charge of defamation, unless the imputation is uttered for the public good. But Kātyāyana (776, q. in *Sm. Ch.* II, p. 327) says that if one warns a man against mixing with a person who is proved to be guilty of a grave sin or of theft, he is not to be punished. ("Yatra syāt parihārārthaṃ patita-stena-kīrtanam/vacanāt-tatra na syāt-tu doṣo yatra vibhāvayet//").

Like Kauṭilya[27] he enjoins that the king should award only half the fine prescribed if the accused said, "What I uttered in abuse, was done through ignorance, carelessness, rivalry or friendship I shall not say so any further". ("mohāt pramādāt saṃgharṣāt prītyā proktaṃ mayeti yaḥ/nāham-evaṃ punarvakṣye daṇḍārdhaṃ tasya kalpayet//". Bṛhaspati also speaks of exemption of punishment, due to verbal injury only in case of a brahmin offending a man without merit. (Guṇa-hīnasya pāruṣye brāhmaṇo nāparādhnuyāt). The laws of other countries may be noted here. In Athens "what may be called ordinary abuse was not punishable. Solon forbade the levelling of abuse at the dead or as to the living, the indulging in it in certain specially protected localities—temples, tribunals and political assemblies. Certain partiality obnoxious terms of abuse were actionable. Magistrates were protected by the severe threat of 'atimia' against any abuse, ... Fines in the cases ranged from the trifling sum of 5 drachmae to heavier penalties".[28] According to the 'Twelve Tables' capital punishment was inflicted for libel or defamation.[29] In Medieval France "insults were generally punishable with fines, though certain insults of graver nature according to the nature of the addresses were punished with heavier fines".[30] In England "libels were punished with fines and corporal punishments and false allegations were subject to heavier punishments".[31]

In modern India defamation is punishable with simple imprisonment up to 2 years or with fine or with both (Sec. 500, I.P.C.); but word, gesture or act intended to insult the modesty of a woman is punishable with imprisonment up to one year or fine or both. (Sec. 509).

REFERENCES

1. II. 3.1 "Śūdṛo dvijātīn-abhisandhāya alhihatya ca vāg-daṇḍa-pāruṣyābhyām-aṅga-mocyo yenopahanyāt".
2. Cf. *Āpas. D.S.*, II. 10.27.15.
3. II. 10.27.14.
4. I, p. 483.
5. III. 18 Sec. 72.1.

6. Manu and Yāj., Calcutta, 1930, p. 151.
7. III. 18.75.9.
8. *C.I.I.*, I, P.E.IV.
9. VIII. 267-77.
10. VIII. 267-68.
11. VIII. 269.
12. XVIII. 7.
13. "Jaghanya-prabhavo" in VIII. 270.
14. Manu and Yāj., p. 150.
15. XVIII. 1.
16. *S.B.E.*, vol. 33, p. 355.
17. II. 204.
18. "daṇḍa-praṇayanam kāryaṃ varṇa-jātyuttarādharaiḥ", II. 206.
19. Varṇānām-ānulomyena tasmād-ardhārdha-hānitaḥ in II. 207.
20. II. 208.
21. II. 209.
22. AŚ. 3.18.9 and 3.19.11
23. II. 211.
24. Manu and Yāj., p. 152.
25. VIII. 274.
26. XVIII. 18.
27. III. 18.
28. *Hist. Juris.* (vinogradoff), vol. II, ch. IX, sec. 5, p. 194.
29. T.T. 8.
30. Contt. Cr. L. I, VI. 39f.
31. Black, IV. ch. XI, pp. 150 & 151.

CHAPTER II

Daṇḍa-Pāruṣya

(Physical Injury or Assault)

Fine for assault is heard of as early as the *Taitt. Sam.*[1] "Yo brāhmaṇāyāpagurātai taṃ śatena yātayāt, yo nihanataṃ sahasreṇa yātayāt, yo lohitam karavadyāvatpraskandya pāṁsūn saṃgrhṇāt tāvataḥ saṃvatsarān pitṛlokaṃ na prajānāditi. Tasmād brāhmaṇāya nāpagureta na nihanyān-na lohitaṃ kuryāt". "He who threatens to strike a brahmin shall be fined with a hundred (cows or niṣkas?) he who strikes a brahmin shall be fined with a thousand; he who draws blood from him shall not behold the pitṛs for as many years as there are particles of dust mixed with the blood that fall on them". Jaimini takes this passage as a recommendatory injunction to all at all times to desist frm assaulting a brahmin.[2] Jayaswal's view that 'danḍa-pāruṣyam' was a common law offence, probably exclusively in the Artha school and that it is not found in Āpastamba, Vaśiṣṭha, Gautama or Bodhāyana, is hardly tenable in the light of its reference, mentioned above in *Tait. Sam.* and Jaimini and particularly for the injunctions of Gautama in this connection.

Let us examine the Artha-laws of Kauṭilya[3] who defines 'daṇḍa-pāruṣya' as (i) touching (sparśaṇam), (ii) striking (avagurṇam) and (iii) severe hurt (prahatam). His rules on touching show the discrimination of punishment in accordance with the spot of the body touched, e.g., a fine of 3 paṇas when the part below navel is touched, its double amount of fine in case of touching above the navel and four times when on the head. The same offence with unclean things, with leg or spittle is punishable with a fine of 6 paṇas but if it is committed with saliva, urine, faeces etc. 12 paṇas. The fine also varies in consideration of the rank of the offended, twice in case of offending a superior person or others' wives but half on persons of lower rank. Plea of mistake, intoxication or loss of sense could be considered to reduce the fine to half the amount.

It is interesting to note that Kauṭilya prescribes that "that limb of a śūdra with which he strikes a brāhmaṇa shall be cut off". (Śūdro yenāṅgena brāhmaṇam-abhihanyāt tad-asya chhedayet"). This is in par with Manu.[4] To R. Shamasastri, however, this passage, singular in character, dealing with an abnormally high punishment for a minor offence is evidently an interpolation as "It is inconsistent not only with the author's principle of gradation in punishments, proportional to crimes but also with his intention to get rid of mutilation of limbs by fines levied in lieu thereof".[5] He thinks that this interpolation is, perhaps due to the hand who in the similar context in Yāj.[6] has formed a scale of punishments under the baneful influence of caste-distinctions and undue partiality to brāhmaṇas, which are assigned no prominence in the *Arthaśāstra*".[7] Jayaswal remarks on the contrary : "The real explanation seems to be that it was pre-Mauryan repressive law which Kauṭilya[8] gives but he modifies it by laying down in the chapter on commutation that where a Śūdra is condemned to have his eyes destroyed for 'rivalling a brāhmaṇa' ...... his sentence can be commuted to a fine of 800.[9] That it was a pre-Mauryan law is taken for granted, because Gaut.[10] and Āpas.[11] ("jihvāchhedanaṃ śūdrasyāryaṃ dhārmikamākrośataḥ") prescribe so; and its influence is naturally felt not only on Kauṭilya but also on later jurists like Yāj.[12] and Bṛhaspati,[13] "Yenāṅgena dvijātīnāṃ Śūdraḥ praharate ruṣā/chettavyam tad-tad-evāsya tan-Mano-r-anusaśānam//". It may not be unlikely that the Śūdras, referred to by earlier jurists included also those Śūdras who turned Buddhists and who proved bitter foes of the brahmins and brahmanism. But Kauṭilya was a jurist of the Artha-school with sufficient softness for the Śūdras whose cooperation he welcomed for the welfare of the state, he is found to have turned his sentence of severer punishment committed to a fine. For mere menacing a ransom was allowed and for mere touching the fine is half. ("avagurṇe niṣkrayaḥ sparśe' rdha-daṇḍaḥ). The rate of fine varied according to the nature of the thing with which menacing was done and also on the basis of the gravity of the injury made.[14] "For one causing hurt without blood the fine shall be 24 paṇas, for causing a bleeding wound double and for one beating another to the point of death, the lowest fine for violence and also for breaking hands, feet or teeth, cutting off ear or nose and opening up wounds. Graver injuries like breaking the thigh or neck or piercing the eye etc. were liable to the punishment of the middlemost amercement and in case of death, the offender should be taken for trial as a criminal by a magistrate.

Manu, compared with Kauṭilya is strict to offenders. Like Gautama and Āpastamba Manu[15] prescribes the punishment of the cutting of that limb with which the Śūdra strikes a twice-born. He[16] extends the same punishment to a Śūdra for merely raising the hand or a stick to strike a twice-born. He[17] enjoins further that a person of a low caste ("apakṛṣṭaja"), defiantly sitting on the same seat with one of a higher caste was to be first branded on the waist and then banished or his hips were to be gashed in such a way that he might not die, that the Śūdra defiantly spitting on the body of a brahmin had his hips cut off, if he urined on him, the penis and if he broke wind against him, the anus. If he laid hold of the hair (of a superior), or his feet or beard or neck or testicles, he would have both his hands cut off. All these texts Jayaswal took to be motivated by Manu's intention to suppress the Śūdras and to raise the dignity of the brahmins. But it should not be missed to note that Manu is strict not only to the Śūdras, offending the brahmins but also to those others offending among the equals, as proved by VIII. 284—"Tvag-bhedakaḥ śatam daṇḍyo-lohitasya ca darśakaḥ/māṃsa-bhettā tu ṣaṇniṣkān pravāsya-stvasthi-bhedakaḥ//", i.e., he who breaks the skin (of an equal) or fetches blood (from him) shall be fined 100 (paṇas), he who cuts a muscle six niṣkas and he who breaks a bone shall be banished". This is evidently general law, applicable to all irrespective of any caste, committing a severe hurt. For the expiation of the sin of murder Manu prescribes the performance of the lunar penance varying in length according to the varṇa of the murdered man. While the penance continues for three years in case of a murder of a brahmin, it does only for $2\frac{1}{2}$ months in the case of the murder of a Śūdra.[18] Manu, like his predecessors prescribes a wergild of 10 cows and a bull[19] for killing a Śūdra and this fine must be given to a brahmin. He prescribes the same penance for killing a Śūdra as for killing a number of small animals and birds.[20] These provisions show Manu's attitude to Śūdras. Elsewhere he declares the murder of women, Kṣatriyas, Vaiśyas and Śūdras to be a minor offence (upapātakam), showing thereby his leniency to the brahmins.[21]

Now let us scrutinize the text of Yāj.[22] in this context. "Vipra-pīḍā-karam Chedyam-aṅgam-abrāhmaṇasya tu/Udgurṇe prathamo daṇḍaḥ saṃsparśe tu tad-ardhikaḥ//"—that means, the limb of a non-brahmin with which he causes any physical injury to any brāhmaṇa (vipra), should be cut off, the first amercement in case of menacing and half of it in case of mere touching. Here Yāj. uses the term 'a-brāhmaṇasya tu' to extend the punishment to Kṣatriyas and Vaiśyas as well, who-soever offends the 'Vipra', thereby reducing them to the same level as the Śūdras. Now about the meaning of 'Vipra' here. It is surprising to note that Vijñāneśvara explains it first as a brāhmaṇa ("Brāhamaṇānām pīḍākaram etc.) but he includes the Kṣatriyas and Vaiśyas within its denotation, following Manu,[23] whose text he quotes therein. Thus evidently Vijñāneśvara, belonging to the orthodox school interprets Yāj. in the light of Manu, though Yāj.'s text itself does not warrant such an assumption. Yāj., however, follows Kauṭilya to pre-scribe 'half punishment' in case of mere touching but he differs from Kauṭ. in case of menacing. Kauṭ.[24] sanctions commutation as an alternative of cutting of the limb but Yāj. insists on the first amercement (prathamo daṇḍaḥ). Here also Vijñāneśvara, following Manu insists on the cutting of the limb concerned in case of menacing on the part of a Śūdra, thus evidently violating the principle of Yāj.

Yāj. takes a more liberal view in cases of offences among the equals, irrespective of any caste. He[25] prescribes that when one menaces the hands or feet, one must be punished with 10 or 20 paṇas' fines respectively and when both parties threaten with arms, the middle amercement would be inflicted on the offender, irrespective of any caste. Mention may be made here of the fact that Yāj. here follows Kauṭ., III. 9.11, who says that "for menacing with the hand the fine shall be 3 to 12 paṇas, double for menacing with the foot, the first amercement for violence with an object causing hurt and the middle one for one's endangering life. Though Kauṭ. is silent on the caste of the offender, we may presume that this rule refers to four varṇas and the Antāvasāyins as in his rule, 3.18.7. Yāj. enhances here punishment to 10 or 20 paṇas in place of Kauṭilya's 3 to 12 and what is more interesting Yāj. reduces the punishment, awarded by Manu in such cases and follows practically the artha laws of Kauṭilya and asserts at the same time that the punishment prescribed would be applicable to all ("parasparaṃ tu sarveṣām"). Yāj.[26] takes into account the position of the aggrieved party relative to that of the offender. In II. 214 he does not mention any caste, though perhaps that is included in the term ("sameṣveva para-strīṣu dviguṇa-s-tūttameṣu ca"). In II. 215 Yāj. mentions that a non-brahmin causing pain to a 'vipra' (Brahmin ?) shall be deprived of his limb and in II. 216 he reaches the climax to prescribe for "all" without any discrimination.

We notice the similarity between Kauṭ.,[27] noted above and Yāj.,[28] though the rate of fine in Yāj. is a little higher than that of Kauṭ. Kauṭ., however, says that in case of death, the culprit shall be taken for trial to a criminal court by a magistrate ("vipattau kaṇṭaka-śodhanāya nīyate"); while Yāj. is silent on the point. While Kauṭ. prescribes the middle fine for violence in cases of graver injuries like breaking the thigh or neck, it should be noted that he enjoins that the criminal should bear the expenses for treatment and cure ("samutthāna-vyayaśca", 3.19.14), thus showing his humanitarian attitude, like Manu,[29] Yāj.,[30] Kātyā.[31] and Viṣṇu.[32] Besides, Yāj.[33] follows Kauṭ. (3.19.16) when he says that if many men inflict jointly any hurt on one man, the offence would be regarded as serious and punishment double. The term "mahājana" of Kauṭ. here means a number of men, signified by "vahūnām" of Yājñavalkya.

Kauṭ.[34] rejects the theory of earlier jurists that "quarrels or assaults of a remote date shall not be complained of" and asserts his own that "there can never be impunity acquired by a criminal" ("nāstyapakāriṇo mokṣa iti Kauṭilyaḥ"). Thus in his eye there should be no period of limitation for lodging the complaint for simple quarrel or assault. Besides, he rejects the theory of his preceptor that "he who is the first to complain of a quarrel wins, in as much as it is pain that drives one to Law"[35] and asserts the ground that "whether complaint is lodged first or last, it is the evidence of witnesses that must be depended upon, in the absence of witnesses the nature of the hurt and other circumstances connected with the quarrel in question shall be evidences. If one does not reply to an accusation of injury, he shall be convicted on the same day".[36] It is interesting to bear in mind that in criminal cases even if the crime is not complained of by any of the parties, it is the king's business to take up the issue on the report of his own spies and try the criminal, hence in a criminal suit the question of complaining first or last should not arise for proper justice. Manu is silent on this point. But Yāj. adopts the artha law and clearly states the rule of procedure in criminal cases like assault etc. In cases when assault is alleged to be made in a secret place and the only direct evidence consists in the allegation of the complaint and the marks of injury, justice should be rendered very carefully on the basis of circumstantial evidences because there is a danger of fabricated marks of injury : "Asākṣita-hate cinhair-yuktibhi-s-cāgamena ca/ draṣṭavyo vyavahāra-s-tu kūṭa-cinhakṛto bhayāt//".[37] Nār.[38] follows practically Yāj. He means to say that when a man is found with a mark of assault upon him and another man with that of committing the assault, such as a sword smeared with blood, we are tempted to connect these two facts but we should remember that people are found sometimes inflicting wounds on their own bodies to put their foes into difficulty and so we must weigh the case very carefully to find out the cause or motive of the assault and the capacity of the offender for such an act. Kauṭilya prescribes heavy penalty on the judge who fails to enquire into the particular circumstances of the case.[39] Besides, Yāj.[40] makes a remarkable improvement on Kauṭ. (III. 19.4) because while Kauṭ. prescribes half of the prescribed punishment in cases of mistakes, intoxication, delusion and so on, Yāj. excuses totally an offence committed under such circumstances.

Kauṭ.,[41] Manu[42] and Yāj.[43] all agree to regard injuries to trees and plants and to animals as well as cases of assault and prescribe rules for protecting them as human beings. Kauṭ. prescribes punishments for varying degrees for causing injury to plants and trees in the city-parks ("purovanaspatīnām"—etc.) and also trees growing in places of pilgrimage, penance-groves and cremation-grounds but he is silent on cases of injury to trees and plants growing elsewhere i.e., in villages and forests, probably for richness of such trees and plants in those areas. Trees and plants of city-parks, holy places etc. are of special interest to Kauṭilya, because they serve a very useful purpose and they are rarely available there. So Kauṭ. might have taken into consideration the entire issue from the standpoint of utility.

It is interesting to note that Kauṭilya, while dealing with the function of the Superintendent of forest produce, says that the Superintendent shall "fix adequate fines and compensation to be levied from those who cause any damage to productive forests".[44] These are evidently penalties for taking fuel or timber from State forests. Some commentator holds that "cutting and carrying off branches of such trees as would be useful for axles of carts etc. is no offence". This standpoint of utility is greater emphasised in the last rule of the section under review when Kauṭ. prescribes the double fines for injuries to trees at the boundaries, in sanctuaries and those which are prominent as well as in royal parks.[45] Manu[46] also ordains that according to the usefulness of all trees, a fine must be inflicted for injuries to them. His term 'vanaspatīnām' (trees) includes all plants, according to Medhātithi and Kullūka and Medhātithi remarks that the position of the trees, whether they are bounday-marks or stand on a cross-road or in a hermitage etc., should be taken into account. The expression "vanaspatīnām sarveṣām" means, according to Manu that the entire kingdom of vegetables should be protected from injuries ("hiṃsāyām). Though Manu has not given us any further minutest details like Kauṭilya, he has guaranteed all plant-world the protection of law from all acts of injury. Yāj. follows Kauṭ. but he enjoins higher punishment for pain to the world of plants and trees, starting with a fine of 20 paṇas in place of Kauṭ. 6 only. Yāj. makes a distinction between trees whose branches, when cut off and re-planted breed fresher trees ("prarohi-śākhinām") like banian trees and others like mango ("upajīvya-drumānām") and cruelty to branches, trunks and main tree was punished with 20, 40 and 80 paṇas respectively. (II. 227) He reproduces the very words of Kauṭ. in 228 with regard to particular trees. Last of all, he reduces the punishment to half of the prescribed amount in cases of injuries to creepers and bushes just like Kauṭilya. The *Matsya Purāṇa*[47] enjoins various amounts of fine for this offence. In most of the ancient countries this offence was treated as a civil wrong, liable to the punishment in the shape of compensation. From Vendidad we learn of seven types of assaults, called in Pahlavi, 'payak vinās' i.e. chief crimes, the first of which is known as 'agerepta' (stroke), Vendi. IV.17, punishable with five stripes. This penalty increases with the repetition of the crime (*E.R.E.* IV., p. 294). In England, however, sometimes this offence was punished with capital punishment. Unlawfully or maliciously cutting down trees in an avenue or a garden etc. was by 9 Geo. III. C. 29 treated as a felony without benefit of clergy. But by 6 Geo.III. C. 36 and 48 & 13 Geo. III. C. 33 the first two cases of intentional destruction of trees, roots, shrubs or trees were punished with fines and the third case of such offences was treated as felony and liable to transportation for 7 years.[48]

Cruelty to animals was likewise treated in the laws of assault equally by Kauṭ., Manu and Yāj. Kauṭ.[49] says that "for causing hurt to small animals with wood and other things, the fine shall be one or two paṇas, double that for causing bleeding. For similar offences to big animals, the fine shall be double and (payment of) expenses for treatment and cure". Manu shows equal interest in cruelty to animals as to men by his juxtaposition of two terms "manuṣyānām" and "paṣūnāṃ ca" in VIII.286. Aśoka's inscriptions show his humane attitude to animals for which he established hospitals throughout his empire. The rule for bearing all expenses for treatment of injuries on animals is nothing but the natural corollary of the new outlook, reflected in Aśoka's inscriptions. The differential rate of fines, inflicted on injuries to small and great animals and specially in cases of bleeding might have been called for and justified from the standpoint of utility. Yāj.[50] follows exactly the same principle of non-injury to animals and prescribes a higher punishment for offences to them. In cases of death by assault on small animals the punishment of middle-most amercement ("madhyamo mūlyam-eva ca"—Yāj.[51]), was inflicted on the offender and the owner of the animal concerned would be paid the actual price. The punishment double this amount was meted out to offenders causing pain to greater animals like a cow, an elephant, a horse etc. (Vijñān. on Yāj. - 226).

Nārada[52] recommends the punishment for injuring or killing animals in proportion to the gravity of the crime. Offence to animals was also treated as a civil wrong in most of the ancient countries. In medieval England, however, this was held as highly criminal. By 9 George III. C 29 to kill, maim or wound any cattle was regarded as a felony without benefit of clergy.[53]

Now we may consider the question of robbery in quarrels. Kauṭ. prescribes that "a person stealing anything during a quarrel shall be fined 10 paṇas. Destruction of articles of small value shall be punished with a fine equal to the value of the articles, besides the payment to the sufferer of an adequate compensation, while that of big things with a compensation equal to the value of the articles and a fine equal to twice the value and for destroying clothes, ornaments, money and gold articles, the same and the first amercement".[54] Yāj.[55] also follows Kauṭ. on this point and prescribes the same thing. ("Kalahāpahṛtam deyaṃ daṇḍaśca dviguṇa-s-tataḥ"). Injury to one's residence in quarrel was deemed to be the same to the owner himself, hence Kauṭ. prescribes the fine of 3 paṇas for damaging the wall of a house and 6 paṇas for breaking or cutting it, besides the cost of repair and 12 paṇas for throwing harmful things in the inside of the house and the first amercement for throwing an object dangerous to life.[56] This mischief, though not on his person told upon his mind because it was deemed as insulting to his sacred right of ownership over his own house and because force was applied there, he took it to be an assault. The Indian jurists took consideration of mental pain equally as of the physical one as cases of assault. Manu is, however, silent on this issue but he prescribes punishments for damages of others' goods in varying degrees in proportion to the nature of the damage done.[57] But Yāj.[58] follows the principle of Kauṭ. in cases of assault to one's house and goods and prescribes a higher punishment than Kauṭ. in similar offences.

The law of assault was also extended to injuries of different types and those to men by one's animals, as pointed out by Kauṭ. in IV. 13.13-26. "Harm due to the construction of unstable houses, carts with no support or with a beam or weapon hung above or with damaged support or with no covering, and harm due to causing a cart to fall in pits or a tank or from a dam, shall be treated as assault. Similarly "cutting of trees, stealing the rope with which a tameable animal is tied employing untamed animals .... raising the arm against chariots or elephants, shall also be treated as assault". But the charioteer who cries out to the passer-by, "Get out" shall not be punished for collision. In cases of injuries to the public on the road Kauṭ. prescribes punishment of varying degrees on the owner of the animal concerned in proportion of his motive of offence. In case of injury when the cart has the nose-strings (of the bullocks) cut or the yoke broken .... the driver is not to be punished, evidently because it is a case of a mere accident without any preplanned motive of injury. Otherwise the driver must be punished as noted in the case of injury to men and animals. When the driver is a minor, the owner, if in the carriage is to be fined and if the owner is not there, the person in the carriage or the driver, if he has attained majority. Thus Kauṭ. is lenient to the driver only when it is an accident case over which he has no control and also when there is no negligence on his part. Manu[59] also adopts Kauṭilya's theory, as stated above. He mentions the cases of impunity of the cart, the cartman and the owner of the cart just in keeping with Kauṭ.'s advice. Yāj.[60] deals with such cases in a separate chapter, "prakīrṇaka" and follows the old law, differing only in the fact that he prescribes a higher punishment than the earlier jurists in cases where the accident is due to sheer negligence on the part of the driver or the owner of carts or of animals. These laws indicate that the society had advanced to a high degree of civilization; and trade and commerce had flourished to no mean degree as that it was found necessary to regulate wheeled traffic, as in the modern age, by enacting laws relating to roads. The ancient Indians realised the distinction between murder and culpable homicide as well as death by mere accident.

Kauṭ.[61] prescribes the punishment for forcible trespassing in another's house, the lowest fine for violence by day and the middle, by night but the highest punishment in case of entrance with a weapon. But he exempts from punishment a mendicant, a trader, an intoxicated and an insane person and also very close neighbours, if they enter the house by force or in a calamity, of course, when no such entrance is specially prohibited.

Nārada[62] defines it as assault to the limbs of another with the hand, foot, weapon and others or striking others with ashes etc. ('para-gātreṣvabhidroho hasta-pādāyudhādibhiḥ bhasmādibhiścopaghāto daṇḍa-pāruṣyam-ucyate"). It is of three kinds, mild, middling and highly serious according as a person merely makes a preparation to assault ("avaguraṇa") or attacks without any qualm (niḥśaṅka-patanam") or causes a wound (Kṣata-darśanaiḥ") and the gravity of the crime depends on the value of the object attacked. ("hīna-madhyottamānāṃ tu dravyānām-anatikramāt:). Bṛhaspati, q. by Aparārka says : "Dvayoḥ praharato-r-daṇḍaḥ samayostu samaḥ smṛtaḥ/ Ārambhako'nuvandhī ca dāpyaḥ syād-adhikaṃ damaṃ//": i.e., when two persons attack each other and when the beginner is not found out, both will be equally punished but he who is proved to have begun the crime of assault or to persist longer than the other, should be subjected to greater punishment. The *Mitākṣarā* on Yāj. II. 212 states the same fact and adds that in cases of assault upon the Āryas by Śvapaca and others the good men (of the locality) are entitled to punish them, and if such punishment is not possible, the king should inflict corporal punishment alone and he should not take fines from them because according to Nārada, these persons are the worst of men and their wealth is also foul ("dhanam-eṣāṃ malātmakam"). Kātyāyana, q. by Aparārka provides the same fact. Bṛhaspati ordains gradation of punishment on the basis of the superiority of the injured ("prādhānyāpekṣayā"), most probably castewise, as Kātyāyana also does the same (786, q. by *Parā. Mā.*). The author of the *Smṛti Candrikā* says that because it is impossible for the *Smṛti-s* to prescribe punishment in cases of crimes of innumerable individuals, punishment should be inflicted on the calculation of the gravity of the crime in each case and he substantiates this by quoting Uśanas—"Yatra nakto damaḥ sarvai-r-ānantyāt tu mahātmabhiḥ/tatra kāryaṃ parijñāya kartavyaṃ daṇḍa-dhāraṇam" and Manu, VIII. 286.

It is interesting to note that the I.P.C. (Sections 350 & 351) defines criminal force and assault and prescribes punishments in the shape of imprisonment, or fine or both in varying degrees in proportion to the gravity of the crimes committed (Section 352 ff).

Now let us turn to the laws of other countries. According to the Babylonian Law "the offender was whipped 50 lashes for striking a man far superior to him. A freeman and a plebeian were to pay the fine of 1 mina and 10 shekels of silver respectively for striking a man of equal rank; but if a slave struck a freeman, his ear was cut off. One destroying the eyes, teeth or bone of a freeman had to lose the same limb; but he had to pay a fine only if he had injured a plebeian or a slave. One striking a man in quarrel had to pay the doctor's bill and compensation in case of death".[63]

The Old Persian law punished the offender for hurt with stripes with each whip in varying degrees according to the nature of the injury from 15 to 200 stripes.[64]

The Mosaic Law prescribed 'lex talionis', i.e., an eye for an eye,[65] but no punishment in case of a quarrel when some compensation was to be paid.[66]

Both civil and criminal actionis for hurt were taken in ancient Athens. In the criminal one the punishment was fine or imprisonment, left to the discretion of the jury.[67] The "Twelve Tables" prescribes retaliation for the fracture of bone or tooth unless compensation was paid.[68]

In medieval France hurts were punishable according to the nature of their gravity, whether blood was made to come out or not and sometimes death was the punishment for grievous hurts. 'Lex talionis' was also sometimes exercised.[69] Retaliation was also in practice in ancient England in such offences but it was soon replaced by fine or imprisonment. In Blackstone's time fine and imprisonment were the punishment for ordinary cases but corporal punishments were inflicted in serious cases.[70]

REFERENCES

1. II. 6.10.2.
2. "Śaṃ yau ca sarva-paridānāt".—Jaim., III.4.17; Śabara's conclusion—"Sarvāvasthasya brāhmaṇasyāyaṃ pratiṣedha uktaḥ na 'darśa-pūrṇamāsa-gatenaiva nāvagoraṇādi kartavyamiti".
3. III. 19.
4. VIII. 279.
5. Ch. X, Book, IV.
6. II. 218.
7. AŚ, p. 220, fn.
8. III. 19.
9. AŚ, B IV. Ch. XII, p. 255.

10. II. 3.
11. II. 10.27.14.
12. II. 205 ff.
13. q. by *Sm. Ch.*, II, p. 328.
14. 3.19. 11-15.
15. VIII. 279.
16. VIII. 280.
17. 281-283.
18. XI. 127, cf. 129-131.
19. XI. 128-131.
20. XI. 132 & 141.
21. XI. 67.
22. II. 215.
23. VIII. 279.
24. "Avagurṇe niskrayāt"—3.19.9 and 4.10.12.
25. II. 216.
26. II. 214.
27. 3.19.12-15.
28. II. 217-220.
29. VIII. 287.
30. II. 222.
31. 781.
32. *D.S.*, V. 75-76.
33. II. 221.
34. 3.19.17.
35. 3.19.19.
36. 3.19.21-22.
37. Yāj. II, 212.
38. IV. 176.
39. IV. 9.
40. II. 214 "moha-madādibhi-r-adaṇḍanam".
41. 3.19.26 ff.
42. 8.285-86.
43. II. 225 ff.
44. II. 17.1
45. III. 19.30.
46. VIII. 285.
47. CCXXVII. 91-95.
48. Black, IV. XVII, pp. 245-247.
49. 3.19. 26-27.
50. II. 225-226.
51. II. 226.

52. 14 Tit., 5 & 7.
53. Black - IV. XVII, pp. 244-45
54. III. 19.23.
55. II. 221.
56. AŚ, 3.19.24-25.
57. VIII. 288 ff.
58. II. 223-24.
59. VIII. 290-295.
60. II. 298-300.
61. 4.13.
62. XVIII. 4.
63. Ham. 196-208.
64. Zend, Vend., Farg. IV. IIIa, 17, 26-42.
65. Exod, 20,[24,25] and Lev. 24,[19,20].
66. Exod, 20,[18,19]
67. Demos, III, Oration against Midias, p. 81; App. VIII, p. 351.
68. 8.[2-4]
69. Cont. Co., Pt. I, ch. IV 39 f.
70. Black, IV, XV, pp. 205-207, 216.

CHAPTER III

Theft

We hear of theft as early as the period of the *Ṛgveda*[1] in which 'taskara', 'stena' and 'tāyu' are frequently mentioned. 'Tāyu' is an Indo-Iranian term. The *Vāj. Saṁ.*[2] and *Taitt. Saṁ.*[3] mention 'malimlu' in the sense of a thief. The *Atharva Veda* (IV. 3) contains charms against wolves, tigers and thieves. Aśvapati, king of Kekaya boasted that his kingdom was free from thieves.[4]

Gautama[5] enjoins that the king should recover the articles stolen by thieves and hand them over to the owner ("caura-hṛtam-apajitya yathā-sthānaṃ gamayet"). Haradatta comments that the recoverer should get some portion of it ("jetu-s-tu jayaphalaṃ kiñcit") when the article is given over to the owner (svāmine eva dadyāt"). But whence this fruit of recovery comes is not made clear whether the thief is to pay something more as fine or the owner would gladly contribute something out of the thing restored. Gautama[6] says further that the king should give the owner the amount equal to the stolen article from his own treasury as a matter of compensation if the king fails to recover it. Thus the jurist shows how the king took it as a matter of duty to extend his protection to the people from all sorts of troubles including thieves etc. and how people enjoyed police-protection and even right of compensation, if necessary. As regards the punishment of thieves Gautama[7] prescribes the amount according to the caste of the thief: the Śūdra thief is to pay the fine of 8 times the value of the article stolen, the Vaiśya, Kṣatriya and Brāhmaṇa thieves are respectively fined 16, 32 and 64 times the price of the article stolen. He puts forward the reason for such castewise distinction "viduṣo' tikrame daṇḍa-bhūyastvam" (*ibid.* 14), i.e. the member of the higher caste is more learned than that of a lower order and because he takes to crimes knowing fully well the demerit of such actions, he should be given higher punishment. ("Niṣedhadoṣam jñātvāpi pravarta-mānasya doṣādhikyaṃ bhavati"). Manu[8] and Nārada[9] follow the old principle of Gautama. Manu is stricter to fine more learned brahmins with 128 paṇas. Gautama is however, lenient to those who steal fruits, green grains and vegetables and prescribes to punish them with a little amount of five Kṛṣṇalas. From the account of Megasthenes we learn the general honesty of the people and the efficient administration of criminal law. Penal law was severe enough to repress crimes of the society. For petty theft of things, the punishments prescribed were a fine of 6 paṇas, shaving the head and exile.

The jurists were not unanimous as to the amount of punishment on thieves or robbers. Kaut.[10] rejects the opinion of earlier jurists and asserts his own that it should be proportionate to the gravity of the crime. He prescribes five grades first 12 to 24 paṇas for articles of small value as flowers, fruits, vegetables etc., 24 to 48 paṇas for articles of great value, such as iron, wood etc., 48 to 96 paṇas—the first amercement for articles of greater value, as copper, brass, bronze etc., 200 to 500 paṇas—the middle amercement for big animals, men, fields, houses, gold, gold-coins and fine fabrics etc. and 500 to 1000 paṇas, the highest amercement for keeping or causing to keep by force men or women in prison or releasing them by force from imprisonment, as sanctioned by his preceptor.

Āpastamba[11] prescribes that the officers should protect a city against theft for one yojana round it and a village for one krośa and that they must return to the owners whatever is stolen within the areas concerned. This rule shows the equal attention to villages and cities, with which the king must protect with the help of his officers from thieves.

Next let us examine Manu's attitude to thieves. We have already noticed his advice to kings that they should restrain the wicked by three means, by imprisonment, by putting them in fetters and by various kinds of corporal punishments (VIII. 310). The king must punish the thief or he takes upon himself the guilt of the thief. The king must not leave even his father, teacher, friend, mother, wife, son or a domestic priest unpunished, if anyone of these fails to do his own duty. Even the king himself should not go with impunity, if he swerves from duty; rather he should be punished thousandfold, compared with ordinary persons. The thief may surrender to the king and appeal for punishment with anyone of the following instruments, a pestle, a club, or a spear etc. and he will be freed from all guilt of theft, if he is punished or pardoned. Here Manu reminds us of both types of punishment, physical and moral and their utility to get all blemishes purged out. Manu also prescribes different grades of punishment, applicable to all, on the basis of the value of the things stolen (8.319 ff). Thus he agrees with Kauṭilya but differs from him because Manu[12] is stricter than Kauṭ., the rate of punishment being definitely higher and being mainly corporal in character instead of being mere fines. Manu[13] prescribes corporal (or capital) punishment for stealing men and women of noble families and the most precious gems. Fines are prescribed only for stealing of things of small value. Manu's method of punishment is preventive in character and with that end in view he enjoins the cutting of the limb which the thief uses in stealing (VIII. 334). Manu[14] (cf. also *Matsya Purāṇa*, 227. 184-85) says that the goldsmith is the worst of all deceitful persons ("sarvapāpiṣṭha-kaṇṭakam") and if he behaves dishonestly, he should be cut to pieces with razors.

Manu speaks of cheat, open and concealed (IX. 257). Open cheats are those who subsist by cheating in the sale of various marketable commodities; whereas the concealed ones are the following, thieves, robbers in forests and so forth. "Those who take bribes, cheats and rogues, gamblers, those who live by teaching (the performance of) auspicious ceremonies, sanctimonious hypocrites and fortune-tellers, officials of high rank and physicians who act improperly, men living by showing their proficiency in arts and clever harlots, these and the like who show themselves openly as well as others who walk in disguise (such as) non-Āryans who wear the marks of Āryans" are the thorns of the society.[15]

Vyāsa[16] speaks of nine kinds of concealed thieves, one who quietly relieves a man of his money when he is absent-minded, a house-breaker, a highway robber, a cut-purse and one who kidnaps a woman, a man, cows, horses or other animals. ("Utkṣepakaḥ sandhibhettā pāntha-muḍ-granthi-bhedakaḥ/ stri-puṃgo'śva-paśu-steyi cauro navavidhaḥ smṛtaḥ//").

Now how to detect thieves and control them. Manu[17] says that the king, having detected them by means of trustworthy persons, who disguising themselves pretend to follow the same occupations and by means of spies, wearing various disguises, must cause them to be instigated to commit violence ("protsāhya" according to Nārāyaṇa instead of the reading "protsādya" according to Kullūka and Medhātithi) and bring them into his power (vaśamānayet). The king should employ spies in various disguises at the following places like meeting halls, refreshment rooms, brothels, wine shops, victualler's shops, cross-roads, well-known trees, festive assemblies, play-houses and concert-rooms, old gardens, forests, the shops of artisans, empty dwellings and natural and artificial grooves. These places should be guarded by companies of soldiers, both stationary and patrolling and by spies. (IX. 266) Moreover, Manu advises the use of old thieves ("pūrvataskaraiḥ"), clever enough who associate with such rogues, follow them and know their various machinations. ("tat-sahayāi-r-anugatai-r-nānā-karma-pravedibhiḥ" in IX. 267). The spies again must make these rogues meet (the officers of justice) under the pretext of offering them various dainties, of introducing them to brahmins and of showing them feats of strength. (268) If they fail to do so, the king must attack the suspected thieves and kill them.

But Manu[18] warns the king not to kill the thief, unless taken with the stolen goods or the implements of burglary in his possession. Yāj.[19] gives us a more detailed account of the possible ways of detecting thieves: "Grāhakair-gṛhyate cauro loptreṇātha padena vā/ pūrva-karmāparādhī ca tathā cāśuddha-vāsakaḥ // anye 'pi śaṅkayā grāhyā jāti-nāmādi-nihnavaiḥ/

dyūta-strī-pāṇa-saktā-ś-ca śuṣka-bhinna-mukha-svarāḥ//" paradravya-gṛhānāṃ ca pracchakā gūḍhacārinaḥ/ nirāyā vyayavantaśca vinaṣṭa-dravya-vikrayāḥ//".[20] The police-officers should arrest the thief, if the stolen goods are found in his possession or when detected by some marks of theft, if the thief is already noted as a criminal for previous acts and if he lives in an unholy place. Others may also be arrested on suspicion when one denies one's name, caste etc. from amongst those who are addicted to gambling, women and drinking, who bear pale faces and different tones, who ask to know others' houses and properties, who live in disguise, who spend a lot though earning a little and who sell stolen goods. Yāj. follows Manu more closely than Kauṭ. in punishing thieves. While Kauṭ. prescribes fines for theft, Manu enjoins that the king should cause not only the thief, detected with stolen goods but also his abettors who help him with food and lodging, put to death, of course, if he is proved to be a criminal. Yāj.[21] says that the thief, arrested on suspicions, should be given a chance to justify his case, if he fails to do so, he must be made to pay the stolen goods and to undergo the punishment due for theft. ("Dāpayitvā gataṃ dravyaṃ caura-daṇḍena daṇḍayet". Manu[22] prescribes punishment on thieves and their abettors, as stated above, and also on others like government officers who are appointed to guard provinces and the king's vassals (sāmantān) if they remain inactive in attacks by a thief or a robber. Professor Louis Renou has rightly remarked that "when an individual charge could not be sustained, the collective responsibility of a village was admitted. It is declared that the guards, the policemen and ultimately the neighbours are chargeable, if the thief is not caught".

Manu's[23] is a very severe code of punishment of thieves. He says that "the king shall cut off the hands of those robbers who, breaking into the house, commit thefts at night and cause them to be impaled on a pointed stake ("tīkṣṇaśūle niveśayat"). He enhances the punishment in cases of repetition of the crime, on the first conviction two fingers of a cut-purse are to be amputated, on the second one hand and one foot and on the third he shall suffer death. Thus Manu's laws are preventive in character and the capital punishment is awarded in incorrigible cases. Manu[24] lays down the general rule that a brahmin offender must not be killed on any account whatever crime he may do. He may be banished from the country and be allowed to go with all his wealth. About theft Manu's rate of punishment on a brahmin was the highest of all. Yāj.[25] lays down the general rule that the thief, irrespective of caste, must be made to pay the stolen goods and must be punished with various types of corporal punishment ("ghātayet vividhai-r-vadhaiḥ"). Vijñāneśvara comments that this punishment is meant for grave offences of stealing things of the highest value and never for lighter ones of stealing things of lesser value like flowers, cloth etc. Yāj.[26] is also in favour of the older theory of not killing a brahmin and agrees with Manu to banish him; of course, after branding him ("sa-cihnaṃ brāhmaṇaṃ kṛtvā svarāṣṭrāt vipravāsayet"). Kātyāyana[27] says that the school of the Mānavas opine that thieves, caught with stolen goods should be at once banished but the school of Gautama rejects this theory on the ground that it entails reduction of people in the country. The *Vivādaratnākara* (p. 332) explains this verse of Kātyāyana as referring to a learned brahmin. Kātyāyana's next two verses[28] are also quoted in the *Viv. Ratnākara* (p. 332). The first verse states that a brahmin, not learned, whether caught with goods or not, should be branded and deprived of all his wealth and the second one provides that a brahmin thief who is neither learned nor rich but of a strong physique should be enchained, fed on a poor food and made to do hard labour for the king till his death. Kātyāyana like Manu (IX. 271 & 278) and Yāj. (II. 276) prescribes punishment for the abettor of thieves like thieves themselves. Manu enjoins the capital punishment ("hanyāt") for the abettors but Yāj. prescribes only the highest amercement for them. ("damauttamaḥ" II. 276).

Nārada says that the capable persons who remain inactive and are indifferent to thieves are equally to blame and they deserve equal punishment. ("Śaktā-ś-ca ye upekṣante te 'pi tad-doṣa-bhāginaḥ"). This rule may be easily compared with sec. 212 on harbouring an offender and Section 411 on receiving stolen property of I.P.C. Manu[29] says that "those who do not give assistance according to their ability when a village is being plundered, a dyke is being destroyed or a highway robbery committed, shall be banished with their goods and chattels". ("grāmaghāte hitā-bhaṅge pathi moṣābhidarśane").

The *Mitā.* on Yāj. II. 268 quotes Nārada and warns that the king should be convinced before punishing anyone whether the alleged person is really a thief; because sometimes an innocent man may have a stolen property with him or may be associated with the marks of theft. ("A-caurasyāpi loptrādi-caurya-liṅga-samvandha-sambhavāt"). Nārada says that the king should carefully examine whether it comes from another hand or it was taken when it was on the ground as an unclaimed property or it has been taken by one as a thief. Nārada is quoted here to have stated that liars often appear as honest men and *vice versa.* ("Asatyāḥ satya-saṃkāśāḥ satyā-ś-cāsatya-sannibhāḥ/ dṛśyante vividhā bhāvā-s-tasmād-uktaṃ parīkṣaṇam//"). It is interesting to note that Nārada[30] speaks of six kinds of disputes in which the marks or circumstances themselves serve as witnesses. Best[31] on Evidence (12th ed., 1922, section 294) gives us an illustration of circumstantial evidence, viz., the fact of one's being armed is taken as a clue to his being the probable murderer in some cases. But Nārada[32] warns us at the same time to be very careful in drawing any conclusion from mere circumstantial evidence, because sometimes, a person, in order to endanger his enemy, may create some marks of injury on himself. The AŚ. seems to recognise the importance of the inquisitorial system. Kauṭ. was in favour of subjecting the accused in cases of theft to a series of interrogations about "the nature of work he did during the day previous to the theft and the place where he spent the night till he was caught hold of" (IV. 8). He says that the suspect should not be generally arrested three days after the commission of the crime because interrogation that may be put of him will not be helpful as he may not answer properly owing to forgetfulness. ("pṛccābhāvāt vismṛti-sambhavena praśnayogāt—ed. Ganapati). He adds that a satisfactory explanation of the criminating circumstances will be regarded as a proof of his innocence, otherwise he will be subjected to 'Karma' (tortures). The interrogation of the accused acts as a moral torture to him and it was applied to extract truth from the suspected person. But it may be argued against this system that "it assumes the guilt of the accused before proof, makes the judge enter into the intellectual fight with him on that hypothesis, impairs his impartiality and thus detracts from the moral weight of the condemnation of the accused, however guilty he is". Kauṭilya[33] warns us of dangers coming out of circumstantial evidence, as illustrated in the case of one Māṇḍavya. That is why Bṛhaspati[34] emphasises on careful reasoning in the decision. ("Yukti-hīna-vicāre tu dharma-hāniḥ prajāyate/ ...... yuktiṃ vinā vicāreṇa Māṇḍavya-ś-cauratāṃ gataḥ//"). The *Mṛcch.* (IX) is a glaring illustration of the danger of the pollution of the judicial procedure simply on the basis of the circumstantial evidence.

Yāj.[35] speaks of the means of restoration of the stolen articles when the thief is not detected. If theft or murder is done in a village, the village-headman is to blame and it is his duty to catch the thief and hand him over to the king. But if he fails to do so, the village-headman must give compensation to the owner; of course, if the marks of the thief's entrance into another village are available, the lord of that village would likewise be liable to compensate. If the crime is committed in any seclusive area outside any village, the owner of that area is to be blame. Whenever the crime is done on the road, whether in or outside a village, the protector of the road who is to uproot the thief is to be punished. Yāj. (272) says further that the entire village must make good the loss, if theft is done either in the village or in the area up to its boundary, another village where the thief is traced to have entered or even sometimes 5 to 10 villages together must bear the compensation amount. Vijñāneśvara reminds us of Gautama's text, already noted, to show that the king is ultimately responsible for the compensation of theft, if the amount is not available from any other source.

Yāj.[36] follows Manu[37] to prescribe impalement (capital punishment) for persons of graver crimes like those who confine others as captives, who steal horses and elephants and who kill others with force. Manu[38] says that those who break into a royal storehouse, an armoury or a temple and those who steal elephants, horses or chariots should be killed without hesitation. Yāj.,[39] like Manu and *Viṣṇu Dh. S.*V.136 prescribes for the cut-purse the punishment of the cutting of the thumb and index-finger for the first offence and the cutting of the hand and foot for the second offence but about death for the third offence, as enjoined by Manu ("tṛtīye vadham-arhati") Yāj. is silent. Vijñāneśvara is an orthodox commentator and so he assumes such punishment on the basis of Manu but it is difficult to read the mind of Yāj. on this issue. Yāj. is in favour of considering factors like conditions of a country, time, age and capacity of the offender before deciding the punishment, though he follows the general principle of Manu (VIII. 320 ff) of inflicting punishment proportionate to the value of the thing stolen in cases of theft of materials, small, middle and great.

Manu has given us a detailed list of things of various cadres, small, middle and great. Yāj. is silent on this point and we may assume that he insists on the principle of classification according to the tradition of Manu and other earlier jurists. Nārada is more clear here to mention three categories: "Mṛd-bhāṇḍāsana-khaḍgāsthi-dāru-carma-tṛṇādiayt/śamī-dhānyaṃ kṛtānnaṃ ca kṣudraṃ dravyam-udāhṛtam// vāsaḥ kauśeya-varjaṃ ca go-varjaṃ paśava-s-tathā/ hiraṇya-varjaṃ louhaṃ ca madyam vrīhi-yavā api// hiraṇya-ratna-kauśeya strī-puṃ-go-gaja-vājinaḥ/ deva-brāhmaṇa-rājñāṃ ca dravyam vijñeyam-uttamam//".

Nārada prescribes three punishments, first, middle and highest amercement in cases of theft or robbery of three types of things proportional to their value. ("Sāhaseṣuya eva ukta-s-triṣu daṇḍo manīṣibhiḥ/ sa eva daṇḍaḥ steye 'pi dravyeṣu triṣvanukramāt/").

In some cases a person was allowed to take possession of some particular things of another even without his permission and with impunity, as evidenced by Gautama:[40] "Go'gnyarthe tṛṇamedhān virudvanaspatīnāṃ ca puṣpāni sva-vad-ādadīta phalāni cāparivṛtānām", i.e., one may take grass, fuel-sticks, flowers of trees and plants for feeding cows and worshipping fire-god from any place as if they belong to oneself and also fruits of trees that are not enclosed. Manu[41] also declares the taking of these things to be no theft ("asteyam"). Though these rules of Gautama and Manu mention no caste-distinction, we may assume that any twice-born is referred to here, because fire-worship was the compulsory duty of the members of the three higher castes alone. Yāj.[42] removes our doubt by the specific mention of the term ('dvija', i.e. the twice-born in the rule: "dvija-s-tṛṇaidhaḥ-puṣpāni sarvataḥ sarvadā haret" i.e., the twice-born may always take grasses, fuels and flowers from all. Aparārka (p. 773) observes that this rule is valid only when there is scarcity of these things (āpadi). Kullūka comments on Manu, VIII. 339 that such a possessor would not be liable to a fine nor does he incur sin. Vijñāneśvara, while commenting on Yāj. (II. 166) says that Gautama's rule "Go'gnyaṃsham tṛṇam-" etc., as stated above, holds good in cases of things, already occupied by others (etacca parigṛhitā-viṣayam), but in cases of unclaimed things, not yet occupied by anyone even the person other than a dvija, i.e., a śūdra is entitled to ownership of the thing which he comes across and possesses. ("aparigṛhīte tu dvija-vyatiriktasyāpi parigrahādeva svatva-siddheḥ"). He quotes a smṛti passage—"Tṛṇam vā yadi vā kāṣṭhaṃ puṣpaṃ vā yadi vā phalam/anāpṛccan hi gṛhṇāno hasta-chhedam-arhati"—meaning that if a person takes possession of grass or fuel or flowers or fruits of another without permission, deserves to have his hand cut off and he explains it to be applicable to persons other than dvija-s or to refer to a case when they are taken by a person who is not in difficulty or when they are not taken for the use of cows or for worship ("tad-dvija-vyatirikta-viṣayam-anāpad-viṣayaṃ vā gavādi-vyatirikta-viṣayaṃ veti").

It is interesting to note here that *Āpas. D.S.*[43] refers to difference of opinion among earlier jurists as to whether taking things of another without permission amounts to theft. Kautsa, Hārīta, Kāṇva and Puṣkarasādi thought that whatever (small or great) one took without the permission of the owner, one was regarded as a thief. Vārṣāyaṇi opined otherwise that one could take such things, if of a small quantity like grains in pods or grass for bulls yoked to carts without being taken as a thief but there would be theft if these things were taken in large quantities. Manu[44] says that "he who has not eaten at the time of six meals, may take at the time of the seventh meal from a man who neglects his sacred duties, without making a provision for the morrow, either from the threshing floor or a field or out of the house or wherever he finds it but if the owner asks him, he must confess to him that deed and its cause. A Kṣatriya must never take the property of a virtuous brahmin but he who is starving may appropriate the possessions of a 'dasyu' or of one who neglects his sacred duties".[45] Both Manu and Yāj. agree on the point that a brahmin's property should under no circumstances be taken but a hungry man, as noted above, may steal from a non-brahmin. ("Brāhmaṇasvaṃ na hartavyaṃ kṣatriyeṇa kadācana", Manu, XI. 18 and "bubhukṣita-s-tryahaṃ sthitvā dhānyamabrāhmaṇād-dharet"—Yāj. III. 43).

Manu[46] enjoins again that "a twice-born who is travelling and whose provisions are exhausted shall not be fined, if he takes two stalks of sugar-cane or two (esculent) roots from the field of another.[47] The *Mitākṣarā* on Yāj. (II. 275) quotes a passage: "caṇaka-vrihi-godhūma-yavānāṃ mudga-māṣayoḥ/ aniṣiddhai-r-grahītavya muṣṭi-rekaḥ pathi-sthitaiḥ//"- showing a traveller's special privilege, mentioned above. Vyāsa[48] permits even theft in case of extreme distress, first from a member of a lower caste, then from one of the same caste and last from a member of a higher caste. ("āpatsu vihitaṃ stainyaṃ viśiṣṭa-samahīnataḥ hīnād-ādeyam-ādau syāt samād-vā tadanantaram"). Here also the Dharma school shows how it accepted the principle of self-defence, as set up in the Artha School. Some think that the Dharma School "took it from the Purāṇa which was the origin of the theory" (Āpas, I. 29.7). There is no question of guilt in protecting one's life and so in repelling force by force and specially in cases where there is no intention of causing injury to others. That is why the AŚ says—"nātatāyi-vadhe doṣo hantu-r-bhavati kaścana" and even the Dharma school asserts in the section of "prāyaścitta:" ("Kāmato brāhmaṇa-vadhe niṣkṛti-r-na vidhīyate") the principle of "no guilt" for want of any bad intention to justify the cause of self-defence. Here the hungry man taking a handful of corn from a field, of course, small enough to satisfy his hunger is not regarded as a thief. Even now this practice is running in India. Bṛhaspati, q. in *Sm. Candrikā* says that a thief, detected by police-officers by means of evil company, marks of theft and stolen goods must be made to restore the articles to the owner and should be punished with amercements, as prescribed by scriptures. Viṣṇu also prescribes that the entire stolen property should be given over to the owner. Bṛhaspati supports capital punishment in cases when one's death brings the benefit of many ("Vahūnāṃ bhavati kṣemaḥ") and prescribes that thieves stealing travellers' goods must be hanged to death on trees and house-breakers should be impaled to death.

It is interesting to note that Daṇḍin[49] refers to the Kirātas of the Vindhya forest who "used to harry the neighbouring country and seize the wealthy villagers with their women and children and having brought them to this forest put them into custody and take all their wealth". It is more curious that the art of stealing was taught to the princes.[50] Daṇḍi[51] describes the manner of theft and the appliances used in stealing. U.N. Ghoshal[52] thinks that the state realised a levy like the modern Chaukidari tax from the people for the maintenance of the Police-staff". It may be noted here that according to the *Agni Purāṇa*, theft (27.53-54 and 258.59), abetment to theft and help to thieves (227.52) are to be punished with capital punishment. The *Agni Purāṇa*[53] mentions the function of an officer-in-charge of protection against thieves. ("Caura-rakṣādhikārī") who is held responsible for theft and the amount stolen is to be realised from him in the case of non-apprehension of the criminal. If the criminal runs away from one village to another, the places where he is suspected to enter are to be brought to account. In case of theft of a horse or an elephant five or ten adjacent villages within the radius of 2 miles from the place of occurrence are to be called for explanation.[54] The above account shows how the village-officers were engaged in charge of peace and order and protection of life and property of the people living in villages. The *Gāthā-sapta-śatī*[55] refers to robbery in villages and the consequent resistance offered by the Grāmaṇī and his men. Besides these village-officers we hear of a 'Sthānapāla' in *Agni Purāṇa* (257.24), as in Yāj. (II. 173) whose duty was to keep in custody lost or stolen things, recovered by him for a year and after that, in the absence of the rightful owner, to restore it to the royal treasury. Gautama also enjoins that the king should wait for a year for the restoration of lost or stolen goods to the real owner. ("Pranaṣṭa-svāmikam ...... saṃvatsaraṃ rājñā rakṣyam") Yāj. (II. 173) also says the same thing: "Śaulkikaiḥ Sthānapālaivā naṣṭā-parhṛtam-āhṛtam/arvāk-saṃvatsarāt svāmī hareta parato nṛpaḥ//". Manu[56] however, extends the period up to three years within which the owner may claim the lost article. Vijñān. comments that this concession is granted only to the learned brahmins.

Let us turn to the ancient laws of other countries: In Babylon theft was treated as a civil wrong and compensation was to be paid to the owner of the stolen articles. But if a man, while extinguishing fire, was found stealing, he was thrown into the same fire.[57] According to Persian Law the thief was punished with fine or imprisonment or hard labour or branding. In the Sassanian period the repeated cases of theft were subject to mutilation of ears and hands and even to hanging.[58]

According to the Mosaic Law,[59] the thief was made to pay the compensation up to 5 times the value of things stolen to the owner. In Athens the thief was penalised with disfranchisement. "Stealing anything in the night time, or from the gymnasia or stealing in the daytime to a greater amount than 50 drachms or from the baths or the harbour to a greater amount than 10 drachms, was punishable with death. When the thief was caught in the act of stealing, the owner of the goods might carry him off at once to the Eleven, and have him sent into prison; or if he was afraid to do it himself, he might bring the magistry to the spot and get them to do it for him".[60] In Rome the Twelve Tables divided theft into two classes, one taken in the act and the other not so taken. Distinction between a freeman and a slave was observed: the former caught red-handed was scourged and handed over to the owner of the goods, while the latter was scourged and hurled from the Tarpeian rock. In Imperial Rome theft was treated as a civil wrong: "The penalty of committing a manifest theft is quadruple, whether the thief is free or bound and the penalty of committing a theft not manifest is double the value of the thing stolen".[61]

Theft or 'larceny' is treated as a capital crime in medieval France and more severely dealt with. In the earlier age the Salic law took it as a private wrong but the Imperial capitularies showed a stern attitude—"The thief was to have his eyes put out; for the second offence his nose was cut off; for the third he was condemned to death". These punishments were retained in the medieval Custumals. According to Bouteiller the thief, caught while stealing a thing of more than 5 sous in value was guilty of a capital crime but if the value was 5 sous or less, he had to lose his ear for the first offence and meet death on repetition. But the thief, not caught in the act was punished either with a fine or whipping in default.[62]

According to the ancient Saxon law, a person stealing a thing of above the value of 12 pence was liable to the punishment of death but he was allowed "to redeem his life by a pecuniary ransom". Since the period of Henry I this privilege of redemption was abolished and the thief was directed to be hanged. But as this was clergyable offence, he was excused the death-penalty for the first offence, though "in many cases of simple larceny the benefit of clergy has been taken away by statute". It may be noted here that larceny in English law was of two kinds, (i) simple, i.e., when theft was unaccompanied with any other atrocious circumstances and (ii) compound, that is when it was accompanied with aggravating circumstances. Simple larceny is again called 'petit' when the value of the thing is 12 pence or less and 'grand' in case of things of higher value. Petit larceny is punished with imprisonment or whipping at Common law but grand larceny is a felony, subject to the withdrawal of the benefit of clergy by 8 Eliz. C. 44.[63]

RECEIVING STOLEN ARTICLES

Laws relating to the stolen property speak of the legal wisdom of the ancient jurists because of their sense of justice to all concerned. Gaut. (XII. 50), as noted before says that he who purchases a stolen article knowing it to be so is guilty of receiving stolen article. But if he does so without such knowledge, he is not guilty. Besides, if the purchaser can produce the vendor, he is freed from guilt; and in such a case the thing will go back to the owner, the purchase-money should be returned to the purchaser and the vendor shall be punished with a fine.[64] The owner also must prove his claim by proper evidence, or he is liable to punishment. From Kauṭ.'s rules on sale without ownership (III. 16, 20) we know that "if the owner takes away a lost or stolen article without informing (the judge), the fine shall be the lowest fine for violence". But Nārada differs from Kauṭ. and allows the owner to keep it, when he recovers the thing, sold by another person without ownership. (N. 7 Tit., 2).

The Babylonian law may be quoted here: "If a lost article is found with another man who says that he has purchased it from another man before the elders, then the purchaser shall produce the vendor and the elders, and the claimant the witnesses recognising his lost property. If the sale be proved and the claimant also establish his ownership, the seller shall be held to be a thief and shall be slain. The claimant shall receive his property from the purchaser who shall receive back his purchase-money from the house of the seller. But in case the purchaser does not produce the seller and the elders, but the claimant proves his ownership by witness, he shall receive back his stolen property and the purchaser shall be held as a thief and shall be slain. If the seller is dead, from his house the purchaser shall claim five-fold as the penalty in the case. If the purchaser has not the elders at hand, the judge shall give him time up to 6 months. If in 6 months his witnesses do not appear he has acted in bad faith; the penalty of that case he shall bear".[65] In English law the receiver of stolen articles with full knowledge of their being stolen, was held guilty as accessory to theft and felony according to 3 and 4 William and Mary C. 9 and 5 Aun. C. 31.[66]

REFERENCES

1. *Ṛ̣V.*, 1. 191. 5; VI. 28.3; VIII. 29.6 and 67.14., X. 4.6
2. XI. 79.
3. IV. 1.101.2.
4. *Chānd. Upa.*, V. 11.5.
5. II. 1.46.
6. *Ibid*, 47.
7. II, 3.12 & 13.
8. VIII. 337-338.
9. Pariśiṣṭa, 51-52.
10. 3.17.5.
11. II. 10.26.6-8.
12. VIII. 319-331.
13. 8.323.
14. IX. 292.
15. Manu, IX. 258-60, cf. also *Nār. Pariśiṣṭa*-2-3; Bṛ. *SBE*, 33, p. 360, verses 3-4.
16. q. by *Sm. Ch.*, II. p. 318.
17. IX. 261-266.

18. IX. 270.
19. II. 266.
20. 266-268.
21. II. 268
22. IX. 272
23. IX. 276.
24. VIII. 380.
25. II. 270.
26. II. 270.
27. 823. q. by *Vi, ra.*, p. 332.
28. 824-25.
29. IX. 274.
30. IV. 172-175.
31. 12th ed., 1922, section 294.
32. IV. 176.
33. IV. 8
34. q. in *Parā. Mā.*, III, p. 39.
35. II. 271.
36. II. 273.
37. IX. 280.
38. IX. 280.
39. II. 274.
40. 2.3.25.
41. VIII. 339.
42. II. 166.
43. 1.10.28. 1-5.
44. XI. 16-18.
45. Cf. Sāntiparvam, 165, 11-13 and Yāj. III: 43.
46. VIII. 341.
47. See also Nārada - XVII. 39 and Śaṅkha, q. by *Sm. Ch.*, I, p. 176.
48. q. by *Sm. Ch.*, I, p. 175.
49. Daśa, Ch. II, Kale's trans., p. 10.
50. Daśa, Ch. I., Kale's trans. p. 14.
51. Ch. III., Kale's trans., p. 56.
52. HRS, p. 211.
53. 223. 22.
54. *Agni Purāṇa.*, 258.60-61 and cf. *Viṣṇu-Dharmottara-purāṇa*, II, 61. 49-50.
55. VII. 28.
56. VIII. 30.
57. Ham, 25, 13, 259 & 260.
58. *Zoroastrian Civilisation*, Ch. XIII & L.

59. Exod. 22.[1, 4]
60. Demos., III, App. VIII, p. 349; Note in P. 147—Orations against Androtion; *Historical Jurisprudence*, IX, p. 177.
61. T.T., 8.[14-16]; Justi, IV. Title, 1, 5.
62. Cont. G.L. , I, VI, 39 f.
63. Black, IV, XVII, pp. 229-241.
64. Manu, 8.198; Kauṭ., IV. VI; Yāj. II. 170; Nār, 7 Tit., 4 & 5 and Bṛh (XIII. 2-4).
65. Hām., 9, 10, 12 & 13.
66. Black, IV. X. 132.

CHAPTER IV

Sāhasa

(Crimes of Violence)

Kauṭilya (III. 17), as noted before defines sāhasa as "sudden and direct seizure (of person or property) as opposed to theft which is coupled with fraud and an act of force not in sight". Nārada[1] defines it as a derivative from 'sahas' meaning force and distinguishes it from theft in the light of Kauṭilya and Manu.[2] Nārada[3] and Bṛhaspati[4] state that sāhasa is of four kinds, viz., killing of man, theft, violence to others' wives and two kinds of 'pāruṣya'. Although these four kinds of crimes are treated under 'sāhasa', yet these are treated separately in the Dharmaśāstras only to distinguish one's gravity from the others and to provide higher punishment for crimes of violence which are regarded as acts of the worst sins.[5] While commenting on Yāj. (II. 230) Vijñāneśvara states emphatically that sāhasa is separately treated for providing a greater punishment. ("Tad-idaṃ sāhasam caurya-vāk-daṇḍa-pāruṣya-strī-saṃgrahaṇeṣu vyāsaktam-api vala-darpā-vaṣṭambho' pādhito bhidyate iti daṇdātirekārthaṃ pṛthagabhidhānam"). The *Vyavahāramayūkha* (p. 2) states that adultery, verbal and physical injury are separately treated, though they are but different kinds of sāhasa on the ground of the maxim of 'cows and bulls' which means that bulls are separately mentioned, though they are included under the general term "gāvaḥ" because they require more attention to be controlled than the cows.

It is interesting to note that Yāska speaks of seven great sins.[6] Āpastamba[7] reduces the number to four: theft, human murder, adultery with the Guru's wife and drinking (wine). He speaks of human murder and theft instead of brahmin-murder and theft of gold. Abortion was amalgamated with the killing of a brahmin. Theft was narrowed down to that of gold. Manu speaks of five kinds of mahāpātaka: killing of brahmin (brahmahatyā), drinking liquor (surāpānam), stealing (steyam), adultery with a guru's wife (gurvaṅganāgamaḥ) and associating with such offenders (Saṃsarga-ś-cāpi taih saha).[8] Yāj.[9] follows Manu. According to the Dharma law penance and punishment makes an offender pure but the later jurists differ and state that men committing great sins, even after undergoing punishment were not held as pure and so not fully admitted into the society. That is why they were debarred from the privilege of competent witnesses.

Gautama[10] condemns a murderer of a brahmin as the ostracised in the society (Brahmahā-patitaḥ). The inciters or abettors who induce others to do the acts of violence or sins are also equally condemned ("pātaka-saṃyojakaśca"). The murder of a brahmin, the drinking of wine and violating the bed of the Guru are, according to Gautama, of so much gravity—that there is no atonement for these crimes (anirdeśyāni) (*Ibid.*, 7). Manu also says that the willful murder of a brahmin knows no atonement—(Kāmato brāhmaṇa-vadhe niṣkṛti-r-na vidhiyate). Gautama[11] prescribes different atonements for murder on the basis of castes and sexes of the murderer and the murdered. The murderer of a brahmin must abstain from food and grow thin and sacrifice himself twice in a pit of fire (III. 4.1). Even an attempt of the murder of a brahmin is condemned as much as the murder itself (*Ibid.*, 11). Gautama (*Ibid*, 12) prescribes the same punishment for murdering a brahmin woman during her menses (Ātreyī) as for murder of a brahmin male. The sexual intercourse with an Ātreyī was condemned as an act of sin in *Śat. Brāh.*, (1.4.5.13). Even the murder of a foetus of a brahmin was similarly looked down upon (*Ibid.*, 13). This shows the supremacy of the brāhmaṇa in the society even long before Manu. The murder of cows and other animals was also condemned as heinous crimes and Gautama prescribes various atonements for the same.

We hear of Aṅgulimulyas, "the unlucky caste (the criminals) of Śrāvasti" who once murdered "men in the towns and country" until they were converted by Buddha.[12] The Jain texts mention various types of thieves: thieves (āmoṣa), robbers (*lomahara*), cut-purses (*gaṇṭhibheya*) and burglars (*takkara*).[13]

(*Uttara,* Sūtra, 9.28). The *Vivāgasūya*[14] mentions a "corapalli" named Sālāḍavī (3, p. 20). Sīhaguhā is another such village, heard of in Rāyagiha.[15] The Jaina texts refer to daring robbers, too difficult for the king to be controlled.[16] The *Vivāgasūya* describes Vijaya of Sālāḍavī, a ringleader of robbers who gave shelter to adulterers, pickpockets, thieves and other undesirable persons and who raided towns and villages (3, p. 20). Punishments for robbery were of various types, imprisonment, mutilation and death-penalty. The robber Vijaya is heard of as being subjected to arrest, blows, throwing over of ashes, dust and filth, imprisonment and starvation to death.[17] Another robber Abhaggasena of Purimatāla was by trick arrested and executed.[18] Even a priest, robbing a purse of a merchant was first subjected to both the punishments of lashes and swallowing human excreta and then his entire property was confiscated.[19]

It has already been noted that Kauṭilya[20] prescribes fines in cases of forcible seizure of things of high or low value in accordance with gravity of crimes (3.17.5) and the highest fine for violence for one who binds or causes another to bind or releases from bondage a woman or man by using force (*Ibid,* 10). He prescribes for the man who incites another to crimes of violence double the punishment to be inflicted on the perpetrator himself and four times for one who incites another to commit violence by saying, "I shall give you as much money as may be required".

Manu[21] defines 'sāhasa': "Syāt sāhasaṃ tvanvayavat prasabhaṃ karma yat kṛtam", i.e., an offence committed in the presence of the owner and with violence is robbery as opposed to theft which is committed in his absence. ("niranvayaṃ bhavet steyam"). He warns the king against any negligence to punish the man committing violence, (8.334) who is, according to him, the worst offender ("pāpa-kṛttamaḥ"), worse than a defamer or a thief or one who commits physical injury.

Next let us analyse the laws of Yāj. on 'sāhasa'. Yāj.[22] enjoins that the king must save his subjects from the hands of Cāṭas, thieves, wicked persons, robbers and kāyasthas. (Cf. *Rājanīti-*

ratnākara of Caṇḍeśvara, ed. K.P. Jayaswal, Patna, 1936, p. 54). The meaning of 'cāta' is controversial, 'royal favourites' according to Bāla Gaṅgādhar and 'irregular troops'[23] in the opinions of Bühler, and Fleet[24] but Prof. Vogel takes it in the sense of a district officer. Vijñāneśvara and Caṇḍeśvara[25] explain it as a cheat ("Cāṭaḥ pratārakaḥ"). According to Aparārka 'cāṭa-s are 'piśunāḥ', i.e., backbiters or betrayers. Cāṭa-s, as associated with thieves etc. in the above text of Yāj. (1.336) are no doubt anti-social beings and oppressors of the people. Yāj.[26] follows practically the artha-laws of Kauṭilya as regards the punishment for forcible seizure of others' articles. But he prescribes special punishments for particular offences, as noted below. A fine of 50 paṇas is imposed on one who violates the order of respectable persons like Ācāryas, who beats the brother's wife, who does not pay the promised amount, who opens the house, closed with a seal and who causes harm to the tenants of his house and to members of his family etc. But the fine of 100 paṇas is inflicted on one who violates the modesty of a widow at his own will, who does not come to the rescue even when asked for help from the hands of thieves etc. and who calls for help without sufficient reason, on the Caṇḍāla who touches the members of the higher castes, on one who feeds the Śūdras and ascetics in sacrifices meant for gods and manes, on one who swears in an ill way, on one who does something which he should not do, on one who destroys the male organs of bulls and lower animals, on one who cheats others from the enjoyment of their things, who causes abortion of his maid-servant and on each of a father, a son, a sister, a brother, husband and wife, a preceptor and a disciple, if anyone of these deserts the other, though not fallen (II. 232-37).

Yāj.[27] prescribes elsewhere the highest amercement for one's striking others with weapons (śastrāvapāte) and for causing abortion (garbhasya pātane ca). Vijñāneśvara, while commenting on this reminds us that this rule holds good only in cases of abortion of women other than maidservants and brāhmaṇīs, because cases of abortion of maidservants are already noted to be dealt with a punishment of 100 paṇas and those of brahmin-females are considered as serious as brahmin-murder ("hatvā garbham-avijañātam"). Murder of men and women in general is to be punished with the highest or lowest fine; considering his or her conduct. Yāj.[28] enjoins further that a woman of a very foul nature like destroying the foetus and causing abortion to herself or a woman who kills her husband and who breaks bridge should be drowned to death with stone fixed in her throat, of course, if she carries no child. The term 'agarbhinīm' indicates that she should be spared her life only in the interest of the child she carries. Similarly if a woman other than a pregnant one commits such crimes as poisoning other's food or setting fire to others' houses or killing one's own husband, preceptor or child, she should have her ears, hands, noses or lips mutilated and then should be killed with the help of bullocks.[29] This punishment is shocking and barbarous. Yāj.[30] again prescribes that the miscreant who burns others' fields with ripe crops, houses, forests or pleasure-gardens, villages or camps (or places with grasses or woods) or who violates the queen must be burnt to death with the fire of the mat with which he is wrapped.

Kauṭ.[31] prescribes the similar punishment for incendiaries. *Viṣṇu*[32], *Agni Purāṇa* (CCXXVII. 32-39) and *Matsya Purāṇa* (CCXXVII 201) also lay down death by burning for persons who set fire to fields, pastures, houses, forests etc. In the ancient world arsoning was very often punishable with death, as for example, in Athens,[33] in Rome[34] and in France.[35]

Robbery was not infrequent in India during Harṣa's rule. Yuan Chwang was robbed of thrice in India,[36] and once his life was endangered by bandits near Ayodhyā. Medhātithi on Manu, VII. 87 says that when robbers and others in sheer disregard of the existing law, attack the people, the king must resort to war against them. Meruturṅgācārya[37] mentions in one of his stories that Gujarata under Vanarāja was known as the depot of robbers and even Vanarāja's sons took to plundering a vessel, anchored in a port of Gujarat. Evidences of robbery in

Indian literature are numerous and the king had to take strong, sometimes even military measures to suppress them.[38]

Nārada[39] divides sāhasa into 3 classes and prescribes punishment proportionate to the gravity of the offence ranging from a fine of 100 paṇas to corporal punishment, confiscation of entire property, banishment and branding or mutilation of the offending limb may be inflicted. Bṛhaspati[40] follows Nārada in classification of and punishment in varying degrees for robbery etc.

The laws of other peoples may be noted here for comparative study. In Babylon a robber was capitally punished but when the robber was not caught, the sheriff in whose jurisdiction robbery was done, had to compensate the victimised.[41] This reminds us of Nārada who also speaks of the duty of the officer-in-charge to trace the robbers etc. and to compensate the loss; and in case of looting of a house, the policemen, guards and the people of the area concerned had to make good the loss, when the robber was not caught.[42] The Mosaic Law enjoins capital punishment for robbery. In Athens the party robbed could arrest the robber and could bring him immediately to the eleven and if required, could have had the help of the magistrates for the purpose. If the robber admitted his guilt, he was at once put to death and if he denied he was tried by the jury.[43] But in Rome robbery was a mere civil offence. It was capitally punished in medieval France, whereas in England it was a felony for which the benefit of clergy was withdrawn by 23 Henry VIII C 1, and other statutes; but up to the period of William and Mary only robbery in a house or on the king's highway was deprived of the benefit of clergy, implying that robbery done elsewhere was exempted from death-penalty.[44]

The highway robbers were severely punished in India, as evidenced by Kauṭ. (IV, XI. 7), Bṛhaspati (XXII, 17) and Kātyāyana. They were also hanged or imprisoned for life[45] (*Zoroastrian Civil.*, Ch. L.) in ancient Persia. They were equally punished according to the laws of Athens[46] and of medieval France.[47] Burglary, i.e. theft at night by breaking into the house was severely punished in ancient India. Kauṭ. (IV. XI), Manu (IX. 276), Bṛhaspati (XXII. 17) and the *Matsya Purāṇa* (CCXXVII. 170) prescribe impaling for burglars. Burglars met the same end of capital punishment in Babylon,[48] and Athens.[49] In England, however, Burglary was, at Common law, a felony with the benefit of clergy.

From the Jaina sūtras we learn that murderer was punished with death-penalty, public execution and fines. The prince Nandivaddhana of Mathura wanted to kill his father-king and engaged a barber for the purpose but the conspiracy failed and the king ordered the execution of the prince publicly. The prince was led by the police officers to a square road, made to sit on a red hot iron, thrown and sprinkled over with hot water etc. and ultimately executed.[50] Even women were not spared and Devadattā, queen of Pusanandi who killed her mother-in-law, was impaled publicly.[51]

Vyāsa prescribes the method of killing the murderer. When the murderer is clearly proved to have committed the crime with his friends or associates, the king should arrange the execution of such criminals in different ways of capital punishment, which may act as deterrent to other people. Bṛhaspati enjoins capital punishment and confiscation of property of the murderer whether the crime is done openly or secretly. Bodhāyana prescribes the same in case of the murder of a brahmin by a non-brahmin. Kātyāyana, however, in case of a joint-attack upon one by many, singles out the man who had hit the heart to be the actual murderer ("marma-ghātī tu ya-s-teṣām sa ghātaka iti smṛtaḥ") so that he may be subjected to death or a befitting punishment. Yāj.[52] penalises not only the thief or the murderer but also his abettors with the highest amercement. He who helps the culprit with food, lodging, fire, water, advice, instruments or the amount of expenses for the crime, knowing well of his intention deserves the highest punishment. Similar laws against abettors are found in I.P.C., Sect. 107 ff. Nārada also says: "Śaktāśca ye upekṣante te 'pi tad-doṣa-bhāginaḥ". Bṛhaspati says the same thing: "Āśrayahśastra-dātā ..... anurūpam tu daṇḍaṃ teṣām prakalpayet". He who commences a crime of violence, who is a helper and who advises as to the way of its performance should be punished according to their ability and guilt. He advises the investigation of cases of murder: "Hata-s-tu dṛśyate yatra ghātakastu na dṛśyate/ pūrva-vairānumānena jñātavyaḥ sa mahībhujā//". The sources of previous hostility of the murdered should be searched after to find out the culprit. The marks like blood etc. must be enquired into. He prescribes the punishment not only for the 'marma-hantṛ' (one who hits the heart) but also for others like the abettors or exciters of the crime according to the gravity of the crime. The following punishments for theft-cum-robbery are prescribed: "Kṣetropakaraṇaṃ setu-mūla-puṣpa-phalāni ca/ vināśayan haran daṇḍyaḥ śatādyam-anurūpataḥ paśu-vastrānna-pānāni gṛhopakaraṇaṃ tathā/ hiṃsayan corayan dāpyo dvi-śatādyaṃ damas-tathā// strī-puṃ-go-hema-ratnāni devavipra-dhanaṃ tathā/ kauśeyaṃ cottamaṃ dravyam-eṣāṃ mūlya-samo damaḥ/ dvi-guṇo vā kalpanīyaḥ puruṣāpekṣayā nṛpaiḥ/ hantā vā ghātanīyaḥ syāt prasaṅga-vinivṛttaye//". Here the terms 'vināśayan', 'haran', 'hiṃsayan', 'corayan' and 'hantā' indicate that these rules are meant for checking cases of theft-cum-robbery. The rule 'hantā vā ghātanīyaḥ' is applicable to non-brahmins. Yama also asserts that in cases of theft-cum-robbery the brāhman should be above corporal punishment, ("Na śārīro brāhmaṇasya daṇḍo bhavati karhicit"). He will be subjected to confiscation of wealth and he may be asked to do acts like cattle-rearing (rakṣākarma) or other condemned acts ("vikarmāṇyapi") in accordance with his crime; but he must not be punished with capital punishment. Bṛhaspati follows Yāj., when he enjoins that the criminal is to pay twice the amount of the value of the thing robbed ("dviguṇo vā kalpanīyaḥ puruṣā-pekṣayā nṛpaiḥ"). Yāj.,[53] as noted before, demands the punishment of twice the value of the thing robbed of like gold, cloth etc. and of four times the value only when the offence was not admitted. The author of the *Mānasollāsa* included under the term 'para-drohaḥ', all cases of injuries, theft and even murder. ("marmodghāṭanam") which are extremely intolerable offences and hence should be avoided. Of 4 or 5 kinds of sāhasa Bṛhaspati[54] considers murder to be the greatest offence ("Vadha-s-tatrādhikaḥ smṛtaḥ") and advises that the culprits connected with murder should not be left with mere fines but they must be awarded death-punishment.

Kauṭilya[55] lets us know the measures adopted for the seizure of criminals on suspicion or in the very act. Criminals like murderers, robbers or offenders, guilty of misappropriation of treasure-trove or knaves living by foul means are to be arrested on suspicion for the following reasons: "Persons whose family subsists on slender means of inheritance, who have little or no comfort, who frequently change their residence, caste and names, ... who conceal their own avocations, and calls, who have betaken themselves to such luxurious modes of life as eating flesh and condiments, drinking liquor, wearing scents, garlands, fine dress and jewels, who have been squandering away their money, who constantly move with profligate women, gamblers .... who hold secret meetings in lonely places .... who hurry on to get their fresh wounds or boils cured, ... who are excessively attached to women, who associate themselves with men of condemnable learning and work ..... who purchase rare or suspicious articles in suspicious times and places .... who, though in charge of villages are terribly afraid of appearing before the prime-minister, ... who pant in fear while sitting alone, who show undue agitation or palpitation of heart, whose face is pale and dry while the voice is indistinct and stammering ..... ". This shows how Kauṭilya takes into account all factors, physiological, psychological and circumstantial, conducive of evil tendencies of criminals.

Care was taken adequately for finding out things lost or stolen. Whenever anything was lost or stolen, it was to be reported to all those who traded in similar goods. Traders who concealed such articles even after proper intimation, were condemned as abettors (sācivyakara) but if they were ignorant about these, they were acquitted on giving the articles. Kauṭilya enjoins strictly (4.6.6) that "no person shall, without giving information to the superintendent of commerce, mortgage or purchase for himself any old or second-hand article". In violation of this law, the person arrested with the article would have to satisfy the superintendent concerned with the right way of acquisition before release. The possessor of the article in question may plead that the article is either borrowed or hired, a pledge or a sealed deposit or one obtained from a particular person for retail sale. He must prove his case by producing the referee for release. He should also produce witness to prove the transfer of the article by gift or otherwise, as stated by him. Even in case of an article, alleged to have been thrown out, lost or forgotten by a third person the possessor must prove his innocence by adducing evidence as to time, place and circumstances of finding the article. Otherwise he shall restore the article, besides paying a fine equal to its value or he may be punished as a thief. It should be noted that this principle is also accepted by Yāj. (2.269): "Gṛhītaḥ śaṅkayā caurye nātmānaṃ ced viśodhayet/ dāpayitvā gataṃ dravyam caura-danḍena daṇḍayet//".

Criminals should be seized on the clue of the following circumstantial evidences. In cases of housebreaking and theft crimes may be due to both types of agencies, internal and external. The circumstances like entrance and exit effected through other than doors, breaking the door by means of special contrivances, breaking the windows with or without lattice-work, pulling off of roofs and houses, breaking the wall and tunelling should be carefully scrutinised. These processes are held necessary "to carry off the treasure secretly hoarded, information about which can only be gathered from internal sources". These circumstances of wear and tear, cognisable in the interior indicate the working of the internal hands in the crime; while those of the reverse nature, external agencies. If the crime is suspected to be committed by an outsider, the following persons shall be examined: a person of miserable appearance, present on the occasion, one associated with rogues or thieves and possessed of such instruments as are necessary for theft, a woman who is born of a poor family or has placed her affections elsewhere, servants of similar condemnable character, any person addicted to too much sleep or who is suffering from want of sleep, any person who shows signs of fatigue or whose face is pale or dry, with voice stammering and indistinct and who may be watching the movements of others or bewailing too much, any person who bears the signs of scaling heights or whose body appears to have been scratched or wounded with dress torn off; anyone whose legs and hands bear the signs of rubbing and scratching, anyone whose hair and nails are either full of dirt or freshly broken, anyone who has just bathed and daubed his body with sandal, anyone who has smeared his body with oil and has just washed his hands and legs, anyone whose footprints can be identified with those made near the house during ingress or egress, anyone whose broken fragments of garlands, sandal or dress can be identified with those thrown out in or near the house during entrance or exit or any person the smell of whose sweat or drink can be ascertained from the fragments of his dress thrown out in or near the house". An adulterer may also break into the house like a thief and he may be suspected on the same evidence, noted above. The 'Pradeṣṭā' (magistrate) with his retinue of 'Gopa'-s (village-officials) and 'Sthānika'-s (divisional officials) shall make a search for thieves outside and the 'Nāgaraka' (City-superintendent) shall try to detect internal thieves, inside fortified towns, according to above indications.

For comparative study laws of other countries may be mentioned here. The Mosaic law divides homicide into two classes, willful and accidental. Willful cases were punished with death, while accidental ones were not so, then the killer must "flee to the city of refuge".[56] In Athens "five tribunals decided cases of homicide. The first tribunal, the court of Areopagus tried cases of murder and poisoning. The proved convicts were punished with death. But except in the case of parricide the accused was allowed to go permanently to another country on a voluntary exile and his property was confiscated. The second tribunal, the court of Palladium tried cases of involuntary homicide. In such cases the person convicted was also allowed to leave the country and remain in exile until he would satisfy the deceased party with compensation. The third court of Delphinium tried cases of justifiable homicide, as in self-defence, which were let off without punishment".[57] The ancient Persian law[58] punished murder with death. The wife killing her husband was subjected to impaling in the Babylonian law,[59] but nothing has been prescribed for other cases of murder. The 'Twelve Tables' enjoin capital punishment for this crime. In medieval France, murder in secret was considered more heinous than an open one. Gradually homicide (meurtre) was defined as killing one's fellowmen with premeditation. Poisoning was counted as a greater crime. Like Roman 'parricide' the murder of husband by wife or of father by son or of son by father was regarded as the most heinous and the culprit was punished with throwing into the river.[60] The English law by the time of Blackstone divided homicide into three types, (1) justifiable, (2) excusable and (3) felonious. Justifiable were the cases committed for the prevention of forcible and atrocious crimes like murder, robbery, arson etc. and also that done by a woman to save herself from the outrage by a man. For these cases there was no penalty. Excusable homicides were again of two types, "by misadventure" and "upto a principle of self-preservation". Felonious cases were also of two classes, man-slaughter and murder. Willful murder was punished with death.[61]

It is worth mentioning that ancient India made distinctions in cases of homicide, as evidenced by the laws. noted elsewhere in connection with the right of private defence.

INQUEST ON SUDDEN DEATH

Kauṭilya[62] dilates in detail on various ways of inquest on sudden death. He gives us the chief features of a person who died suddenly by different processes, being victimised to crimes like suffocation, hanging, drowning, throwing down, poisoning, administration of a stupefying mixture or murder. Hence these symptoms are to be carefully watched for the proper investigation of any of these crimes, committed.

Poisoning was done by the administration of poison or of a stupefying mixture. Sometimes a person was killed by hanging, obviously to make it appear as a case of suicide either by hanging or by cutting the throat. Cases of murder by poison are confirmed by the examination of the meal taken by the murdered through birds (vayobhiḥ), or by milk (payobhiḥ ?). The meal extracted from the belly and thrown on fire is taken to be poisoned, if it makes 'Ciṭciṭa' sound and assumes the rainbow colour. The investigation of the case of murder is to be made through the dead-man's servants who might have received violent and cruel treatment at the hands of the dead, ("vāg-daṇḍa-pāruṣyāti-labhdham), or through the relatives of the deadman like a person of miserable life, a woman with affections placed elsewhere or a relative defending some woman that has been deprived of her inheritance by the dead man. It is interesting to note that this principle of Kauṭilya is followed by Yāj. who advises the following measures for finding out the culprit in case of a murder by an unknown man: "A-vijñata-hatasyā-śu kalahaṃ suta-vāndhavāḥ/ praṣṭavyā yoṣita-ś-cāsya para-puṃsi ratāḥ pṛthak//" (II. 280)—The sons and other near relatives and also the wives of the murdered person, who are attached to other persons should be separately asked the details of the quarrel whether the deadman was addicted to women, or he had special desire in anything or interest in a particular occupation and with whom he went to another country and also the officer-in-charge of administration of the place of occurrence of death should also be confidently asked to ascertain the criminal and penalise him properly. ("Strī-dravya-vṛtti-kāmo vā kena vāyaṃ gataḥ saha/ mṛtyu-deśa-samāsannaṃ pṛchhed-vāpi janaṃ śanaiḥ//")—II. 281.

Sometimes a man is first murdered and then hanged and Kauṭilya advises the same method of examination of such crime. Again one hangs himself either for wrongs he committed to others or for wrongs done to him and in such cases these wrongs should be investigated into. Murder is also caused by anger centering round an offence to women or property etc.

and in all cases investigations should be made from the relations first as follows: "who called the deceased, who was with him, who accompanied him on his journey and who took him to the scene of death".[63] Those outsiders staying at the spot of murder should be separately asked about the process of the actual occurrence, and any clue afforded by them shall be followed in further enquiry. Yāj.[64] also accepts the same principle of enquiry as Kauṭilya. Kauṭilya insists on finding out whether the witnesses "saw any armed person lurking in the place and showing signs of troubled appearance". Yāj.[65] also advises enquiry from the sons and nearer relatives about the dispute and from the unchaste wives of the deceased and next from others meaning outsiders who might have witnessed the scene—whether the murdered was interested in woman, wealth or any profession. Kauṭ. insists on the scrutiny of the personal property like travelling requisites, dress or ornaments of the murdered and on investigation with those who supplied these as regards "associates, residence, cause of journey, profession and other calls of the deceased".

SUICIDE

Kauṭilya[66] is very strict to those who commit suicide. If anyone under the infatuation of love, anger or any other sinful passions commits or causes to commit suicide by means of ropes, arms or poison, he or she shall be dragged by means of a rope along the public road by a Cāṇḍāla. Kauṭilya also forbids all funeral rites to such wretches and if any relative performs such rites, he shall either himself be deprived of his own funeral or be abandoned by his kith and kin. Thus Kauṭilya denounces suicide like all acts of murder or inducement to murder under the influence of passions because life is sacred. The measures, mentioned above, in cases of suicide were taken only to demonstrate to the people the ugliness and immorality of suicide. The I.P.C., Sec. 309 prescribes the punishment of simple imprisonment for one year or with fine or with both for one who attempts to commit suicide; with Sec.

306 is more strict to punish the abettor of suicide with the imprisonment for 10 years and also fine. Thus compared with modern law Kauṭilya is definitely severer to both those who commit or cause to commit suicide.

POISONING

Kauṭilya[67] prescribes that the man giving poison to another should be drowned in water and that the woman should be torn by bullock for this crime. (*Ibid.*, p. 181). Yāj.[68] follows Kauṭ.'s principle of punishing the woman concerned. Manu[69] warns the king against poisoning and Kauṭ.[70] cites some cases of kings being poisoned to death. Hence the ancient jurists of India like Vaśiṣṭha (Cf. Viṣṇu V, 191-192) deemed all such criminals as 'ātatāyin's ("agnido garadaścaiva" Vaś. II, 16) .... Poisoning was also practised in other countries in ancient period and was treated as a heinous crime in Athens and Med. France. In England it was counted as a treason by 22 Henry III, C. 9. According to Nārada, if a man kills another by applying poison, he is guilty of the sāhasa of the highest degree as in cases of rape etc. affecting life, punished with a fine of not less than 1000 paṇas, corporal punishment and confiscation of entire property etc.

REFERENCES

1. XVII. 1.
2. 8. 332.
3. XVII. 2.
4. *S.B.E.*, 33 p. 359, V. 1. q. *Sm. Ch.*, II, p. 312;
5. Manu, 8.345 and *Mitā.* on Yāj. II, 230.
6. "mahāpātaka", Nir. ch. VI. 27.
7. II, 27, 1 ff.
8. Cf. also Manu, IX. 235.
9. III. 227.
10. III. 3.1.
11. III. 4.
12. Beal, II. p. 3.
13. Uttara, Sutra, 9.28.

14. Ed. A.T. Upadhya, Belgaum, 1935.
15. Nāyā, 18, p. 209.
16. Panhavagaranaim, ed. A.C. Sen, 1936, 3 pp. 43a ff.
17. Nāyā, 2., pp. 53 f.
18. *Vivā*, 3, pp. 24 f.
19. Ācārāṅga Chūrṇi, 2, p. 65.
20. 3.17.5.
21. 8.332.
22. 1.336.
23. *I.A.*, V, p. 115.
24. *Gupta inscriptions*, p. 98.
25. *Rājanīti*, p. 54.
26. 2.230-32.
27. II. 277.
28. II. 278.
29. Yāj. II. 279; Cf. Kauṭ. IV. 11.19.
30. II. 282.
31. IV. 11.20.
32. V. 9-11.
33. Demos, III, App. VIII, p. 328.
34. T.T. 8, 5, 10.
35. *Cont. Cr.L.*, Pt. I, ch. VI, 39 f.
36. Beal, pp. 87 and 200.
37. P.C., p. 14.
38. Cf. *Vivā.*, 3, pp. 24 f.
39. 14 Tit, 3-10.
40. XXII, 23-28.
41. Ham. 23 & 24.
42. Nārada, Nep. man., 16-18.
43. Demos. III, App. VIII, p. 350.
44. Black, IV, XVII, pp. 242 & 243.
45. *Zoroastrian Civilisation* ch. L.
46. *ERE*, Greek, Cr. & Pun.
47. *Cont. Cr. L.*, *I*, VI, 39 f.
48. Ham., 21.
49. Demos. III, p. 154, Note 3.
50. *Vivāgasūya*, 6 pp. 36-39.
51. *Vivā.*, pp. 49 and 55.
52. II. 276.
53. "nihṇave tu caturguṇaḥ", II. 230.
54. "Tat-kāriṇo nārtha-damaiḥ śāsya vadhyaḥ prayatnataḥ", as quoted by *Viv. Chint.*, p. 105; Cf. also *Sm. Ch.*, Vya. Kāṇḍa, p. 722.

55. AŚ, IV. 6.
56. Exod 21^{12-14} Levi, 24. 17. 21, Deu, $19^{2-6, 11-13}$ and Ezek. 18^{10-13}.
57. Demos, III, App. VIII, pp. 327-336; Orations against Aristocrates, pp. 189-192.
58. *Zoroastrian Civilisation*, ch. L.
59. Ham., 153.
60. *Cont. Cr. L.*, pt. I, ch. VI, 39 f.
61. Black, IV, XIV, pp. 177-203.
62. IV. 7.
63. AŚ, 4.7.20.
64. II. 280-281.
65. II. 281.
66. IV. 7.5.
67. IV. 11.18.
68. II. 279.
69. VII. 217-220.
70. 1.20.16 f.

CHAPTER V

Strī-Saṃgrahaṇa

(Adultery)

Kauṭilya[1] deals with the offence of sexual intercourse with immature girls. Before examining them let us trace the views of earlier jurists on the issue.

Gautama[2] enjoins that in case of a wife's adultery the king shall cause her to be devoured by dogs in a public place, when she commits adultery with a man of inferior caste. (Śvabhiḥ khādayet rājā hīna-varṇa-gamane strīyaṃ prakāśam"). Similar punishment is prescribed by Manu:[3] "If a wife, proud of the greatness of her relatives or (her own) excellence, violates the duty which she owes to her lord, the king shall cause her to be devoured by dogs in a place frequented by man;" and also by the author of the *Mahābhārata*: "Śreyāṃsaṃ śayanaṃ hitvyā 'nyaṃ pāpaṃ nigacchhati".[4]

Āpastamba[5] prescribes the penalty of cutting the penis and testicles for the male, if guilty of adultery with a married woman but only confiscation of property in case of adultery with an unmarried woman. His laws on adultery provides the severest punishment for the Śūdra: "If a Śūdra commits adultery with an Ārya, he should be put to death. ("Vadhyaḥ Śūdra Āryayā II. 10.27-29) and the woman concerned would be purified by a penance if no child was born for their adulterous intercourse (*Ibid.*, 10). But if an Ārya commits the same offence with the Śūdra woman, he would be banished. ("Nāsya Āryaḥ Śūdrāyām—II. 10.27.18). Thus Gautama, Āpastamba and Manu—all the jurists show the policy of caste-discrimination applied in punishing cases of adultery.

Adultery in woman (that is, man is never referred to as something punishable in the Jātakas) was punishable with "death, imprisonment, mutilation or even cleaving asunder".[6] When once a headman of a village intrigued with a villager's wife, he was seized by the lock of hair on the top of his head, dragged into the courtyard and thrown down as he cried: "I am the headman". He was thrashed till he fainted and was made to remember the lesson.[7]

From the Jaina Sūtras also we learn that like robbery, adultery was punished severely with death, imprisonment, mutilation and banishment. Ujjhiya, a merchant's son of Vāṇiyagāma used to visit a courtesan named Kāmajjhayā who was also the object of love of the king. The king turned Ujjhiya out and kept her as his mistress. But after some time Ujjhiya met her secretly and was caught and belaboured by the king's officer. His hands were tightly bound behind his back, ears and nose mutilated, his offence was publicly announced and ultimately executed.[8] Elsewhere Sagaḍa is also heard of as being executed for committing adultery with a courtesan Sudamsanā.[9] Again, Bahassaidatta, a minister of king Udayana was impaled for a similar offence along with the queen.[10]

Both the *Mahābhārata*[11] and Manu[12] prescribe expiatory rites for the offences of an unchaste wife. "If one's wife misbehaves, she shall be kept confined and made to perpetrate the same penance that has been prescribed for a man committing adultery". (*Mbh.* XII. 165.63). Manu[13] also says the same thing. Thus these two sources show that the unchaste wife should be given a chance to correct herself and for the purpose should be kept confined and be allowed to practise penances. To engage dogs to devour her was the most cruel punishment prescribed by Gautama, Manu and the *Mahābhārata,* most probably in graver offences, specially when the wife committed adultery with a member of an inferior caste. Against those laws of the Dharma School, the artha-laws of Kauṭ. were definitely lighter and their influence on Yāj. is distinctly clear.

Kauṭ. recommends that the offender, for having sexual intercourse with an immature girl of equal caste before she has reached her puberty, should have his hands cut off or must pay a fine of 400 paṇas but if the girl dies, he shall be put to death.

The punishment would be lighter, i.e, cutting of fingers instead of hands or a lighter fine of 200 paṇas when the girl concerned attained maturity, though, of course, the offender was made to compensate to the father. Kauṭ. laid stress also on psychological factors for determining the amount of punishment, as for example, whether the offence was done against the will of the maiden or with her consent. The girl, if inclined was also made to pay half the fine of the male, i.e, (27 paṇas). He who violated the girl;, already promised to another with the price paid to her father, was punished with the cutting off of his hands or a fine of 400 paṇas, besides the compensation of the price to be returned to the previous suitor.

Kauṭ. shows a softer attitude to offenders in some cases and thus makes a realistic approach to the problem of the society for psychological reasons. The maiden, remaining unmarried even after menstruation for consecutive seven months would be enjoyed by the male, the groom-elect, according to his will—without any fear of compensation to her father for her father loses his right of authority over his daughter. Kauṭ. goes further to enjoin "no offence" for a man of equal caste and rank for his connection with a maiden lying unmarried three years after her first menses and also for a man of a different caste in case of connexion with a maiden remaining unmarried for more than three years and having no ornament on her person because "taking possession of paternal property under such circumstances shall be regarded as theft". (p. 259).

Kauṭ. prescribes the fine of 200 paṇas for an offender, who intending a maiden for another secures her (for a third person) and cancels his right to her if she is unwilling. Thus the cheat is punished and the girl's freedom to marry a different man altogether is sanctioned.[14] Similarly other cases of cheating like showing one maiden and giving another are also restricted by punishment of 100 paṇas, if the girl is of the same varṇa and by that of the double amount, if she is of a lower varṇa. Thus Kauṭ. fixes the amount of punishment according to caste.

Virginity was, as is always, held very important in the matter of marriage and so if any girl was proved to be not a virgin at the time of consummation, she had to pay a fine of 54 paṇas and even double the amount, if she failed to prove it even after maintaining that kind of condition. Similarly the man was also punished for accusing the girl of the loss of virginity.

Kauṭ.[15] also tries to check adulteration of girls not only by males but also by females; and the punishment prescribed is determined by consideration of castes and willingness of the party concerned. He is very strict to the maiden who deflowers herself and enjoins that she shall become "the king's slave" (*Ibid.* 22). He enhances the fine to double the usual amount in case of violation of a girl outside the village and for spreading false report regarding such things. The fine is 200 for abducting a maiden by force and the highest fine is prescribed, if she is abducted with gold (ornaments). For many persons abducting a maiden each of them shall be fined as above.

It is interesting to note that Kauṭ. guards the interests of daughters of a courtesan or of a slave who is not a slave by herself by prescribing three grades of fines, 12 paṇas for one violating a female slave due for redemption, along with the payment of clothes and ornaments, 28 paṇas for deflowering the daughter of a slave and 54 paṇas along with a dowry to the mother for molesting a courtesan's daughter (26-28). The Dharma-śāstras were written with the motive of maintaining the morale of the society and so their authors regarded the courtesans as the fallen and were blind to their merits, as noted in the *Kāmasūtra*. Kauṭ., belonging to the Artha School was aware of the utility of the courtesans and prescribed their different functions. (*AŚ*, p. 44 and 123); hence it is quite natural that he would not neglect their interests to save their daughters from any molestation. Kauṭ. holds that "when having received the requisite amount of fees, a gaṇikā dislikes to yield her person, she shall be fined twice the amount of fees. ("bhogaṃ gṛhītvā dviṣatyāḥ bhoga-dviguṇo daṇḍaḥ"—AŚ, II. 27.20). This shows how the gaṇikā was regulated to serve the society, as agreed upon without cheating anybody. That the gaṇikā-s played a prominent role in the society is vouchsafed by the *Mahābhārata*[16] which shows that when Kṛṣṇa came to the Kaurava court on peace mission, he was welcomed by thousands of public women who were noted there as "Kalyānyaḥ" or auspicious. Kauṭ.[17] ordains that "for enjoyment of a prostitute by force, the fine shall be 12 paṇas and for many men enjoying (forcibly) one prostitute, the fine shall be 24 for each one separately.

Kauṭilya was also equally liberal to the slaves and enjoined to set them free under certain conditions (AŚ, III, XII. 182) one of which was that when a child was begotten on a slave by her master. He strongly advocates for the humane treatment of the slaves: "violating the chastity of a female slave shall cause the forfeiture of the value paid for him or her and shall at once earn their liberty for them. When a master has connection with a pledged female slave against her will, he shall be punished with the first amercement; a stranger doing the same shall be punished with the middlemost amercement. When a man commits or helps another to commit rape on a girl or a female slave pledged to him, he shall not only forfeit the purchase value but also pay śulka to her and a fine of twice the amount" (p. 182). This shows Kauṭilya's intention that a slave, when molested, would be automatically free and the offender would be punished with the fine, specifically mentioned above.

Compared with earlier jurists Kauṭ.[18] takes a lenient attitude to a wife committing adultery, when he prescribes that "the husband's kinsman or his servant should keep under guard the wife who misbehaves when the husband is away on a journey. Kept under guard she should wait for the husband. If the husband were to tolerate, both should be set free. In case he does not tolerate, (the punishment shall be) the cutting off of the ears and nose for the woman and the lover shall meet with death". ("Proṣita-patikām-apacarantīṃ pati-vandhu-s-tat-puruso vā saṃ-gṛhṇiyāt. Saṃgṛhītā patimākāṃkṣeta, patiścet kṣameta, visṛjyeto 'bhayam-akṣamāyāḥ striyaḥ karṇa-nāsa-chedanaṃ vadhaṃ jārasya prāpnuyāt").

Kauṭ.[19] holds that the sexual intercourse with the sister of one's father or mother, maternal aunt, the preceptor's wife, daughter-in-law, daughter or sister is incestuous and the punishment prescribed is the excision of the penis and death. The woman, if willing is also subject to similar punishment. Manu[20] also prescribes some expiatory penances ("guru-talpa-vratam") for the sins of approaching the women, the same as mentioned in the above list of Kauṭ., because he regards such women as unapproachable ("agamyā"). The punishment Manu prescribes for violating the Guru's bed is that after confessing the crime the offender must extend himself on a heated iron-bed and die (XI. 104). Yāj. (III. 231-233), Nārada (XV, 73-75) and the *Matsya Purāṇa* (227. 139-141) also prescribe the excision of penis and death by way of punishment (except for a brāhmaṇa) and expiation and for the woman, if willing, death-sentence.[21] Kauṭ. prescribes the same punishment even for the woman "having relations with a slave, servant or a pledged man".[22] It may be noted here that sexual intercourse with a near relation was also considered a heinous crime by the Hebrews and the Babylonians. The Babylonian law punished incest with death or banishment. Hammurabi prescribes banishment for a person who knows his daughter, death by drowning for him who knows his daughter-in-law and by burning for him who holds incest with his mother. The mother involved has also to share the same penalty.[23] The Mosaic Law prescribes death for both the parties involved in such incest.[24] In 1650 incest was made a capital offence in England but after the Restoration the offence was left to "the feeble coercion of the spiritual court".[25]

It is worth remembering that Kauṭ. (IV. 13. 32 ff) prescribes fines as punishment for adultery with an eye to caste distinction, the first amercement for a Kṣatriya, the confiscation of the entire property for a Vaiśya and burning to death for a Śūdra in case of relations with a brahmin woman, not guarded. Cooking in a big jar was meant for one having relations with the king's wife. For adultery with a Śvapāka (cāṇḍāla) woman the male was to be banished with the mark of a headless trunk branded on his head, while the Śvapāka male, committing adultery with an Ārya woman had to meet death. It is surprising that Kauṭ.[26] and Yāj.[27] prescribe a fine of only 24 panas for adultery with a female ascetic; whereas Nārada[28] and *Matsya Purāṇa*[29] take it to be a heinous crime. It may not be unlikely that Kauṭ. and Yāj. refer to nuns of lower classes, not following the orthodox path, while Nārada refers to nuns of a higher order. Kauṭ. does not allow such a female ascetic, if willing, to go with impunity. She is also ordained to undergo the same punishment.

Kauṭ.[30] allows circumstantial evidence to be placed for proof of adultery. Adultery is taken to be committed when there is mutual caressing of the hair ("Keśākeśikaṃ saṃgrahṇam") or from indication of bodily enjoyment (upaliṅganāt) or from the opinion of experts (tajjatebhyaḥ) or from the woman's statement (strī-vacanāt).

It is interesting to note that Kauṭ. acknowledges the right of a rescuer over a woman, either a stranger or one belonging to others under certain sets of circumstances when he has rescued her from the greatest peril of her life; the rescuer "may enjoy her as agreed upon". But she has the right to be ransomed if she belongs to a superior caste or she is unwilling or she has children. This shows the deep regard of the society for mothers and also for woman of higher order and the jurist is careful to control the torture of criminals on an unwilling woman. The woman, saved through the power of the king ("rājā-pratāpena") or by his kinsman was also likewise restored to her kinsmen in return for a suitable ransom.

The punishment for rape and adultery varied according to the caste of the male or female or according to the woman's state of being married or unmarried or according as she was guarded or not.[31] Kauṭilya's and Yājñavalkya's attitude to women might have been influenced by Bodhāyana and Vaśiṣṭha. Vaśiṣṭha[32] and Bodh.[33] say the same thing: "Strīyāḥ pavitramatulam naitā duṣyanti karhicit/ māsi māsi rajo hyāsāṃ duṣkṛtānyapakarṣati//", i.e., women possess an unrivalled means of purification, they never become (entirely) foul; for month by month their temporary uncleanness removes their sins". Manu[34] says that the husband must be constantly worshipped as a god by a faithful wife under all circumstances, but Yāj. makes provision for the escape of a wife from the clutches of a criminal husband (I. 77 and 87). Manu prescribes the duties of man and wife, whether they be united or separated (XI. I). He says that "women must be guarded against evil inclinations" (IX. 5 and 7-9) in order to ensure the purity of the issue. Hārīta. q. by *Sm. Ch.*, II, p. 239 and Śaṅkha-Likhita, q. by *Sm. Ch.*, II, p. 241 also advise so. Manu (IX. 10) devises the means as well how to guard the wife, not confining her in seclusion but by keeping her engaged in family work (IX. II).

Now let us examine Manu's laws on adultery. He (IV. 134) like the Anuśāsanaparvan, 104.21 and the *Mārkaṇḍeya Purāṇa*, 34. 62-63 forbids a man to have sexual intercourse with another's wife ("para-dāro 'pasevanam"), which is, according to him, the most detrimental to long life. But such illegitimate sexual intercourse was in practice in his days as in the earlier period, as already pointed out. By the way it may be mentioned that such ill practice was in vogue as early as the period of the *Ṛgveda*.[35] By adultery is caused a mixture of the castes (Manu, VIII. 353) and so Manu, an orthodox exponent of the caste theory prescribes that "man who commits adultery with the wives of others, the king shall cause to be marked by punishments which cause terror and then banish" (*Ibid.*, 352). That is why he restricts even the secret conversation of one, already once accused of such offences, with the wife of another person by enjoining punishment of the first amercement (VIII. 354). He also makes it clear that such secret talk with a person, not accused before, does not incur guilt (355).

Manu (VIII. 356) enjoins as a preventive measure that one must not address the wife of another man ("para-strīyam") at a "tīrtha" (a place on the river-bank where women fetch water, according to Medhātithi), in a forest or at the confluence of rivers perhaps because these places are generally lonely and fit for such illegitimate transactions. Medhātithi holds that the term "tīrtha" means such places which are generally frequented by people for fetching water and which are sometimes utilised by criminals for preparing the ground for committing adultery.

Āpastamba, however, advises us that women should never be passed over without proper address but in the light of this context his advice should be taken in the sense that women should be properly addressed only when many people are present so that there is little chance of any such illegal transaction. Medhātithi interprets the use of the term "para-strīyam" here, though the entire issue is concerned with talk with another's wife ("parasya patnyā") in the sense that talk with one's mother, sister and wife of the Guru in such places is not prohibited. Manu[36] also forbids the following acts, offering presents to a woman, romping with her, touching her ornaments and dress and sitting with her on the same bed, because these acts are, according to him, all adulterous ones. He again prescribes that one must not touch a woman in a place ("strīyam spṛśed adeśe") which ought not to be touched or must not allow oneself to be touched in such a spot because these acts, done with mutual consent are held to be adulterous (VIII. 358). Govindaraja means by 'adeśa' a lonely place. It is interesting to note that Medhātithi's contention that mere touching of even the private parts of the body is not always an act of adultery because adultery depends on the motive of the person concerned, which should be carefully assessed. Manu (VIII. 362) says that "the above rules making talk with another's wife in lonely places punishable do not hold good in cases of wives of actors and singers and of those who live on the earnings of their wives, for such men send their wives to others or concealing themselves, allow them to hold criminal intercourse". Yet he who secretly converses with such women or with female slaves kept by one master and with female ascetics shall be made to pay a small fine.[37]

Manu[38] emphasises on the care to be taken to guard the wives of each caste and prescribes death sentence on all except the brahmin for adultery. The brahmin should under no circumstances be killed, the highest punishment inflicted on him in lieu of death sentence for adultery is tonsure of the head. ("Mauṇḍyaṃ prāṇāntiko daṇḍyo brāhmaṇasya vidhīyate", VIII. 379). He should be banished with (without according to some) all his property and with his body unhurt. Elsewhere the question of death sentence for a brahmin has been dealt with and it is quite clear that Manu is lenient towards the brahmin, most probably because he belonged to the period of brahmanical revival, as Jayaswal would like to place him in the Śuṅga period.

Now about the non-brahmins. Manu says emphatically that one who violates an unwilling maiden ("Yo'kāmāṃ duṣayet Kanyām" VIII. 364) or who enjoys a maiden of the highest caste ("Uttamāṃ sevamanāstu", VIII. 366), even if willing shall suffer corporal punishment. The girl again, if approaching a man of the highest caste is not to be fined but if going to a man of lower caste, must be confined in her house until she is cured of her attachment. Medhātithi says that the girl, committing adultery with a low person must remain so until death. Manu again prescribes that a man who through insolence forcibly contaminates a maiden, shall have his two fingers cut off instantly and shall be made to pay a fine of 600 paṇas (VIII. 367). This rule is applicable, according to Medhātithi, to the case of a maiden, inclined to the man concerned without the consent of her guardians and this punishment is due for his insolence, because in the next verse (368) Manu ordains that a man of equal caste, defiling a willing maiden shall not suffer the amputation of his fingers but must pay the fine of 200 paṇas in order to deter him from the repetition of the crime. This is, therefore, not a case of insolence but a case of defilement in secret without the knowledge of her guardians.

Manu is also equally aware of another type of adultery, i.e., defilement of a maiden by another maiden or by another woman and so he prescribes the punishment of the fine of 200 paṇas with the double of her nuptial fee plus ten lashes with a rod in the first case and that of shaving her head or cutting of two fingers and riding on a donkey (VIII. 370). Medhātithi and Nārāyaṇa opine that these three punishments are meant for three castes, a female brahmin offender is to be shaved, a Kṣatriya woman to be led through the streets on a donkey, while a woman of other castes is to lose two fingers. Kullūka and Govindarāja think that the punishment is to be regulated by the circumstances. We have already noted Manu's stiff attitude to the woman who violates the duty to her husband showing his prescription of severe punishment, i.e., the adulteress must be devoured by dogs in the public place and the adulterer must be burned to death. His measures of punishment were determined by the castes of the offender and of the offended. Adultery with a woman of a higher caste is to meet higher punishment and with that of a lower order, a lighter punishment. His attitude to Śūdras is also very stiff as is natural for one who frames laws in keeping with a brahmanical revolution after the long Śūdra's rule of the Mauryas. That is why he like Gautama prescribes the excision of the penis and the loss of entire property of the Śūdra for intercourse with an unguarded woman of the twice-born caste and the loss of everything, even his life, if she was guarded (VIII. 374). Likewise a Vaiśya would forfeit all his property after imprisonment for a year and a Kṣatriya shall be fined 1000 paṇas and be shaved with the urine of an ass (375) for intercourse with a guarded woman of the twice-born caste, but for connexion with an unguarded brāhmaṇī the Vaiśya and Kṣatriya will be fined 500 and 1000 paṇas respectively. The Kṣatriya is to meet higher punishment than the Vaiśya because the former's duty is to protect all from injuries and so if he violates this principle, he should be punished more. But even these two, if they offend a brāhmaṇī, (not only) guarded (but the wife of an eminent man), shall be punished like Śūdra, as mentioned above in VIII. 374. or be burnt in a fire of dry grass (377).

It has already been pointed out that a brāhmaṇa is immune from death-sentence, even if he commits all the wrongs. The brahmin who has intercourse with a guarded brāhmaṇī against her will, is to pay the fine of 1000 paṇas but if he has connexion with a willing one, he has to pay only 500 (VIII. 378). He is to pay 1000 paṇas for intercourse with a guarded woman, belonging to all castes (Vs. 383 and 385); but he has to pay only 500 for connexion with an unguarded woman of the lower castes (385). The Kṣatriya and the Vaiśya are to pay 1000 and 500 paṇas respectively for intercourse with a guarded woman of the Vaiśya and Kṣatriya castes respectively. But the Vaiśya is to pay only 500 if the Kṣatriya woman is unguarded and the Kṣatriya is to pay the same amount or shall be shaved with the urine of an ass for similar offence with a Kṣatriya or Vaiśya woman. Thus the entire survey of Manu's laws shows that the society maintained a sharp distinction of castes and punishment was inflicted on the criminals on the basis of caste-distinction. The higher the caste of the offender, the higher punishment and *vice versa*. Punishment was determined also by the character of the woman concerned, whether she was guarded or unguarded.

Next let us examine the laws of Yāj. Vijñān. defines "saṃgrahaṇa" as the unlawful coming together of a man and a woman for sexual enjoyment.[39] Vyāsa classifies it under three heads, the first, the middling and the highest in accordance with three types of punishments, due for this: conversation with another's wife in improper place and time, side-glances and laughter constitute the first category, the sending of fragrant objects and garlands, incense, ornaments and cloths and enticement by food and drink form the middling one and the highest one consists in mutual catching hold of hairs. Bṛhaspati[40] also speaks of three kinds of adultery: "Valopadhikṛte dve tu tṛtīyam-anurāgajam/ anicchantyā yat kriyate mattonmattapramattayā// pralapantyā ca rahasi valātkārakṛtaṃ tu tat/ chadmanā gṛham-ānīya datvā ca madya-kārmaṇam// saṃyogaḥ kṛyate yatra tat-tūpadhikṛtaṃ viduḥ/ anyonya-cakṣu-rāgeṇa dūtī-saṃpreṣaṇena vā// kāma rūpārtha-lobhena jñeyaṃ tad-anurāgajam/" (Cf. Bṛh., q. by Aparārka, p. 854; *Sm. Ch.*, II, p. 8 and *Parā. Mā*, III, p. 462)—The first (rape) takes place when intercourse is had in a secluded place against the will of a woman or with a woman, intoxicated or unbalanced in mind or who is under a mistake or when she raises a cry. The second occurs when a woman is brought to one's house by some trick, wine is given to her and she is brought under control by chants etc. and then intercourse takes place and the third happens when intercourse is had by arousing passion in each other by means of glances, the use of a go-between and by means of the temptation of beauty or of wealth.

The I.P.C., Sec. 375 defines 'rape' of 5 categories and Sec. 376 prescribes punishment in the shape of imprisonment for life or for 10 years plus fine. The I.P.C., Sec. 493 again restricts cohabitation caused by a man deceitfully inducing a belief of lawful marriage by the prescription of the punishment of imprisonment up to 10 years with liability to fine. The Sections 497 and 498 prescribe for adultery with and enticing another's wife with the intention of illicit intercourse with her punishments in the shape of imprisonment up to 5 years and 2 years respectively or with fine or with both.

Now let us examine the laws of other ancient peoples. According to the Babylonian law "if the wife of a man is found lying with another male, they shall be bound and thrown into water; unless the husband lets his wife live and the king lets his servant live". But when the man is taken captive, the wife may enter the house of another man under dire need of food, without any punishment.[41] "Violation of a virgin wife dwelling with her father entailed death to the man but exile to the woman".[42] According to Persian law a man committing adultery with the wife of a noble man was banished, while the woman had her nose and ears cut off.[43] In all cases of adultery the Vendidad (XV. 18) requires that the person seducing a woman, shall maintain her and the children that may be born of her until they come of age. The Hebrew law prescribes capital punishment for both, man and woman for this offence.[44] The Athenian law treated it a serious crime, subject to the punishment at the discretion of the jury. A man could lawfully kill on the spot "one whom he caught in adultery with his wife, daughter or sister, mother and even with his concubine".[45] The first adultery was not held as a crime in Rome but by the end of the Republic immorality became so rife that by 'lex Julia' it was made so by Angustus and the culprit was liable to capital punishment.[46]

In Medieval France sexual intercourse with the consent of the maiden was not treated as a crime. Generally the punishment for adultery in modern sense was very light—a small fine. But the husband had the right to kill his wife if caught in the act.[47] It was so in early England but since the Restoration adultery is regarded as a private injury.[48]

The Hindu jurists treated kidnapping and abduction as a kind of theft and suitable punishments are noted before, as varying in degrees in proportion to the nature of the circumstances and rank of the victim. Kauṭilya[49] prescribes the alternative punishments of death with torture or highest amercement for abducting man and woman but he enjoins the cutting off of the left hand and two legs or a fine of 900 paṇas for kidnapping a maiden or a female slave together with money. Manu[50] also lays down corporal punishment or death for abducting higher people but only punishment for theft in cases of slave girls. Yāj.[51] follows Kauṭilya more than Manu. Later jurist like Nārada, Bṛhaspati and the *Agni Purāṇa* and *Matsya Purāṇa* prescribe capital punishment for this. Kidnapping was punished with the confiscation of the entire property, as evidenced by the statement of the Public Prosecutor in Daśakumāracaritam.[52]

The Babylonian, Mosaic and Athenian laws prescribe capital punishment for kidnapping or abduction.[53] In the Roman Empire also this crime was punished with death but sometime mildly treated.[54] In medieval France the abductors were capitally punished but they were allowed to go free by marrying the girl.[55] In England it was punishable at Common law with fine, imprisonment and pillory.[56] It may be noted here that rape was also treated as a heinous crime in ancient India as in other countries. It was punished with death according to the Babylonian and Mosaic laws, and in ancient Athens and Rome and in medieval France.

England under the Saxons punished rape with death. But William the Conqueror replaced it by castration or loss of eyes, but if the woman accepted the man as her husband, no punishment was inflicted. By 18 Eliz. C. 7 rape became a felony without clergy.

Yāj.[57] mentions the circumstantial evidences for the proof of adultery which should be judged before punishing anyone, viz., the sports of touching hairs of another's wife, the recent marks of passion like those made by nails or teeth and the confession of both the parties, touching the knots of dress, breast-cover, the hips and hairs, talk in improper place and time and sitting on the same seat. He[58] prescribes first of all, punishment for adultery with the wife of another: the highest fine ("sajātauuttamo daṇḍaḥ", i.e., 1080 paṇas) for the male in case of a woman of the same caste, half of this in case of a woman lower in caste ("ānulomye tu madhyamaḥ") but when adultery is committed with a woman of a higher caste, the male will be put to death ("prātilomye vadhaḥ puṃsaḥ") and the woman shall have her ears etc. cut off. Vijñāneśvara, while commenting on this raises the question of "guarded" or "unguarded" character of the woman concerned and substantiates the distinction of punishments for this reason with relevant question from Manu but it is difficult to say what was Yājñavalkya's opinion on this point. It is interesting to note that Vijñāneśvara observes that the direction for death sentence comes from the king and not from the twice-born because the king is the appointing authority to protect the kingdom but when lodging complaint to the king entails delay or loss of interests, then the twice-born should himself kill the paramour and others for the maintenance of dharma, as Manu sanctions in VIII. 348.

Now let us consider Yāj.'s attitude to adultery with maidens. His prescription of punishment is of different types and is determined on the basis of caste distinction and of willingness of the maiden concerned. He (II. 287) prescribes the punishment of the highest amercement for the male for stealing a maiden of equal caste, bedecked with ornaments, that is, when she is going to be married ("alamkṛtāṃ haran kanyām-uttamām"); otherwise the lowest amercement ("anyathādhamam") that is, when the maiden concerned is not inclined to marriage, that means, when the maiden is willing to be so stolen. But in case of stealing a maiden by 'prātilomya', that is, when the male (except a brāhmin) steals a maiden of a higher caste suffers corporal punishment. Vijñāneśvara remarks that besides this punishment, the maiden should be recovered from the (culprit) thief and given to another deserving hand. Yāj., however, finds no fault in case of stealing a maiden, if willing and belonging to a lower caste. But if the maiden, even of a lower order is not inclined, the punishment of the first amercement is inflicted on the male stealing her (II. 288). Here Yāj. follows *in toto* Kauṭ. who prescribes the punishment of the highest fine for abduction of a maiden, with ornaments by force and also accepts his principle of punishing the culprit more in case of an unwilling maiden and less in other cases. But Kauṭ.'s discrimination of punishment on the caste-basis is not so acute as we find in Yāj. Here Yāj. is more a follower of Manu than of Kauṭilya.

It is interesting to note the attitude of the ancient jurists towards rehabilitation of abducted or outraged women in India. Vaśiṣṭha[59] enjoins that a wife who is the victim of an outrage or of thieves is not to be cast away and assures that she will be purified by her courses. Atri holds that a woman, ravished by mlecchas and evil men (pāpa-karmabhiḥ) is purified by performing the 'prājāpatya' penance and by her courses (Cf. also *Parāśarasmṛti*, X. 25). Yāj.[60] enunciates that in adultery, purification accrues from the recurrence of the courses but not if there has been conception and that in the later case, the wife should be put away. ("Vyabhicārād-ṛtau śuddhi-r-garbhe tyāgo vidhīyate"). Vijñāneśvara shows the spirit of reaction against the lenient treatment of the woman when he points out that purification is rendered by her courses, if she commits only mental adultery (mano-vyabhicāra) but she must be cast away, if she becomes pregnant by a Śūdra; and he quotes Manu and Vyāsa in this context. But he shows the soft corner of his heart for such unfortunate woman by prescribing that 'casting away' here means only deprivation from the privilege of cohabitation and share in religious rites and not driving away from the house. ("tyāga-ś-copabhoga-dharma-kāryayoḥ na tu niṣkāsanaṃ gṛhāt-tasyāḥ"). She should be confined in a single house. Aparārka[61] also takes the same stand. It may be noted that Al-Biruni[62] reports that "an adulteress is driven out of the house of the husband and banished" and this shows that the rule had hardened by his time.

Manu, an orthodox jurist of the Dharma School is more conscious of the caste distinction of the society and so his laws are shaped in greater detail accordingly. Manu as already pointed out, prescribes corporal punishment for defiling an unwilling maiden of equal caste, and no punishment in case of a willing maiden of the same caste. Yāj. substitutes lighter punishment of fine in lieu of a corporal one in such cases but Yāj. follows Manu in cases of 'prātilomya' by prescribing capital punishment, in cases of defilement of maidens of lower castes. Yāj.[63] provides a severer punishment of the cutting off of the hand in place of that of two fingers only along with a fine of 600 paṇas, as enjoined by Manu (366) in inflicting corporal punishment for defiling the brahmin girl. He (II. 289), however, strikes a new chord when he prescribes the fine of 200 paṇas for the false accusation of a woman in public that she is suffering from a bad disease or is of bad character and that of 100 only if she actually possesses such demerits. Manu is silent on this point but Kauṭ. is aware of such wrongs and prescribes punishment only for the false accusation of a girl about her virginity.

Next let us turn our attention to the question of carnally approaching the female slaves and the ordinary courtesans. Yāj.[64] prescribes the fine of 50 paṇas for approaching them so.

The female slaves are of two types, the first ("avaruddha") who are confined in one's own house for one's own enjoyment and the second "bhujiṣya" who are not so confined in the house but who are specially meant for a particular man. Vijñāneśvara includes here also the cases of even unchaste women like public women, Svairiṇī and others; if they are associated with one man, they are to be regarded as his wife and so they should not be approached by any other men, as evidenced by his text which makes it clear: "Para-parigṛhītatvena tāsāṃ para-dāra-tulyatvāt ... tāsu ca sarvapuruṣa-sādhāraṇatayā gamyāsvapi gaccan pañcāśat paṇān daṇḍanīyah". Nārada also says the same thing: "Svairinyabrāhmaṇī Veśyā dásī niṣkāsinī ca yā/ gamyāḥ syu-r-ānulomyena strīyo na pratilomataḥ// āsveva tu bhujiṣyāsu dosaḥ syāt para-dāra-vat/ gamyāsvapi hi nopeyāt yat-tāḥ para-parigrahāḥ//". It may be noted in this connection that the inscription at Jambai (South Arcot) during the 28th year of the rule of Rājarāja I[65] refers to "a merchant of Jambai" who "had a concubine whom a native of Nāvalūr (now Tirunāmanallūr) attempted to outrage at night. The latter was stabbed by the merchant. The merchant could not be prosecuted. He combined with a relative of the deceased and gave gold for a lamp to burn in the Tānṛonṛiāḷvār temple at Jambai". This shows some sort of ownership over the concubine who was to be protected like one's wife from all molestations. The merchant, though not prosecuted for stabbing the native outrager atoned for the sin by the dedication of a lamp in the said temple.

It is remarkable to notice that even any of these unchaste women, if restricted under a particular man is to be protected by law from molestation by anybody else but if she is not so, she may be approached by anybody without any punishment, as evidenced by even Manu's texts like "Kanyāṃ bhajantīm-utkṛṣṭaṃ tu na kiñcidapi dāpayet". Vijñāneśvara mentions the courtesans or prostitutes (veśyā) as a separate class growing in the society from time immemorial out of the mixture of a female courtesan and a male of either equal caste or a superior caste as evidenced by the *Skandapurāṇa*: "Pañcacuḍā nāma kāścana Apsarasa-s-tatsantati-r-veśyākhyā pañcamī jātiḥ". He observes that this class of women incurs no unseen demerit or no punishment by approaching any man, equal and superior and a man, approaching such unrestricted prostitutes is also free from punishment but incurs an unseen demerit, because of violation of the principle "Sva-dāra-niyataḥ sadā" - i.e., one should be interested in one's wife alone. Besides, the penance of Prājāpatya is also enjoined to be practised for approaching an animal or a prostitute.

Vyāsa also prescribes the same amount of punishment for carnally approaching a woman, confined in the house of another. ("Paroparuddhāgamane pañcāśat-paṇako damaḥ"). But for forcible intercourse with a prostitute against her will without paying the usual fee Kauṭilya[66] and Yāj.[67] prescribe a fine of 12 and 10 paṇas respectively. And if many men enjoy one unwilling prostitute by force, both the jurists impose the fine of 24 paṇas for each one separately. Here the culprit deserves punishment for forcible intercourse against the will of the prostitute, though she is ordinarily approachable without any punishment, as shown above. But if she takes her fee willingly and then disallows anybody, then the use of force is not punishable.

Nārada, however, reminds us of the different possibilities of the prostitute when she may not respond to the call without any fear of punishment, viz., when she is ill, tired, busy or engaged in royal duty. Yāj.[68] in the earlier period says that a prostitute under normal conditions who takes her fee but does not yield to the payee must pay back twice the amount, already accepted and if the fee is not paid, she must pay back the same amount, already pledged to the person. The *Mitākṣarā* points out that the man who pays the due to the prostitute but even under the normal state of health does not wish to enjoy her, shall lose the amount already paid. For unnatural intercourse with a woman elsewhere than in the female organ and also for one misbehaving with a man Kauṭ.,[69] Yāj.,[70] *Viṣṇu. D.S.*.[71] and Nārada[72] prescribe fines of 12, 24, 100 and 500 paṇas resectively.

While Kauṭ.[73] prescribes the fine of only 12 paṇas, Yāj.[74] enjoins that of 100 paṇas for carnally approaching lower animals and double that for misbehaving with images of gods. Yāj. is stricter to those who had intercourse with a cow and with a woman of a lower order ("hīnāṃ") by enjoining the fine of the middle amercement. Now it is hard to say what Yāj. means by "hīnāṃ" here. The *Mitākṣarā* means by it a woman of the lowest class known as "antyāvasāyinī". From Manu (X. 39) we hear that a niṣāda woman bears to a Cāṇḍāla a son called 'antyāvasāyin', employed in burial grounds, corresponding to "Doms or Cāṇḍāla-s" of the present day. But the term "hīnāṃ" may be better taken in the sense of any woman of a lower caste because Yāj. (II. 294) himself prescribes like Kauṭilya (IV. 13.34), already noted before, the far bitterer punishment of banishment after branding the foul mark on the body of the culprit for sexual intercourse with the woman of the lowest caste (known as Cāṇḍālī). Hence to justify the anomaly of degrees of punishment it may not be unjust to take "hīnāṃ" in the sense, suggested above. The survey of Manu's texts shows that if a brahmin approaches carnally a woman of the "antyajā", i.e. .owest class, he must pay the fine of 1000 paṇas. The *Smṛti Candrikā*[75] states that the term 'antyajā' means the caste of cobblers ("Antyajaḥ prasiddhaś-Carma-kārādiḥ"). Manu is, however, silent on the culprit other than the brahmin going to such a woman. We may easily surmise that in the society of Manu's days when the brahmins were granted far greater privileges, the punishment on the non-brahmin offender must have been far more serious. Manu, however, enjoins (XI. 176) that the brahmin, having intercourse with a caṇḍālī without the knowledge of this fact, becomes an outcast; but if he does it intentionally, he becomes her equal. Yāj. follows practically Kauṭ. *in toto* on this issue, because he says that the Śūdra becomes a caṇḍāla by approaching a cāṇḍālī and that the member of this lowest caste shall be put to death for intercourse with an Ārya woman. Vijñāneśvara, however, an orthodox commentator quotes Manu's text of punishment of

1000 paṇas and applies it to the twice-born offender who is indifferent to the expiation and who must be branded and banished. He is in favour of mere fine on one, inclined to undergo penance of expiation. But it is hard to say whether Yāj. intends to make any such discrimination.

Yāj.[76] prescribes the punishment of 500 paṇas on one who allows the adulterer to go free for fear of blasphemy of one's own family and that of eight times of this amount on one who takes bribes from the adulterer. "Jāraṃ cauretyabhivadan dāpyaḥ pañca-śataṃdamaṃ/upajīvya dhanaṃ muñcaṃstadevāṣṭaguṇīkṛtam//". This rule shows the prevalence of this evil practice even among the high circles who were eager to maintain the prestige of their own family and Yāj. was keen to check it by such a high rate of fine, specially in cases of acceptance of bribes from the adulterer which evidently indicates their ignoble nature.

Let me add a brief note on the attitude of the ancient jurists towards sexual crimes. Gautama prescribes positive laws only for checking a Śūdra's intercourse with a twice-born woman. But he is silent on such connection between a Kṣatriya or a Vaiśya and a brāhmaṇī and it is more likely that Gautama wished these wrongs to be expiated by penances or punished by the community. He regarded the intercourse by a Śūdra with the woman of the higher caste as a great outrage on Dharma, which required the king's justice. Āpastamba prescribes punishment for the man offending a woman but a mere penance for the woman. Niyoga is, according to him, a form of adultery. He condemns not only adultery of a Śūdra with a twice-born woman but also that of a brāhmaṇa with a woman of his own caste. However, he prescribes death for the former but mere penances for the latter. Viṣṇu regards adultery with a woman of one's caste as punishable but only less so with a woman of the lowest caste. However, he prescribes death sentence for intercourse with an antyajā woman.

The unnatural sexual crime with cattle is held punishable with a fine of 100 paṇas; in the case of a cow the second amercement is recommended (Viṣṇu).[77] While Kauṭ. enjoins a fine of 12 paṇas only for one's carnally approaching lower animals, Viṣṇu, Yāj. (II. 289) and Nār. (12 Tit., 76) show a stiffer attitude by prescribing a heavier punishment of fine of 100 paṇas, if not more. The *Matsya Purāṇa*[78] prescribes shaving of head for intercourse with a donkey but a fine of one gold piece for that with a cow (CCXXVII, 141 & 142).

In ancient Persian law such unnatural offence was held as an unpardonable offence for the person, if he were a teacher of the religion of Mazda but if not, he could have cleaned himself of the sin, if he confessed the said religion and resolved never to commit again such heinous act.[79] This offence was punished with death, according to Mosaic law.[80] In Athens, however, sodomy was not punishable, unless committed with violence and it was punished even up to death according to the discretion of the jury, if done with violence.[81] This offence was punished with capital punishment in Rome.[82] In medieval France and in ancient England it was punished with burning[83] but by 25 Hen. VIII. C. 6, confirmed by 5 Eliz. C. 17 it was treated as felony without the benefit of clergy.[84]

Thus compared with laws of other countries in the ancient world Indian laws prescribe a very mild punishment only in the shape of fine or shaving the head. Even in modern India such unnatural offences are liable to imprisonment for life or for the term up to 10 years plus fine.[85]

Manu[86] deals in greater detail not only with all sorts of criminal intercourse but also with other kinds of forbidden association with women. He is very severe to adulterers of both sexes, prescribing punishment in varying degrees for different castes including ghastly penalties besides fines. Kauṭilya, Yāj. and Nārada show softer attitude towards women. Nārada prescribes remarriage for widows and for women, either abandoned or with impotent husbands (XII. 95-101); but his laws on adultery are in conformity with those of Manu and Yāj. Bṛhaspati prescribes three grades of fines for adultery and a higher amount of fine for a very rich man and he rises up to death penalty in case of a man, connected with a woman of a higher caste. He prescribes strict chastity, forbids niyoga and provides for a strict supervision of a married woman by her mother-in-law etc., reflecting a social picture of the subsequent period (*S.B.E.*, 33, XXIV, 2). Kātyāyana speaks of nine varieties of adultery and prescribes death for the man forcibly enjoying a woman. *Śūkranīti*[87] regards adultery and offences against women as crimes in which the king prosecutes (IV., V. 83 ff) because these grave immoral acts lead to Varṇa-saṅkara.

ABORTION

Kauṭilya[88] prescribes that "for one causing abortion with a blow ('prahāreṇa') the fine shall be the highest, with medicine (bhaiṣajyena) the middle, by causing suffering (parikleśena) to the woman the lowest fine for violence". Elsewhere[89] he enjoins the lowest fine for violence even "for one causing the abortion of a female slave by medicines". Manu (XI. 88) prescribes the performance of the vow of 'brahma-hatyā' (brahmin-murder) as an expiation for the destruction of the embryo (of a brāhmaṇa the sex of which was) unknown. Yāj.[90] says, as noted before that one causing miscarriage to a female slave ("dāsīgarbha-vināśa-kṛt") must pay a fine of 100 paṇas ("śata-daṇḍa-bhāk") and thus practically follows Kauṭilya (III. 20.17). But elsewhere (II. 277) he prescribes the highest punishment for causing abortion ("garbhasya pātane chottamo damaḥ"). Vijñān. comments here that the highest punishment is to be inflicted only in cases of abortion of women other than a female slave or a brāhmaṇī; because the fine of a hundred has already been noted for cases of female slaves and the expiation of 'vrata-s' has been just in the above-mentioned fashion of Manu, prescribed by Yāj. ("garbhahā ca yathāvarṇam"— II. 251). Thus while Manu is silent on the punishment for this offence, mentioning only the expiation, Kauṭ. and Yāj. are careful to note specific punishments in varying degrees, showing thereby the gravity of such offences in the period concerned. Nārada[91] enjoins banishment for the women who procure abortion. The *Matsya Purāṇa* (CCXXVII, 196) prescribes like Yāj. a fine of 100 paṇas for causing abortion.

The Babylonian law prescribes compensation for causing abortion to plebeian women and female slaves.[92] The Old Persian law regarded abortion as grave as murder and one causing it by medicines was guilty of murder.[93] The Mosaic law prescribes death sentence on one causing abortion to the extent of mischief.[94] The early English law also took it as murder but in Blackstone's time it was only misprison.

Thus ancient law in India as elsewhere was very strict to those causing miscarriage. Even in modern India the I.P.C. (Sec. 312 ff) treats it punishable, of course in varying degrees under different sets of conditions. One "voluntarily causing a woman with child to miscarry shall, if such miscarriage be not caused in good faith for the purpose of saving the life of the woman, be punished with "imprisonment" up to 3 years or with fine or with both. The imprisonment may be extended up to 7 years when the woman is quick with child. Abortion without the consent of the woman concerned shall be punished with imprisonment up to 10 years plus fine. The same penalty is meant for cases of death caused by such act done intent to cause miscarriage. Abortion done with intent to prevent child being born alive or to cause it to die after birth and causing death of quick unborn child by act amounting to culpable homicide are equally punishable in the same way (Sec. 315 & 316). Unlike ancient Indian law modern law of India is also equally watchful to punish offences like exposure and abandonment of child under 12 years by parents or persons having care of it with imprisonment up to 7 years or with fine or with both. Concealment of birth by secret disposal of dead body is also subject to punishment of imprisonment up to 2 years or with fine or with both.

REFERENCES

1. IV. 12.
2. XXIII. 14.

3. VIII. 371.
4. XII. 165. 63.
5. II. 10.26.20-21.
6. J.II., p. 309 and V, p. 444.
7. J. II., p. 136.
8. *Vivā.*, 2, p. 18f.
9. *Ibid.*, 4, p. 31.
10. *Ibid*, 5, p. 35.
11. XII. 165.53.
12. XI. 177.
13. XI. 177.
14. IV. 12.12-13.
15. IV. 20-21.
16. V. 86.15.
17. IV. 13.38-39.
18. IV. 12.30-33.
19. IV. 13.
20. XI. 170-171.
21. "Liṅgaṃ chhitvā vadha-s-tasya sakāmāyāḥ strīyā api". Yāj III. 233.
22. IV. 13.31.
23. Ham., 154, 155 and 157.
24. Leviticus, 18, 20.
25. Black, V, IV. p. 65.
26. IV. 13.36.
27. II. 293.
28. XV. 74.
29. 227. 141.
30. IV. 12.35.
31. Gaut. XII. 2; Vaś. XXI. 1-5; Manu, VIII. 359; *ViṣṇuD.S.*, V. 41; Yāj. II, 284, 294; Kauṭ., IV. 12 & 13 and Nārada, XV. 70.
32. XXVIII. 4.
33. II. 4.4
34. V. 154.
35. *ṚV*, II. 29.1, X. 34.4; *Vāj. Sam.* XXX. 22 and *Tait. Sam.* V. 6.8.3.
36. VIII. 357.
37. Manu, VIII. 263; Yāj. II. 293 and AŚ, IV. 13.36.
38. VII. 359.
39. "Strī-puṃsayo-r-mithunībhāvaḥ saṃgrahaṇam—*Mitā.*, on Yāj., II, 283.
40. *S.B.E.*, 33, p. 365, verses 1-2.
41. Ham. 129, 133 and 134.

42. *ERE*, IV. p. 259.
43. *Zoroestrian Civilization*, Ch. L.—Moral wrongs.
44. Ezek. 18, [11,13]
45. Demos. III—Oration against Aristocrats, p. 184 and App. VIII, pp. 348-349.
46. Justinian's Institute, IV, Title, XVIII, 4.
47. Cont. C.L., Pt. I, ch. VI, 39 f.
48. Black, IV, p. 64.
49. IV. X. 14.
50. VIII. 323 & 342.
51. II. 287 & 288.
52. Uttara, Ucchvasa VI.
53. Ham., 14; Exod. 21.16; Deu 247; Demos. III, p. 154 Note 3; *Encly. Religion and Ethics*, vol. IV, Cri. & Pun.
54. Just. IV. Tit. XVIII, 10.
55. Cont. C.L., I, VI, 39 f.
56. Black, IV, XV, pp. 208-9 & 219.
57. II. 283-84.
58. II. 286.
59. 28. 2-4.
60. I. 72.
61. "etaccha mānasa-vyabhicāre" etc., pp. 98-99. See also Nandapaṇḍita's commentary on Parāśāra, X. 27.
62. Ed. Sachau, 1910, II, pp. 162-163.
63. II. 288.
64. II. 290.
65. Cf. *"The Cholas"*, vol. I, p. 521.
66. IV. 13.38.
67. II. 291.
68. II. 292.
69. IV. 13.40.
70. II. 293.
71. V. 44.
72. XV. 76.
73. IV. 13.41.
74. II. 289.
75. III. pt. II, 745.
76. II. 301.
77. V. 42 & 44.
78. CCXXVII, 141 & 142.
79. Zend, Vend. Farg. VIII, 27 and 28.
80. Lev. 20[13-19], and Exod. 22[19]

81. Demos. III, against Midias, p. 73, Note 2.
82. Just. IV - Tit. XVIII, 4.
83. Cont. C.L., Pt. I, Ch. VI. 39 f.
84. Black IV, XV. p. 215.
85. I.P.C., Sec. 377.
86. VIII. 374-85.
87. IV, V. 83 ff.
88. IV. 11.6.
89. III. 20.17.
90. II. 236.
91. 12 Jit., 92.
92. Ham. 214.
93. Zend - Vendidad - Farg. XV - IIa, 9-12; and 11b, 13-16.
94. Exod. $20^{22, 23}$

CHAPTER VI

Gambling

Gambling was a vicious game, practised in the Vedic age, as evidenced by the *Ṛg-Veda*[1] and the *Atharva Veda.*[2] It appears to have been a proto-Aryan institution, prevalent not only in ancient India but also in ancient Germany. Tacitus speaks of its vogue among the Germanic tribes. Pānini[3] refers to the loss, caused by one dice being cast in an unfavourable way and to the enmity caused by dice in gambling (IV. 4.19). *Vāj. Sam.*[4] mentions 'akṣa-rājāya kitavam'. Gambling was practised even in sacrifices like Rājasūya.

Āpastamba[5] enjoins that players should be men of three higher castes, pure and devoted to truth . The story of Yudhiṣṭhira's gambling in the *Mbh.* is glaring example to show how this game proves ruinous and degrading even for a man of strong morality like Yudhiṣṭhira. The above references show that gambling was resorted to by men of the higher order of the society in the earlier period as a game. Even women took part in gambling, as evidenced by the Ajanta fresco[6] depicting some women in a royal palace as engaged in dice-playing. But for its evil consequences it was denounced by all belonging to both Dharma and Artha Schools.

Kautilya says emphatically that "gamblers indeed are generally fraudulent players" and hence he wishes it to be controlled by the state under the supervision of the Director of gambling (III.20). Gambling, according to Kauṭ. and Yāj. (II. 203) should be carried on only in one place, obviously for the reason, stated distinctly that it would be helpful for finding out the persons who follow a secret profession.[7] Kauṭilya differs from the earlier teachers on the amount of fine to be imposed in a suit concerning gambling. While the teachers prescribe the lowest fine for violence on the winners and the middle on the loser. Kauṭ. rejects it and opines that "if the loser is punished with a double fine, no one will approach the king for justice. He enjoins that "masters of gambling halls shall provide for the gamblers clean chowrie-shells and dice" so that his game may be held in a right way as far as possible and prescribes the fine of 12 paṇas for substituting other chowrie-shells, the lowest fine for violence along with confiscation of winnings for fraudulent play and also the fine for theft in addition for cheating. These evidences show how gambling was practised with dishonesty and how the poor souls were cheated. That is why Kauṭ. prescribes elsewhere (4.10.9) the punishment of cutting off of one hand or a fine of 400 for one's cheating with false chowrie-shells, dice, leather-straps, ivory-cubes or by sleight of hand. It should be noted that though Kauṭ. admits that gamblers are generally fraudulent players and advises measures for the restriction of this game, he is full aware of its economic aspect as a source of revenue and enjoins that "the master of the hall shall take 5% of the winnings as well as hire for articles or instruments, necessary for the act of gambling".[8] The Director of gambling is empowered to carry out the pledging and sale of articles and he shall be punished with twice the amount of the fine, mentioned above, levied from the deceitful gamblers, for not prohibiting offences concerning dice, ground or the use of hand.

Manu[9] condemns and prohibits the practice of gambling and betting in the kingdom because these two vices lead to the destruction of the kingdom. He opines that these two vices amount to open theft ("prakāśam-etat tāskaryam", IX. 222) because honest people are deprived of their property only; and so the king shall always exert in suppressing them. He[10] enjoins that the king should corporally punish all those persons who either gamble or bet or afford an opportunity for it. Manu makes a distinction between gambling (dyūtam) and betting (samāhvaya); in the former inanimate things are used for staking money on them but in the latter only animate beings are used for the same purpose.[11]

It is interesting to note that samāja or samāhvaya (of Manu), i.e., fighting together between living beings, between animals or between animals and men was stopped in the Mauryan age. Gladiatoring or duels between animals was a sort of national diversion in the period of Megasthenes. Aśoka stopped it and allowed only shows of single performances ("Ekatya-samāja") by the R.E. No. I. Manu, a puritan jurist vied with the Buddhist rule of the Mauryas in puritanism. So he[12] denounced royal hunting, gambling, drinking, dancing and music. It is quite natural that he wanted to stop gambling and betting; and he advised gamblers ("Kitavān" in IX. 225) to be expelled from the town instantly. (Kṣipram). The author of the *Sm. Ch.* comments that the gamblers are mentioned along with dancers and singers in Manu (IX. 225) only to indicate their ignoble character. Daṇḍin paints the picture of a cock-fight in the *Daśakumāra Caritam* Uttarapīṭhikā, Ucchvāsa V.

Cock-fight was also widely prevalent in Suvarṇadvīpa as attested by the account of this country by Ibin Khordadzbeh (844-848 A.D.) who speaks of "about 50 maunds of gold" a revenue per day, realised out of this game by the king of Zabag, named Mahārāja.[13]

Yāj.[14] follows the Artha-laws of Kauṭilya to regulate gambling under the state-monopoly. He speaks of the function of the 'Sabhika', i.e., the Superintendent employed by the state ('Samyak-pālita') who must realise for his own maintenance from the cheat players 5% of the amount, won, if of course, the gambler wins either the amount of hundred or more but 10% of the amount won when the gain amounts to only hundred: "Glahe śatika-vṛddhe-s-tu sabhikaḥ pañcakaṃ śataṃ/ gṛhnīyād-dhūrta-kitavād-itarād-daśakaṃ śataṃ//". (II. 199). Vijñān. comments that the sabhika must extract the above-mentioned shares for his own sake ("ātmavṛttyartham"). But the differentiation of shares requires careful scrutiny because what Yāj enjoins is explained by Vijñān. in the sense that 5% of the amount of gain in gambling should be accepted by the sabhika from the gambler who wins a hundred or more ("Śatika-vṛddheḥ") but 10% in case of gain of just one hundred only ("pūrṇa śati-ka-vṛddheḥ"). Parāśara-Mādhava notes ("a-pūrṇa-śata-vṛddheḥ kitavāt", i.e., whose gain has not reached a hundred (p. 390). The term 'Dhūrta-kitava" is applicable to both the cases. So the differentiation of shares seems to be justified in the sense that when a gambler is expert enough to gain a hundred or more, the indefinite amount, he is granted a concession of payment of only 5%, that is, 1/20th of the amount gained but in other cases of inefficient gamblers the rate of payment is 10% i.e., double the amount. This indicates that the state encourages the act of gambling only to extract some revenue, because in the next verse Yāj. says distinctly that the Sabhika must pay to the king something out of his earning, though however, the amount payable to the king is not made clear ("sa-samyak-pālito dadyād rājñe bhāgaṃ yathākṛtam"). This payment is again explained as a return in lieu of protection from the king from the cheat players. The Sabhika (II. 200) is also enjoined to take the responsibility of recovering to the winner from the vanquished party the amount of gain ("jitam-udgrāhayajjetre") and must create confidence in the minds of players by truthful words (dadyāt satyaṃ vacaḥ kṣamī). If the Sabhika is unable to recover, the king should arrange the recovery of the amount won, if the game is performed in public under the supervision of the sabhika and the king's due is paid. This shows the interest and responsibility of the king in the administration of gambling. In cases of disputes the evidences of gamblers who are eye-witnesses are to be accepted. Bṛhaspati says the same thing and adds that if the said witnesses are malicious, the king himself should decide.

Yāj. awards punishment on cheat players: "Rājñā sacinhaṃ nirvāsyaḥ kūṭākṣopadhi-devinaḥ" i.e., those who play with false dice or with fraud are to be branded with marks and banished from the state and in order to regulate their activities advises that gambling should be made only in one place. ("ekamukhaṃ kāryaṃ") so that a thief may be caught. A thief who has won wealth by stealing is naturally inclined to take to this game. Thus the above survey shows that Yāj. follows Kauṭ. in regulating gambling with an eye to the revenue available from this source, while Manu does not take into account this economic aspect and he prohibits strictly the performance of this game and enjoins banishment of all gamblers whom he thinks to be secret thieves (pracchanna-taskarāḥ). Bṛhaspati sums us the views of Manu because it destroys truth, purity and wealth but it is approved by others when it is accompanied with the king's share and it should be supervised by the Sabhika for finding out thieves".

Nārada prescribes that cheat players should be banished from the realm after the garland of dice-beads is placed on their neck. Thus he adds insult to the actual punishment. But he adds: "Let the gamblers pay to the king the share due to him and play in public, thus no wrong will be committed". This rule indicates a larger vogue of gambling leading to relaxation of restrictions. The rules once contemplated control of the game, obviously to prevent offences by catching thieves but in the period of Nārada the control is practically reduced to one for revenue purposes. Kātyāyana allows time of three weeks for the payment of the pledged amount ("tri-pakṣakam").

Both Kauṭilya and Yāj. regulate "a challenge" or bet in the same way as gambling. Manu prohibits it just like gambling. Bṛhaspati says: "Dvanda-yuddhena yaḥ kaścid-avasādam-avāpnuyāt tat-svāminā paṇo deyo yas-tatra parikalpitaḥ//" i.e., he who is defeated in the bet is made to pay the agreed amount. Nārada adds that gambling is sometimes done for the sake of the fun only for diversion in moments of idleness and if so, the winner must receive any amount (nāpnuyāt kāmam) or he may receive only the amount, agreed upon before the actual play (athavānumataṃ tayoḥ). It is interesting to note that Kauṭ. allows challenges with bets concerning learning or skill in art, which are not subject to state-control and may be freely indulged in ("anyatra vidyā-śilpa-samāhvayāt"). Kāmandaka[15] states that hunting, gambling and wine in the case of kings must be condemned, since calamities befell Pāṇḍu, Nala and the Vṛṣṇi-s respectively by being addicted to these. This shows that gambling was practised in his days and kings are warned against it. The *Mṛcch.*[16] refers to a gambler fleeing from the gambling house after losing all the games and without paying ten suvarṇas due to the keeper of the gambling house. It depicts the surprising way by which the culprit was caught in a deserted temple by his pursuers.

It may be noted here that in medieval France the government took care to control gambling by various ordinances. According to Bouteiller the keepers of the gambling houses were to be fined 60 sous.[17] In England by 9 Ann. C. 14 cheating in games was made punishable with corporal punishments and infamy. Gambling was punished with pecuniary penalties under George II and racing was regulated by 13 George II. C. 19.[18]

REFERENCES

1. 1.41.9; VII. 86.6; X. 34; 42.9 and X. 43.5.
2. IV. 16.5 and IV. 38.
3. II. 1.10.
4. 30.18.
5. "Āryāḥ śucayaḥ satya-sītlā dīvitāraḥ syuḥ", II. 10.25.13.
6. Yazdani, E.H., Deccan, Pl. II, pt. XXXV.
7. "Gūḍhājīvi-jñāpanārtham" in AŚ, 3.20.1 and "taskarajñāna kāranāt" in Yāj. II. 203.
8. 3.20.10.
9. IX. 221: "Dyūtaṃsamāhvayaṃ caiva rājā rāṣṭrān-nivārayet".
10. "Tān sarvān ghātayet". IX. 224.
11. IX. 223.
12. VII. 47 and 50.
13. *Hindu Col. in F.E.*, by R.C. Majumdar, p. 35.
14. II. 199 ff.
15. 1.54.
16. Act. II.
17. *Cont. Cr. Law,* 1, vi, 39 f.
18. Black, IV. XIII, pp. 170-172.

CHAPTER VII

Crimes in the Field of Commerce and Industry

Let us first examine Kauṭilya's measures for the suppression of criminals in the sphere of trade and commerce and crafts and industries (IV. II). The evil effects of capitalism and cornering in the pre-Mauryan age are heard of in the early Dharma-sūtras which denounce usury and the raising of prices. Hence the Mauryan government had to frame laws for enforcing "a just price in the case of traders, a just profit in case of manufacturers and a just remuneration for labourers". Consequently commerce and industry was thoroughly regulated by the state and the state even started business, creating some monopolies and thereby subjecting the private enterprisers to a keen competition with the state. No trader was allowed to keep any stock without a licence. This put a stop to speculation in commodities of everyday use. Anyone except a licensed trader making purchases to the excess of his own needs had his goods confiscated. Kauṭilya regarded traders, artisans and others as thieves in theory, though not in name because they cheated the people very often. ("Evaṃ caurān-acaurākhyān vaṇik-kāru-kuśilavān .... vārayed-deśa-piḍanāt"); and hence made laws for strictly regulating them. The profits of merchants were regulated. The government forbade all sales except in markets only to ensure just prices and profits. Cornering was checked and steps were taken against the fluctuation of prices, dependent on abnormal demand or unusual supplies. Merchants' guilds attempting to raise prices were heavily fined. The government regulated weights and measures and took steps against adulteration of food stuffs. Kauṭilya mentions five controlling officials presiding over boards for the proper upkeep of the entire machinery to enforce the above regulations, viz. Śulkādhaykṣa, Paṇyādhyakṣa, Saṁsthādhyakṣa, Pautavādhyakṣa and the Anta-pālas. The government did its best for improving internal trade. Foreign trade was encouraged by inviting merchants from abroad and granting special privileges to them as testified to by Kauṭilya and Megasthenes. The security of trade in trading in the later period can be imagined from Kalhaṇa's *Rājataraṅgiṇī*[1] where we learn that the queen Sūryamati removed the disgrace of the country under the king Bhoja, caused by one foreigner Padmarāja by handing over the savings of her own treasury; and also from the report of Muslim historian Al-Idrisi (*Hist. of India,* by Elliot and Douson, Vol. I, p. 88) who speaks of the Chalukya kingdom as frequented by a large number of Muslim traders.

It should be noted that customs-duties were an important source of the state; and Kauṭ. framed elaborate rules to ensure their proper collection under the supervision of Paṇyādhayakṣa. For facilitating the collection of tolls and making the evasion of duty difficult Kauṭ.[2] prohibited the sale of the commodities in the place of their production or manufacture and he who violated this rule was punished. Manu (8, 400) prescribes a fine of 8 times the defrauded duty as punishment for the merchant who avoids the toll-house, buys or sells at an improper time and makes a false statement in enumerating his goods. Viṣṇu[3] is severer to prescribe the confiscation of the entire goods of such merchant. Yāj.[4] and Nārada[5] however follow Manu on this issue. Kauṭilya[6] was careful to control the evading of duty by hiding commodities on the part of the smugglers and punish them with forfeiture of the smuggled quantity and an equal amount as fine. It is worthnoting that smugglers were similarly dealt with by the earlier statutes of England, sometimes daring cases were subjected to transportation for 7 years. But the subsequent law 19 Geo. II C. 34 treats all forcible acts of smuggling as felony without benefit of clergy.[7] In Medieval France evasion of duty was punished with more fines.[8] (Cf. *Trade and Commerce in Ancient India* by myself).

Kauṭilya[9] begins his chapter four on the suppression of criminals with his laws for the regulation of the artisans or their guilds. He recommends the creation of a Board, presided over by three Amātyas or Pradeṣṭr-s. He enjoins that "employers of artisans capable of making good an article (arthya pratīkārāḥ Kāruśāsitāraḥ), those good at entrusting material (sannikṣeptāraḥ) and artisans working with their own capital (sva-vitta-kāravaḥ) should accept entrusted material with the guarantee of the guild (Śreṇi-pramāṇāḥ nikṣepaṃ gṛṇhīyuḥ) and in case of death the guild shall be responsible for the entrusted material".[10] This passage shows at least two classes of artisans, 'Kāruśāsitārah' who are apparently employers of artisans, i.e., some sort of master-artisans with assistants working under them and 'sva-vitta-kāravaḥ', i.e., those who work on their own capital and deal directly with customers. Thus the guilds of artisans had to work under the directions of the Board which settled wages and work. "The artisans shall carry out the work with the place, time and work stipulated, without stipulation as to place or time if the nature of the work can be pointed out (as the reason)". Failure to do the work, as prescribed meant the reduction of wages and punishment. "For exceeding time-limit there shall be a reduction in the wage by one-quarter and double that as fine. They shall be liable to what is lost or destroyed except in case of deterioration of a sudden calamity. For carrying out the work otherwise than as ordered (there shall be) loss of wage and double that as fine.[11] It is interesting to note that the guilds framed their own rules and they were recognised by the state. The state tried to safeguard the interests of the guilds and wished that the guilds did not suffer from internal quarrels and breach of rules by their members.

Manu prescribes the punishment of banishment for the members of the guild violating its rules.[12] Sometimes such a breaker is advised to be imprisoned and fined.[13] Viṣṇu[14] enjoins banishment only in such a case. Yāj. recommends banishment and total forfeiture instead in such a case and in case of embezzlement of the guild's property. He enjoins milder punishment of fines for higher offences.[15] Nor is he in favour of an exemplary punishment for one who creates dissensions in the guild.[16] Bṛhas.[17] follows Yāj.

Kauṭilya (IV. 1) gives us details of regulations on the act of weaving. Weavers were supplied materials by capitalists, they turned the raw material into the fabric required and were paid according to their outturn. The wage for weaving shall be equal to the value of the yarn, $1\frac{1}{4}$ times in the case of Kṣauma and Kauśeya and double in the case of patrorṇa, blankets and dukūla. Weavers had to pay the fine for diminution in the increase of the yarn and also their wages were reduced for shortness in measure. Reduction in carding and spinning wool was, however, allowed to the extent of five palas.

Next Kauṭilya's laws on washerman. They must wash garments on smooth boards of wood or of stone. Any damage to clothes for washing elsewhere should be compensated and a fine of six paṇas was levied. They must wear their own garments and if they used others', they had to pay the fine of three paṇas. For selling, hiring out or pledging the garments of others the fine was 12 paṇas and for change of garments the fine was double the price and the return of the garment. Washermen were allowed 1, 2, 3 and 4 days respectively for producing the different grades of whiteness of the garment to be washed. The dyeing makes a longer period necessary and so 5, 6 and 7 days were given for the purpose. After that they shall lose their wage. In cases of dispute concerning dyeing experts mediated and fixed the wage. Wages were fixed for washing garments in proportion to their quality (IV. 1.22). Kauṭilya regulates tailors by the above rules in connection with washerman.

Now about goldsmiths. Kauṭ. (2.13) speaks of the superintendent of gold in the workshop and his functions in detail. For the manufacture of gold and silver the goldsmith of good birth and conduct should be stationed in the middle of the market highway. Artisans working in gold were thoroughly searched before entering and leaving the workshop and everyday in the morning and evening they deposited the gold and the articles, marked with seals of the maker and the overseer. This implies that works were carried on even in night shifts as well. Kauṭilya is very careful in regulating the goldsmiths who were, as still now, very often cheats. Hence all his rules were meant for keeping them in right path. The goldsmiths were fined 12 paṇas for purchasing silver or gold in the same form from the disreputable person without informing the state officers, 24 paṇas if in a changed form and 48 paṇas, if taken from a thief. The punishment for theft will be inflicted on a goldsmith, if he purchases gold at a low price in secret or what is changed in appearance; and if he plays any deceit in the manufacture of articles.

The goldsmith had to pay fines of different grades for stealing gold while in manufacturing any golden article. Sometimes people were cheated by an artificial enhancement of colour or by practising removal or mixture of gold with base metals and Kauṭ. prescribes the fine of 500 paṇas for this sort of cheating. Goldsmiths were given the wages in proportion to works done in gold or silver and one was paid double for one's special skill. The above laws show how gold business was strictly regulated by the state, with proper justice to artisans and customers alike and how all ill-practices were checked by the board of magistrates, appointed for the suppression of all criminals of the country.

In cases of copper, steel, bell-metal, Vaikṛntaka and brass the wage was fixed 5 paṇas per hundred palas while working in these metals, the artisans were allowed a certain amount for reduction but if they reduced more by dishonesty, they had to pay double the value of the loss. The examiner of coins should establish the currency of paṇas, obviously two sets of currency, one for trade and the other for receipts in the treasury (II. 12.25). " He should also fix a coining fee of 8% (rūpikam), a commission of 5% known as Vyāji (which was a sort of excess in measure or weight charged when goods were received in the treasury or stores), an inspection fee of 1/8% (atyayam) and a penalty of 25 paṇas for those who manufacture, purchase, sell and examine in other places" (i.e., not in royal mints). Some think that this 'atyaya's is perhaps restricted to penalty for violation of state regulations, while 'daṇḍa' is a fine imposed by judges and magistrates only. Sometimes an established currency of paṇa-s which does not deserve to be rejected is wrongly rejected and again that currency which deserves to be rejected is not rejected and for this deception the examiner of coins has to pay the fine of 12 paṇas and he has to pay the similar fine for accepting one māṣaka as a bribe on a paṇa, sent into circulation[18] ("paṇān māṣakam-upajīvataḥ"). A heavy fine of 1000 paṇas is inflicted on one causing a counterfeit coin to be made or receiving it or sending into circulation and for inserting it in the treasury the penalty is death.

Then let us examine Kauṭilya's laws on finds of precious things or gems or mines or treasure-troves regulating criminals who tried to misappropriate them, to the heavy loss of the treasury. Sweepers who came across precious things were allowed to take one-third, the rest must be given over to the king. Precious gems, when found, must be wholly surrendered to the king, otherwise for stealing the one he would be punished with the highest amercement. Kauṭilya is stricter than Manu (VIII. 33) who says that the king, instead of taking two-third may take 1/6, 1/10, 1/12th of the property lost. Medhātithi comments that the amount due to the king depends on the length of time for which it has been kept or on the trouble which it gave or on the king's compassion; while according to Kullūka and Nārada the amount depends on the virtue of the owner. Kauṭilya prescribes that the finder of mines, gems or treasure-troves shall, on supplying the first information to the king, receive 1/6th of it as his share but if the man happens to be a peon or servant of the state, he shall have 1/12th of it. The king will take the whole of the treasure-trove, if valued over one lac of paṇas, but will pay 1/6th to the finder of the same of less value.

Definitely this amount is paid to the finder as a prize for his attempt to search such things as a matter of encouragement. Of course such treasure-troves as referred to here are those which belong to nobody and hence are unclaimed properties. But if any man of pure and honest life claims and proves his ownership over such treasure-troves as belonging to his ancestor, he is allowed to take them entirely. However, if anyone takes possession of such treasure-troves without establishing his claim, he must pay the fine of 500 paṇas and for taking possession of the same in secret, he will be punished with the fine of 1000 paṇas. Manu[19] says that the property lost and afterwards found by the king's servants shall remain in the custody of special officials (Yuktai-r-adhiṣṭhitam) and those whom the king may convict of stealing it, shall be slain by an elephant. Manu does not allow anyone, like Kauṭ., to take the whole of the treasure-trove, if he claims and proves his ownership. He enjoins that the king may take 1/6th or 1/12th of it in such cases. But if he falsely "claims so, he would be fined 1/8th of his property or a smaller portion of the value of the treasure." It is interesting to note here that Manu[20] unlike Kauṭilya grants a special privilege to a brahmin who may take the whole of the treasure because he is held to be master of everything. Even if the king himself finds treasure of gold concealed in the ground, he would give half of it to the brahmins and place the other half in his treasury. According to Nārada even a brāhmaṇa must give notice to the king about the finding of any treasure-trove, or he will be treated as a thief.

In England concealment of a treasure-trove was punished with death in the earlier period but in the period of Blackstone, with fine and imprisonment, because it was recognised that it was to go to the king. Yāj.[21] follows Manu[22] in this connection.

Kauṭilya[23] regulates medical practice in the state. For the physician undertaking treatment without intimating to the government the dangerous nature of the disease, the fine is the first amercement in case of death, the middlemost amercement in case of death through a mistake in treatment and in case of injury to a vital part or causing a deformity ("marmavadha-vaiguṇya-karaṇa") the magistrate shall treat it as a case of physical injury. Some read 'karma-vadha' in place of 'marma-vadha' to denote the sense of negligence or indif ference for which the physician is liable to punishment as due in case of assault. Manu[24] prescribes that "all physicians who treat (their patients) wrongly (shall pay a fine; in the case of animals, the first; in the case of human beings the middlemost amercement)". Viṣṇu[25] enjoins for this offence the highest amercement for a patient of a high rank like king's officers, the middlemost for others and the lowest for animals. Yāj.[26] also recommends like Viṣṇu the punishment of quack physicians the first, middlemost and the highest amercements for treating birds or beasts, men and government-servants respectively. Nārada adds in connection with Manu (IX. 284) that "this (punishment) refers to cases when death is not (the result of the wrong treatment); for if that is the case the punishment is greater (Bühler's ed. of *Manu*). Bṛhaspati[27] again says that "the physician who, though unacquainted with drugs and spells, or ignorant of the nature of the disease, yet takes money from the sick, shall be punished like a thief. The *Matsya Purāṇa*[28] prescribes the punishment of the highest amercement for the physician who intentionally treats a patient wrongly.

The Babylonian law[29] prescribes mutilation of limbs as the punishment for the doctor whose operation caused the death of the patient or the loss of his eyesight. He had to pay compensation if the patient was a slave or an animal. The old Persian Law[30] treated the unsuccessful operation as murder. Blackstone[31] points out, "if a physician or a surgeon gives his patient a lotion or plaster to cure him, which, contrary to expectation, kills him, this is neither murder nor-slaughter, but misadventure; and he shall not be punished criminally, however liable he might formerly have been to a civil action for neglect or ignorance; but it hath been holden that if he be not a regular physician or surgeon, who administers the medicine or performs the operation, it is man-slaughter at least".

Kauṭilya[32] regulates the activities of actors, dancers, singers, musicians, story-tellers and minstrels. They must work in such a way as not to disturb the work of the people specially agriculturists. Hence they are required to live in one place during the rainy season. They must avoid "excessive gifts of love by one person and excessive praise of one" and for the transgression of this rule, they must have to pay 12 paṇas. The same laws are applicable to dancers, dumb-players and other mendicants. For them, the punishment shall be many lashes with an iron-hand and the number of paṇas the judges may impose as the fine.

The above rules indicate how the artisans were tried to be brought under the state-control specially under the Mauryas. They were also mobilised by the state to help agriculture. They seem to have been employed by the state in weaving, mining, store-keeping, manufacture of arms, metal work etc.[33] Artisans like weavers were in the earlier age employed by Gahapati but in the Mauryan period by the state and they worked under the guidance of the state-superintendents, mainly in the cities. But Megasthenes refers to the work of wood-cutters, carpenters, blacksmiths and miners under the supervision of great officers, which indicates some sort of control over these artisans even in the country-side. Kauṭilya prescribes rules regulating the relation between the employer and the employed. Artisans were regarded as sources of troubles and so measures are prescribed in the section on the Kāru-rakṣaṇam. The artisans must fulfil their contracts as to time, place and nature of work. Failure except under situations of "troubles and calamities" involves not only the forfeiture of a quarter of their wages but also a fine twice the amount of wages and the payment of damages into the bargain. Of course, the interests of artisans were also safeguarded. Anyone seeking to deprive them of their just earnings by minimising the quality of their work or hindering the sale and purchase of their goods was fined 1000 paṇas (IV. 2). An employer not taking work from his labourer was fined 12 paṇas. Kauṭilya recommends the privilege of extension of grace-period of seven nights over and above the period agreed upon for the execution of the work to the artisans, combined into guilds. It has already been noted that wages were fixed according to the time and quality of the work and in cases of disputes over wages, the decision of the experts must be accepted.

Manu[34] is also, like Kauṭilya, very severe to a negligent worker. A hired workman who fails to perform his work according to the contract, out of pride, without being ill shall be fined 8 Kṛṣṇalas and no wage shall be paid to him. But if he gets ill and finishes his work after recovery, he shall be paid his wages even for the period of absence and if he does not finish it even after recovery, wages shall not be paid to him even for the period he worked.[35] Thus Manu is not in favour of penalising any *bona fide* workman who is forced to suspend work for illness and who finishes it after recovery. New guilds of artisans, formed in the post-Mauryan age helped to secure the comparative freedom of artisans, leading thereby to the improvement of their status, as evidenced by numerous inscriptions recording gifts of smiths, perfumers, weavers, goldsmiths and even leather-workers, dyers, jewellers, sculptors and fishermen. (Lüd. Nos. 53, 54, 68, 76, 95, 331, 345, 381, 495, 857, 986, 1006, 1032, 1051, 1061, 1177, 1203-4, 1210, 1230, 1273, 1298). The artisans including gamblers, dancers and singers, men following forbidden occupations and sellers of spirituous liquor were found to have constantly harassed the good people by their forbidden practices and so they were regarded as secret thieves by Manu.[36] deserving banishment by the king.

Let us now consider the rules of earlier jurists on breach of service contract. Viṣṇu[37] recommends that if a hired workman or servant leaves his work before the expiry of his term, he shall be fined 100 paṇas and given no wage. Thus he is sterner than even Kauṭ. (III. XIV). Yāj.[38] treats breach of service-contract as a civil wrong and lays down that the servant who has received wages, if proved negligent, must return twice the amount of wages to his master; if he has not been paid wages, he must compensate the same amount as the wages. Nārada[39] follows like Manu practically the same principle as Yāj. Bṛh.[40] enjoins like Manu that "he who promised (to do a work) and does not perform it, shall be compelled to do so by forcible means even; and if, through obstinacy, such a servant should not still do it as engaged for, he shall be fined 8 Kṛṣṇalas and his wages shall not be paid to him. This rule is also followed in the *Agni Purāṇa*.[41] Thus breach of service on the part of the employee was punishable in ancient India only when it was due to insolence, impertinence or any other unreasonable cause. Similarly any breach on the part of the master was liable to punishment as evidenced by Viṣṇu[42] who provides for the fine of 100 paṇas, to be paid to the king. The *Agni Purāṇa*[43] prescribes a fine of one suvarṇa for such a master. The master was fined in varying degrees for non-payment of wages as enjoined in Kauṭ.,[44] Bṛhas.,[45] and *Matsya Purāṇa*.[46] From Kauṭ.,[47] Viṣṇu[48] and the *Agni Purāṇa*[49] and the *Matsya Purāṇa* it is evident that the seller was punished a fine of 12, 100 or 600 paṇas respectively for non-delivery of goods paid for or agreed upon.

Breaches of marriage-contract were also equally regulated in ancient India (AŚ, III. XV). Marriage was looked upon by the Hindus mainly as a sacred sacrament, though the idea of contract was not wanting in the Artha-school. However, both the Dharma and Artha schools took care to punish the breakers of marriage-ties in ancient India, as indicated by the ancient jurists.

The breach of contract was always treated as a crime in ancient India, but it should be noted that only in cases where the default was intentional and not providential, the breaker of contract was liable to punishment. The jurists of ancient India insisted on the sanctity of contract so much that even the breach of contract on the part of a prostitute or her paramour did not escape their keen attention, as already noted in the section on adultery.

REFERENCES

1. 7. 190-7.
2. II. XXII.
3. 3.15-16
4. II. 262
5. 3 Tit. 12-13
6. II. 21.20
7. Black, IV, Ch. XII., p. 154.
8. Cont. Cr. L. I, VI. 39 f.
9. AŚ, Ch. 4.

10. AŚ, tr. by R.P. Kangle, pp. 294-95.
11. AŚ, IV, 1. 4-7.
12. VIII. 219
13. VIII. 220.
14. V. 168.
15. II. 187-190.
16. Nār, 10th Tit; 6.
17. XVII. 5. 13-16.
18. AŚ, IV. 1.46.
19. VIII. 34
20. VIII. 37.
21. 7th Tit, 6
22. II. 34-35
23. IV. 1.56.
24. IX. 284.
25. V. 175-177.
26. II. 242
27. XXII. 8
28. CCXXVII. 175
29. Ham., 218-220, 225.
30. Zend. Vend, Farg. VII-VII a. 36, 40
31. IV, XIV. p. 197.
32. II. 1.34
33. AŚ, II. 12-13
34. VIII. 215
35. VIII. 216-217
36. IX. 225-226.
37. V. 153-154.
38. II. 193
39. 6 Tit, 5.
40. XVI. 14-16.
41. CCXXVIII, 1-17.
42. V. 157-159.
43. CCXXVIII, 1-17.
44. III. XIII.
45. XVI. 18
46. CCXXVII, 18
47. 3.15
48. V. 127 & 128
49. CCXXVII. 18

CHAPTER VIII

The Law of Treason

The law of Treason, prescribed in the AŚ may be compared with that of England, introduced during the reign of the Plantagenets. The following offences were counted as treason in England for which the highest punishment, i.e., death was inflicted.[1]

(i) Waging war against the king or adhering to his enemies;

(ii) Attempting the death of the king, queen or their eldest son;

(iii) Violating the queen, eldest unmarried daughter of the king or the wife of his eldest son;

(iv) Counterfeiting the king's seal or money or importing false money; and

(v) Slaying the Chancellor, Treasurer, or Judges, while engaged in duty.

Kauṭilya (IV. XI) also prescribes the law of Treason in the following words: "rājya-kāmukam-antaḥpura-pradharṣakam-aṭavyamitrotsāhakaṃ durga-rāṣṭra-daṇḍa-kopakaṃ-vā śirohasta-pṛādīpikam ghātayet", ... "brāhmaṇam tam-apaḥ praveśayet"—that means, the following were condemned as acts of treason deserving the capital punishment: (i) coveting the royal domains, (ii) violating the modesty of the harem, (iii) exciting the enemies or forest tribes, and (iv) inciting revolt or tampering with the defensive forces or exciting revolt in the army or among the people. This shows the similarity between the laws of Kauṭilya and those of England.

Besides, the forging of royal seals and edicts were also punishable with death-sentence. ("Kuṭumvādhyakṣa-mukhyasvāminaṃ kūṭa-śāsana-mudrā-karmasu pūrva-madhya-mottama-vadha-daṇḍaḥ yathāparādhaṃ vā" (Kauṭ IV. IX).

Kauṭilya also prescribes that one should be punished with the loss of tongue for (i) slander on the king, and (ii) divulging the secrets ("rājā-krośakamantra-bhedakayor-aniṣṭa-pravṛttikasya. ...... jihvāmutpāṭayet"). Even the brāhmaṇa who was ordinarily immune from capital punishment was liable to be drowned. "This law even suspended or abrogated civil rights arising out of the old traditional laws".[2] Hence through the operation of the law of treason a wife could renounce her husband if he was proved to be a traitor to the king. ("nīcatvaṃ paradiśam vā prasthito rāja-kilviṣī prāṇābhihantā patita-s-tyājyaḥ klīvo 'pi vā patiḥ"). Women also lost all rights to their property, if they incurred the displeasure of the king. ("Rāja-dviṣṭāticārābhyām-ātmāti-kramanena ca/strī-dhanānīta-śulkānām-asvāmyaṃ jāyate striyaḥ").

Manu[3] ordains that the king shall inflict various kinds of corporal punishment on those who rob the king's treasures and who persevere in opposing (his commands), likewise on those who conspire with his enemies. He[4] prescribes death penalty on those who break into a royal storehouse, armoury etc. With the development of the king's power the later jurists were more strict on the law of treason. Yāj.[5] also prescribes the penalty of cutting off of tongue plus banishment on those, guilty of treason. He (II. 282) says that one violating the modesty of the queen should be burnt alive. ("Rāja-patnyabhigāmī ca dagdha-vyāpta-kaṭāgninā"). Elsewhere he[6] prescribes the fine of 800 paṇas in cases of one's predicting evil of the king, i.e., one who speaks ill of the king or who divulges the secret of the state affairs. Nārada deems treason as a graver crime than even a brahmin-slaughter (15 & 16) and enjoins banishment as the punishment. It is interesting to note that in ancient societies of the world, specially in Babylon and Persia treason was treated as a grave offence, punishable with death sentence. The ancient Roman law also treated treason likewise. Treason in any shape, exciting the rebellion and the role of an abettor was also the gravest offence in ancient Athens. In the medieval France the man held suspicious of treason was sentenced to death, if he denied the crime.[7] The Indian Penal Code, Sec. 121 is severe against treason: "Whoever wages war against the Govt. of India or attempts to wage such war or abets the waging of such war shall be punished with imprisonment for life. (Sec. 124 A) and (Sec. 132 in connection with abetment of mutiny). It may be noted that the I.P.C. used the term 'offence' in place of treason, felonies and misdemeanours.

The punishments prescribed by ancient Indian jurists are no doubt less cruel and barbarous than those, practised in other countries in ancient or medieval period. The punishment in medieval and early modern England was more shocking. "The offender was first of all hanged by the neck, next he was brought down while still alive, then his entrails were taken out and burnt, the head was next severed and the rest of the body was cut into four parts, and all these were to be placed at the disposal of the king".[8] In India the children were not punished for their father's sin. The offender's property was not forfeited to the State or his family reduced to starvation or begging as in Athens or France. It may be noted that the earlier jurists of India did not give any particular name to the crime against the king or the state. Only in a later period Śukra mentions 50 chhalas or offences against the king, many of which might have been new creations. Attempt on the life of the king was regarded a very heinous crime, punishable with death in a very cruel manner, as evidenced by Nārada.[9] Hostility to the king was similarly treated, as evident from Manu (IX. 275), Kauṭ. (IV. ch. XI. 227) or Viṣṇu (VII. 18 & 19). Bṛhas.[10] is more lenient to enjoin banishment for the person, inimically disposed towards the king. Obviously this punishment was meant not for active hostility. The *Matsya Purāṇa*[11] enjoins capital punishment in an aggravated form for the hostility to the king. In medieval France, a man revolting against the king was denied even a form of trial and was flayed alive, his property confiscated and children exiled.[12] Even his advisers or abettors would share the same fate. Manu[13] and Kauṭ.[14] and *Matsya Purāṇa.*[15] recommend capital punishment for those who help or instigate the enemies of the king. Manu is silent on the question of violating the modesty of the queen, but Kauṭ.[16], Yāj.[17], *Agni Purāṇa*[18] and *Matsya Purāṇa*[19] prescribe death-sentence by burning for this offence. Nārada[20] softens the punishment to the extent of the excision of the organ. Manu and *Matsya Purāṇa* prescribe death sentence for one who destroys or breaks open royal treasury or arsenal or steals royal treasures, horses, elephants etc.[21]

Kauṭ.[22] enjoins tongue-cutting for betraying or disclosing the King's counsel, while Yāj.[23] prescribes banishment in addition. Nārada lays down death penalty for using abusing words to the king but he recommends the cutting off of the tongue or confiscation of the entire property for one who censures the king, "devoted to the discharge of his duties".[24] Does it imply that the king, indifferent to his duties might have been censured without the fear of any penalty ?

The law of treason has already been discussed above. It may be added in this connection that Yāj.[25] enjoins the punishment of the highest amercement on one who sits on the royal conveyance or on the throne and on one who sells clothes and flowers etc. belonging to the dead body and who beats, the 'gurut's like father or preceptor. It is interesting to note that the *Smṛti Candrikā* (p. 773) quotes Yājñavalkya wrongly as advising the middle amercement in such cases and Kātyāyana as ordaining the corporal punishment on those who are addicted to royal games. ("Rājakrīḍāsu ye saktāḥ .... vadhaṃ teṣāṃ pravartayet").

REFERENCES

1. Cf. 25 Edward III, St. 5
2. Kaut. by N.C. Bandyopadhyaya, p. 85
3. IX. 275
4. *Ibid.*, 280.
5. II. 302.
6. II. 304.
7. *Cont. Hist. Criminal Law*, Pt I. Ch. VI.
8. Blackstone, Bk IV, Ch VI, p. 92.
9. 15 & 16 Tit, 31.
10. XVII. 16.

11. CCXX. VII. 185
12. *Cont. Hist. Cr. L.*, Pt. I, Ch. VI, 39 ff.
13. IX. 232 & 275.
14. IV. XI, 227.
15. CCXXVII. 165-170.
16. IV. XIII. 234.
17. II. 282.
18. CCXXVII. 56-58.
19. CCXXVII. 201.
20. 12 Tit, 73-75.
21. Manu, IX. 275 & 280.
    Matsya Pureṇa, - CCXXVII, 165-170 & 172.
22. IV. XI. 228.
23. II. 302.
24. 15 & 16 Tit., 30.
25. II. 303.

CHAPTER IX

Prakīrṇaka (Miscellaneous Crimes)

It is interesting to note that the eighteen topics into which Manu classified first the various offences did not include any miscellaneous section. Later development of law made it more difficult to squeeze all topics into Manu's eighteen heads. Viṣṇu uses first the term 'prakīrṇaka' with reference to the law of penance ("yad-anuktaṃ tat prakīrṇakam") and advises that the wise man must perform penances for Prakīrṇa sins under the guidance of brāhmaṇas.

Yāj.[1] deals with different crimes in a separate section known as Prakīrṇaka. Vijñāneśvara, after examining the characteristics of Prakīrṇaka cases as noted in Nārada says that these cases are all 'nṛpāśraya'-s, i.e., the king should take up these crimes and punish the culprits so as to bring them back to the traditional path of justice. ("Nṛpa eva tatra smṛtyācāravyapeta-mārge vartamānānām pratikūlatām-āsthāya vyavahāra-nirṇayaṃ kuryāt"). Nārada includes[2] the following matters in the section called 'Prakīrṇaka': transgressions of the king's commandments (rājñām-ajñā-pratīghātaḥ), sitting on the royal throne etc. ("tat-karma-karaṇaṃ tathā", Cf. *Sm Ch.* p. 771), grants of towns ("pura-pradānam as read in the *Mitā.* on Yāj. II. 295) or evidences like written records of a municipality ("pura-pramāṇam" as read in the *Sm. Ch.*, 772), dissensions among the constituent elements of the state ("saṃbhedah prakṛtīnām, tathaiva ca"), breaches of duties of heretics, followers of the Veda, guilds of merchants ("pāṣaṇḍi-naigamaśreṇi-gaṇa-dharma-viparyayāḥ"), quarrel between father and son, neglect of penances (prāyaścitta-vyatikramaḥ), abstraction of gifts made to worthy persons (pratigraha-vilopaśca), the wrath of hermits (kopa-ś-cāśraminām api), sinful confusion of castes (varṇa-saṅkara-doṣaśca), and the rules regarding their maintenance (tad-vṛtti-niyamā-s-tathā) and in short whatever else has been omitted in the preceding sections on law (na dṛṣṭam yacca pūrveṣu).

Yāj.[2] prescribes the highest amercement for offences like the following—"one who writes wrongly, either more or less than the actual amount of the land donated by the king and one who catches the adulterer or the thief but lets him go free without bringing him to the king. If the Brahmin, Kṣatriya, Vaiśya or Śūdra is forced to take forbidden food, the culprit must be punished with the highest, middlemost, the lowest and its half amercement respectively. This is exactly like the law of Kauṭilya.[3] Kauṭilya, however, adds that "those consuming such things of their own accord, shall be banished from the country " but Yāj. is silent on this issue. But the question may be raised as to the significance of the term 'a-peyam' and 'a-bhakṣyam'. Some scholar thinks that it "does not seem to refer to food etc., forbidden in the Smṛtis on sacramental grounds, that has mostly to do with brahmins only". But there being no specific mention of the items of forbidden food or drink here, it may not be wrong to surmise that the traditional list of food or drink, as prescribed in the Smṛtis may be referred to here. Vijñāneśvara's comment on Yāj. may be borne in mind in this connection, intending the distinction of degree of punishment proportionate to the nature of the forbidden article like garlic etc. ("laśunādyabhakṣya-dūṣaṇe tu-"). The I.P.C., Sec. 295A may be noted in this connection, as it prescribes the punishment of imprisonment upto 2 years or of fine or of both for deliberate and malicious acts intended to outrage religious feelings of any class by insulting its religion or religious beliefs. Manu[4] prescribes death penalty for one destroying temples, fine of 500 paṇas for breakers of images of gods and banishment for heretics, i.e. non-believers in Vedas. Viṣṇu enjoins death-punishment on one who defiles a brahmin by making him drink wine[5] and even on a Śūdra who touches the body of the twice-born.[6] But Kauṭilya[7] advises the punishment of fine of 100 paṇas on a cāṇḍāla touching an Āryan lady. Yāj.[8] however, says that the cāṇḍāla must be fined one hundred for touching the twice-born ("cāṇḍāla-ś-cottamān-spṛśet") and thus for the offence of untouchability only. Manu[9] prescribes corporal punishment for the Śūdras bearing the marks of the twice-born like the sacred thread. Kauṭilya[10] advises in such cases the punishment of making him blind or the fine of 800 paṇas. Yāj.[11] is however, more lenient to prescribe the fine of the same amount only instead of any corporal punishment.

It may be noted that the ceremonies called 'abhicāra' meaning incantations and sacrifices, intended to destroy life were in wide practice during the period of Manu and so Manu[12] regulates such activities by the prescription of a fine of 200 paṇas.

Kullūka means by 'abhicāra' all such actions, taught either in the Veda or in secular works. Kullūka and Medhātithi think that if the 'abhicārika'-s are successful, they would be liable to the punishment of murder. Kauṭilya[13] also regulates witch-craft and black magic. Bṛhaspati[14] enjoins the punishment of banishment for such activities.

Kauṭ.[15] warns against hindrances like damage caused to agriculture by misuse of tanks, rivers etc. Persons, letting out the water of tanks etc. in any other place than their sluicegate, must be punished with a fine. He enjoins punishment in varying degrees for breaking the dam of a tank (Manu, IX. 279; Yāj. II. 278). The inscription,[16] found at Malūrpaṭna (Mysore) mentions the fine of 50 Kaḻañju for obstructing the irrigation. Yāj. prescribes drowning for a woman who breaks the embankment (of a tank) but he is silent as regards men. Śaṅkha enjoins a fine of 800 paṇas for this offence. But while *Matsya Purāṇa*[17] prescribes death by drowning for obstructing the cause of water in a tank, *Agni Purāṇa*[18] recommends imprisonment for a month for "diverting the water of a stream into another channel". In England, by 9 George III C. 29 maliciously breaking down a fish-pond for the destruction of fishes was regarded as felony without benefit of clergy.[19]

(i) Crimes connected with public health

Sanitation attracted the attention of the government in the Mauryan age, as evidenced by Kauṭilya. Hence all measures were adopted as far as possible for preserving the health of the people. Physicians were stationed in villages and towns. Aśoka's edicts show his interest in public health, not only of men but also of animals, not only here in India but also outside India. Strong steps were taken to combat outbreaks of pestilence or epidemic.

Adulteration of foodstuffs was strictly prohibited. Royal officials supervised the cleaning of roads and laws were very severe against the culprits who caused nuisance or injury to public health. Kauṭilya[20a] prescribes the fine of 1/8th of a paṇa for throwing dirt on the road and double this amount on the royal highway. Fines for voiding faeces in a holy place, in a place for water .... are one paṇa rising sucessively by one paṇa and half these for passing urine except when these are due to medicine, illness or fear. For throwing the dead body of a cat, a dog, an ichneumon or a serpent inside the city the fine shall be three paṇas, for throwing the deadbody of a donkey, a camel, a mule, a horse or cattle six paṇas, and for a human corpse, 50 paṇas. For depositing and burning a corpse elsewhere than in a cremation ground, the fine shall be 12 paṇas. Constant inspection of places supplying water, roads, watercourses etc. was the main duty of the city-superintendent (2.36.43). The Paṇyādhyakṣa was appointed to regulate the supply, sale and price of commodities and to check cornering and he punished the adulteration of foodstuffs.

Kauṭilya is very strict to those who sell unclean meat because he enjoins the punishment of the mutilation of the left hand and both feet on them and in case of sale of human flesh, the death is the punishment.[20b] The Sūnādhyakṣa was appointed to supervise the sale of meat because meat-eating was the fashion of the day in ancient India and the sale of bad or adulterated meat or of meat of diseased animals was severely punished. Manu[21] is stricter than Kauṭilya in cases of dropping filth on the king's highway when the culprit is made to pay two paṇas instead of 1/8th paṇas, as prescribed by Kauṭilya. He ordains the fine of the first amercement for adulterating unadulterated commodities.[22]

Yāj.[23] is very strict to those traders who sell gold and meat with adulteration. ("kūṭasvarṇa-vyavahārī vimāṃsasya ca vikrayī") and prescribes that such culprits should be punished with the mutilation of three limbs, noses, ears and hands and also with the highest amercement. It may be noted that Manu is stricter than Yāj. with respect to a goldsmith. Manu[24] says that "the king shall cause a goldsmith who behaves dishonestly, the most noxious of all the thorns, to be cut to pieces with razors", Vijñāneśvara, however, says that such severe punishment was imposed only in cases of gold belonging to a god, a brahmin and the king ("deva-brāhmaṇa-rāja-svarṇa-viṣayam"). Kauṭilya[25] prescribes the fine of 12 paṇas for adulteration of foodstuffs and others. ("Dhānya-sneha-kṣāralavaṇa-gandha-bhaiṣajya-dravyānāṃ samavarno'-padhāne dvādaśa-paṇo daṇḍaḥ"). The modern law of India is also very strict against adulteration of food or drink intended for sale and sale of noxious food or drink which are punishable with imprisonment up to 6 months or a fine up to 1000 rupees or with both.[26] Adulteration of drugs and sale of adulterated drugs are likewise penalised.[27]

It should be noted that Kauṭilya's laws[28] in connection with the throwing of dead bodies inside the city are meant for preventing the outbreak of any epidemic through the putrefaction of a dead body. Similar laws were enforced in ancient Persia.[29] The Persian law was—"The worshippers of Mazda shall carry the dead to the highest summits where there were corpse-eating dogs and birds. If they shall not fasten the corpse, so that the dogs and birds may carry the bones to water and to trees, they shall be Peshotanu and punished with 200 stripes"—with each whip.[30] The 'Twelve Tables' of Rome also declared it unlawful "to burn or bury the dead within the city".

The sale of noxious or forbidden food was also punishable in ancient India, as already evidenced by Kauṭ. and Viṣṇu. We come across a similar law in England[31] prohibiting the sale of corrupted wine, contagious or unwholesome flesh etc. The sale of noxious and unwholesome articles was also forbidden in India, as noted in Kauṭilya,[32] Yāj.[33] and *Matsya Purāṇa.*[34]

This shows that the ancient Indians were not blind to the danger of spreading germs of diseases, carried by articles lying on a dead body. They were equally alive to the importance of pure water for health, as evident from the laws of Kauṭilya prescribing fines for fouling water of public springs and reservoirs, already noted. Śaṁkha's severe step enjoining death or mutilation for defiling tanks etc. deserves mention. Committing nuisance in the highway or in a public place was equally tried to be checked by the ancient jurists who prescribed fines plus the removal of the filth. In England also, according to Blackstone, for this offence the culprit was indicted to amend the wrong and sometimes fined.[35]

(ii) Miscarriage of justice

Yāj.[36] makes us aware of the king's duties that he should protect the people from all harassments from the hands of the cheat or secret thieves and robbers and specially of the clerks or accountants of the state. That is why he enjoins that the king should know through spies the movement of the government employees and honour the good, punish corporally the bad and banish after confiscation of all wealth those who are bribed. Nārada[37] means to say that the submissive people should be honoured by the king and the insolent ones must be treated in a reverse way. Vyāsa prescribes the same punishment as Yāj. on officers-in-charge of law and justice ("nyāya-sthāne ye' dhikṛtāḥ"), if they are proved guilty of taking bribes.

To maintain the impartial standard of justice the judges themselves were asked not to violate justice by their own misconduct. We have already noted that Kauṭilya prescribes rules for keeping watch over officers of all departments of government in AŚ. IV. 9. The Samāhartā with the Pradeṣṭṛ-s working under him should keep in check all heads of departments and their subordinates and even the judges were under his surveillance. The judges were punished for the following offences, viz., for threatening, or rebuking a litigant without reason, the lowest fine for violence, double that in case of verbal injury; for improper question like questioning one unnecessarily and omission of questioning to one who should be questioned the middlemost fine and the highest fine for violence for improper way of handling evidences, granting undue privileges to either party, allowing time more than necessary or tampering with the normal course of justice (4.9.13-16). In case the judge repeated the same offence, he was punished with double the fine and removal from office. ("punaraparādhe dviguṇaṃ sthānādvyaparopanaṃ ca"). He was also punished for unjust sentence (lighter or heavier than that laid down for the offence). Scribes were also punished for their negligence to write the correct evidence or tampering with it intentionally. Manu[38] also enjoins that in cases of unjust settlement by ministers or the judge the king should resettle and fine (them) one thousand paṇas. Medhātithi and Kullūka think that this rule refers to cases where the cause of the unjust decision is not a bribe because the punishment of corrupt judges has previously been prescribed. But Nārāyaṇa and Rāgh. think that it applies to cases of bribery also. Yāj.[39] also refers to re-trial by the king of the cases, improperly decided by judges. Someśvara[40] also warns that the king should never accept anything as bribery from any litigant. The Kuhūr (Tanjore Dist.) inscription[41] of the period of Rājarāja I (10th cent. A.D.) mentions the harassing of royal officials in collecting the fine. The *Agni Purāṇa*[42] shows how corruption of officers and undue harassment of the people by them are severely punished. Officers charged for these offences get the punishment of the highest amercement and they are to be banished from the kingdom after the confiscation of all their property. Thus compared with Manu (IX. 234) this Purāṇa is more strict. The *Agni Purāṇa* asks the king to refund thirty times an unjust fine levied on an innocent man (258.82). This Purāṇa (258.83) holds the same view as Nārada (1.26-27) that the administration of proper justice brings seven benefits: piety, wealth, fame, popularity, respectability, influence on the people and at last a place in heaven.

Kāmandaka[43] speaks of five types of fear of the people from the Āyuktaka, thieves, royal favourites, enemies and the avarice of the king. Chaṇḍeśvara (Gr. R. p. 54) holds that royal officers are very liable to become knaves. The Prime Minister Guṇavarman is also painted as plotting against the king in the *Kathā-saritsāgara.* Kalhaṇa gives us clear examples of corrupt royal officers like that of a scribe during the reign of Yaśaskara (939-48 A.D.) who was bribed to falsify a deed only to dispossess an innocent merchant of his belongings.[44] Another king named Pārtha is also heard of in the Rājatara[45] as appointing only those officers as councillors etc. who brought more and more money into the royal treasury at the cost of poor peasants. Harṣa of Kashmira oppressed his subjects by employing Kāyasthas who were adept in the art of oppression. This shows that sometimes kings were not solicitous for rendering proper justice to their people, as evidenced by Kalhaṇa's statement that Chakravarman of Kashmira (936 A.D.) appointed thieves and robbers as government officers, though, however, it is used in the figurative sense.

(iii) Crimes relating to weights and measures

The *Kāśikā* on Pāṇ. II. 421 informs us that weights and measures, probably existing in its time were first introduced by the Nandas. ("Nandopakramāṇi mānāni"). The proper use of standard weights and measures is necessary for the protection of people from cheats. Kauṭilya[46] enjoins the employment of the Superintendent of weights and measures, ("pautavādhyakṣa) whose duty was to get manufactured weights from half māṣaka onwards up to one hundred suvarṇas, weights being made of iron or of stones found in the Magadha country and the Mekala mountain in Madhya Pradesh. The term 'māṣaka' is the name of a weight (equal to 1/16th suvarṇa and also referred to as māṣa) and of a copper coin (equivalent to 1/16th of a paṇa). A Karṣa or suvarṇa is the weight of the paṇa as well as of the coin māṣaka. It may be noted that Karṣa is the name of a weight in ancient Iran as well. F.W. Thomas thinks that the weight in India was imported from western Asia like the Vedic Mānā or Minā.[47] Kauṭ.[48] enjoins that the Superintendent "should cause a stamping of the weights and measures to be made every four months. The penalty for unstamped weights etc. is 27 paṇas and a quarter. Traders shall pay a stamping fee amounting to one Kākaṇī everyday to the Superintendent of Standardisation".[49] The Saṃsthādhyakṣa was employed to punish the use of false weights and measures. Kauṭilya advises the king to supervise weights and measures so that no fraud be committed on the people by dishonest persons. He prescribes proportionate fines rising from 3 paṇas upwards foı possessing or forging false weights and measures (IV. II-2 ff). He enjoins (4.2.13f) again that for using false weights and measures the trader must pay double the fines imposed on forgerer or possessor of false weights and measures.

Vyāsa[50] and Manu[51] say that all weights and measures must be duly marked, they must be re-examined every sixth month and those meant for objects for householders' use must be guarded against falsification. Yāj.[52] and *Viṣṇu Dh. S.*[53] prescribes the punishment of the highest amercement for those who fabricate false balances, edicts, measures and coins and also for those who use them in their transaction. (Cf. *Nītivākyāmṛta*, p. 98 "paṇya-tulā-māna-vṛddhyau rājā svayaṃ jagṛyāt/na vaṇigbhyaḥ santi pare paśyatoharāḥ//; See *Alberuni*, tr. by Sachau, Vol. I, ch. XV). The *Matsya Purāṇa*[54] prescribes the highest amercement for using false weights. It may be noted here that in medieval France one using false weights and measures was often punished with the loss of the thumb.[55]

(iv) Crimes connected with Coins

The early jurists of India say little about counterfeiting coins. Kauṭilya was very cautious to make coinage the monopoly of the state and tried his best to maintain the purety and accuracy of coins. He mentions one examiner of coins (rūpadarśaka) and prescribes that no gold coin should be accepted by the treasury officer unless its purity has been attested to by the examiner of coins. Yāj. follows Kauṭ. in penalising counterfeiting of coins. Great care was taken to regulate the goldsmiths, employed in the state-mint so that they might not falsify the standard weight and quality of coins. While Kauṭ.[56] enjoins banishment for private manufactures or counterfeiting of coins, Yāj.[57] prescribes merely the highest amercement for the same offence.

(v) Negligent conduct in respect of vicious animals

Kaut.[58] prescribes that "for the owner not rescuing a person being injured by a horned or tusked animal of his, the lowest fine for violence (shall be the punishment); the middle if he was called to come to the rescue". "For one allowing horned or tusked animals to kill one another, the fine shall be that and as much again".[59] Yāj.[60] says the same thing. We are not told whether the owner was liable to punishment if the animal attacked a man in his absence or whether the owner was made to control his animal of vicious nature from injuring others. Nārada[61] says that "the owner of a horse, dog or monkey is not responsible for any injury, made by these unless he should have set them to do it. We may compare here the laws of ancient India with those of other countries. According to Babylonian law, if an ox, known to be vicious, be not bound, nor its horns blunted, the owner must pay half a mina of silver if it gores and kills a freeman and one-third mina if a slave. There is no punishment in case of an injury by a mad bull.[62] The Persian law is barbarous in nature when it provides for the punishment of mutilation of limbs of a mad dog committing injury.[63] It is really surprising to hear of criminal prosecution against animals even in the medieval French law.[64]

(vi) Religious offences

It is interesting to note that the ancient Indians were not only tolerant of other religions but their treatment of religious offences also was generally lenient. It is due to the spirit of toleration among them that so many religious systems took their rise in India. While in other countries heresy and apostacy were punished with extreme severity, the Hindus allowed so many to reform and preach new religions. Though there was rivalry between different religious sects, in no period of ancient Indian history do we hear of religious persecution. Rather Aśoka or Harṣa stands as an example of religious toleration to the entire world. Yuan Chwang and other foreign travellers speak highly of India's spirit of religious toleration. This spirit is better appreciated when we compare the laws of other peoples. Death was the punishment for heresy in ancient Persia. Mani, the heretic was flayed alive.[65] The heretics winning over the Israelites from the true God were stoned to death.[66] "He that sacrificeth unto any god save unto the Lord only, shall be utterly destroyed".[67] In Athens the preaching of false philosophy was known as 'impiety', punishable with fine, banishment or death.[68] The history of Rome both in the Imperial and Republican periods shows criminal prosecution against upholders of rival cults.[69] Better silence on the religious history of medieval Europe and England. But no harassment is heard of in ancient India on the Cārvākas or on Buddha or Māhavīra. However, measures were taken to safeguard the temples or idols of gods. Manu prescribes death for the destroyer of temples.[70] Kātyāyaṇa enjoins a higher punishment in the stage of a fine of 250 paṇas for this offence. Manu[71] prescribes a fine of 500 paṇas for the destruction of an idol, while Viṣṇu[72] enjoins the highest amercement for this. Manu and *Matsya Purāṇa* (CCXXVII, 176-179) insist that the broken idol should be repaired and restored. Kauṭilya prescribes the punishment of death or the highest fine for stealing the idol of a god (IV. 11.16).

Gautama[73] and Bṛhaspati (XX. 12) are strict enough to punish a Śūdra by cutting out his tongue for recital of the Veda or teaching the religious lessons. Defiling others by giving prohibited food and drink was regarded as a criminal offence and different punishments have been treated earlier. It is really regretable that Viṣṇu[74] enacts that an untouchable, willfully defiling a member of higher caste by simple touch would be punished with death. Yāj.[75] softens this punishment to a fine of 100 paṇas. Similarly Śūdras wearing the insignia of brāhmaṇas were also subjected to corporal punishment.[76] The later lawyers like Yāj.[77] enjoin a fine of 800 paṇas only.

(vii) Witchcraft and sorcery

Like all ancient and medieval peoples the ancient Indians believed in witchcraft and sorcery. Even today they are practised in India. But ancient India was tolerant of these black arts and did never try to render wholesale massacre of witches and magicians as was done in medieval Europe. They were, however, punished for their criminal activities. Compared with other countries witches were treated leniently in India. Death[78] was the penalty for 'a man who wrongfully casts a spell on another' in Babylon. The Mosaic law[79] prescribed for a witch death by stoning. Death sentence was also the punishment for this offence in Athens. (Demons., III. App. VIII, p. 350), and in the 'Twelve Tables' (T.T., 8[21]). Witches were burnt to death in medieval France[80] and England.[81]

Kauṭ.[82] enjoins that "what a magician brings about to another by witchcraft and black magic, that small be meted out to him. The use of love-winning magic may be allowed towards a wife who does not like her husband or towards a maiden by a suitor or towards the husband by the wife. Else, in case of injury, the middle fine for violence shall be imposed". Manu[83] also prescribes a fine of 200 paṇas for a person attempting to kill another by this black art. Kullūka explains that this punishment is to be inflicted when death has not resulted, otherwise the punishment of murder shall be inflicted. Bṛhas.[84] says that one procuring gain by spells or medicine shall be made to disgorge it, but one practising incantations with roots shall be banished.

(viii) Forgery

Forgery was treated as a serious crime in ancient India as elsewhere. Manu says that "forgers of royal edicts .... the king shall put to death". Viṣṇu[85] prescribes the same punishment for forging not only royal edicts but also private documents. But Yāj.[86] makes the punishment lighter in the shape of the highest amercement. Kātyāyana follows Yāj.

Rome punished a slave capitally for this offence but a free man, guilty of forgery was punished with deportation, according to the law of Cornelia de falsis. In medieval France it was generally punished with pillory but an officer or a notary, was capitally punished for this offence.[87] In England, however, by Eliz. C.14 forgery was punished with fines, payable to the injured party, with pillory, mutilation of ears and nose and imprisonment; but for the second offence capital punishment was inflicted. By acts in the later period it was made capital offence even for the first time.[88]

REFERENCES

1. Yāj. II. 295.
2. Yāj. II. 295.
3. 4.13.1
4. IX. 280 & 285.
5. V. 98-103.
6. V. 104.
7. 3.20.16.
8. 11.234.
9. IX. 224.
10. 4.10.13.
11. II. 304.
12. IX. 290.
13. 4.13.27.
14. 22.16.
15. III. 9.
16. *E.C.*, ix. p. 127; 506 of 1911.
17. CCXXVII, 171.
18. CCXXVII, 32-38.
19. Black, IV, XVII, pp. 244-246.

20a. 2.36.26 ff, Cf. Manu, IX. 282.

20b. 4.10.14-15, 2.26.12.

21. IX. 282.
22. Cf. Yāj. II. 245.
23. II. 297.

24. IX. 292.
25. Cf. also Manu. IX. 287.
26. I.P.C., Sec. 272 & 273.
27. Sec. 274 & 275.
28. II. 36.30.
29. Vendidad, Farg. VI-II. 10 ff-Zand Avesta.
30. Vend. Farg. VI-V-44-48.
31. 51 Hen. III. st. 6 and the ordinance for bakers.
32. IV.X.
33. II. 303.
34. CCXXVII, 204.
35. Black, IV. ch. XIII. p. 167.
36. 1.336; 1.338-339.
37. *Sm. Ch.*, p. 772.
38. IX. 234; IX. 231.
39. II. 305.
40. *Mānasollāsa,* vol. I, p. 143; Vim. 2, Adhy. 20; Sl. 1274.
41. Cf. *The Cholas* by N.K. Sastri, p. 484.
42. 227, 47-49.
43. V. 82-83.
44. *Rājat.*, vi, 38-41.
45. V. 275.
46. II. 19.
47. *JRAS,* 1916, p. 366.
48. II. 19.40 ff.
49. AŚ , ed. Kangle, p. 157.
50. 19.13.
51. VIII. 403.
52. II. 240.
53. V. 122.
54. CCXXVII, 199.
55. *Cont. Cr. L.*, Pt. I, ch. VI, 39 f.
56. IV. IV. 210.
57. II. 240.
58. 4.13.18.
59. *Ibid.*, 4.13.19.
60. II. 300.
61. 15 & 16 Tit. 32.
62. Ham, 250-252.
63. Vend. Farg. XIII. 29.34.
64. *Cont. Cr. L.*, Pt. I, ch. VI, 3.

65. *Zoroastrian Civilisation,* Ch. L., Religious offences Sassanian period.
66. Den. 13.1-10.
67. Exodus, 22[20], Ezek. 18[12.13]
68. (Demosthenes, 111, App. VIII, p. 347 and App. IV, p. 258.
69. *Cont. Cr. L.,* Ch. 1, 16.
70. IX. 280; cf. *Matsya Purāṇa,* CCXXVII, 172.
71. IX. 285.
72. V. 174.
73. XII. 4 & 5
74. V. 104.
75. II. 234.
76. *Manu,* IX. 224 & 260.
77. II. 304.
78. Ham. 2.18.
79. Exod. 22.
80. *Cont. Cr. L.*, I, VI, 39 f.
81. Black, IV.IV, p. 60-61.
82. 4.13.27 ff.
83. IX. 290 cf. also *Matsya Purāṇa* CCXXVII, 183.
84. *S.B.E.* Vol. 33, p. 361, verse 16.
85. V. 9.11.
86. II. 240. (damam - uttamam).
87. *Cont. Cr. L.*, I, VI, 39 f.
88. Black, IV. XVI, pp. 247-249.

CHAPTER X
Conclusion

Now let us conclude with a brief note on the modern criminologists and their views on crime and punishment only to judge the entire picture of the penal system of ancient India, as presented in this treatise from their standpoint.

Modern jurists are aware of the utility of the study of criminology as a science, because they think that the treatment of crimes and criminals can be no more machine-like and indiscriminate than the treatment of a disease by a doctor of medicine (cf. Dr. Healy, "Present-day aims and methods in studying the offender", *Journal of Criminology*, Vol. IV, p. 204). We must bear in mind that a criminal is as much a unit of the society as a law-giver or a judge; and punishment should be individualised as far as practicable. Dr. Holmes points out the following orthodox classification of the theories on the object of punishment: (i) retributive, (ii) preventive, and (iii) reformative. It may be mentioned here that the last two theories have had little response from the European jurists, saturated as they have been with Kantian and Hegalian Absolutism. These jurists seem to think that the relation between crime and punishment is absolute and that the punishment should always be proportionate to the objective gravity of crimes. (*Law Quarterly Review*, 1918, Mr. C. Keany). The fundamental principle of the objective school is that since desire for vengeance is inborn in human nature, the law should try to make the gratification of the spirit of revenge an object of punishment. In the words of Sir James Stephen "the criminal law stands to the passion of revenge in much the same relation as marriage to sexual appetite". (*General View of the Criminal Law of England*, p. 99).

It is interesting to note that Prof. Ferri in his "Criminal Sociology" divides criminals into five classes: (i) insane, (ii) born, (iii) habitual, (iv) occasional, and (v) criminals actuated by passions. But this is more or less an empirical classification and it is not based on psychological principles. Prof. Ellwood of Missouri classifies on the basis of the psychological principle of habit criminals into three classes: (i) defective, (ii) habitual and (iii) occasional. But how to incorporate the political offenders ? The social and sociological school of criminology such as Tārde, Colajamis, Benger, Karl Marx and others suggest that social and economic causes bring about cases of criminality. But it may be equally argued that these factors do not so much cause criminality as give a particular shape to it. Some others think that the modern system of non-moral education, by raising false hopes, never to be fulfilled and by putting false values upon things breeds discontent and discontent is the father of criminality.

Now whatever may be the reasons, we cannot deny that crimes still exist in the society and they are rather on the increase in India and specially in different countries of Europe, as evidenced by the available statistics, shown by Garofal.[1] The reports on the Police Administration in the Presidency of Bengal in 1914-16 also corroborate the same fact. The high rate of criminality in the modern India, particularly in Bengal is beyond any question. But the question is why and how to tackle the problem. Some scholar points out that not only the number of criminals but also that of recidivists are on the increase both in India and Europe[2] and he tries to explain this phenomenon as the result of many potent factors like economic depression, particularly among the lower order of the society, political upheavals of nations and mainly the indiscriminate and mechanical treatment of criminals by the classical method, as for instance, German law imposes a heavier penalty for deceitful offences than for violent ones.[3] The main objection against the classical method he puts forward is that it ignores altogether the subjective personality of the criminal and it takes into account only the objective fact of the crime.

The Italian jurist Beccaria, however, urged in 1764 that no punishment should be greater than what is warranted by the crime and that all men should be treated as equal in the eye of law. That means, law is no respecter of persons and it must punish the crime according to its character. He stood against the differential system because it would lead to the infliction of different punishments for the same offence. But it cannot be gainsaid that even under the attractive garb of equality of law gross injustice may be sometimes done if a particular crime is not properly analysed with respect to different circumstances of the crime. The most essential duty of the state is to punish a criminal for the preservation of the society but its right to punish is ultimately based on its duty to protect the individual and surely it would be the highest inequity to insist on the right without fulfilling the duty. The criminal is after all a man of the society and given proper opportunity he may be restored to the right path. But this demand of the criminal is most unfortunately not properly met and hence the soulless penal system is held according to such thinkers, responsible for the ever increase of cases of criminality. To take for example, in India the substantive penal law is fixed in the Indian penal code and the procedural law in the criminal procedure code. Both these codes, it must be admitted show attempts to individualise punishment, in the former a particular offence is considered in the background of the mental state of the delinquent and in the latter trial is made by the judge with the aid of the jury. But as a matter of fact punishment depends ultimately on the discretion, of course, judicial discretion of the judge or jurors, exercised solely with an eye to the objective gravity of the offence and not to the subjective or social personality of the criminal. Hence some of modern jurists insist on the subjective study of the crime which may be due to biological, social and physical reasons; that means, punishment should be individualised. Besides, Prof. Ferri in his *Criminal Sociology* suggests some preventive measures, known as "penal substitutes" and stresses on educational, industrial and moral reforms instead of on mere repressive and retributory measures. Prof. S. Banerjee, also puts forward some measures, preventive and repressive and reparative in character as possible remedies against all sorts of delinquency.[4]

Now about the penal system of ancient India, it may be noted that though not without defects, it was not altogether blind to the points, raised by modern jurists. Of course, it will be unwise to judge the past by the standard of the present. According to modern jurists a man is liable to be punished only when he commits an offence intentionally or out of criminal negligence. That means, he is immune from punishment in the absence of these factors. The ancient Indian jurists also cherished the same view, as already noted before. It has also been noted that the ancient Indian theory of punishment insisted on four motives, deterrent, preventive, corrective and purificatory. Besides, the subjective analysis of the crime with particular attention to the different circumstances of the crime was also not neglected by the ancient jurists like Kauṭilya, Manu, Yāj. and others; as already discussed before. The differential treatment of punishment on the basis of the caste may sound bitter to the ear at present but in a caste-ridden society of ancient India it was an unavoidable necessity for the maintenance of social stability and it evolved itself gradually in a better way as far as possible. Discrimination of punishments in cases of lunacy, infancy, ignorance, negligence etc. suffices it to show that at least humble attempts at individualisation of punishment were made in hoary antiquity. At the first sight punishments mạy apear to have been rigid and inelastic and the judges appear to be absolutely bound to the laws of the land, but the ancient jurists permitted the judges to exercise their own discretion or reasoning. The superiority of equity or reason was expressed in clear-cut terms by the ancient lawgivers of India.

REFERENCES

1. *Criminology*, pp. 210-211.
2. Cf. *Calcutta Law Journal*, Vol. XXXI, p. 11n.
3. Kohler, *Philosophy of Law*, p. 290.
4. Sir Asutosh Mookherjee Silver Jubilee Volumes, Vol. I, p. 375.

Appendix A
Sources of Hindu Law

The Mīmāṃsā school holds the Vedas as the first source of 'Dharma' (cf. Jaimini's sūtra "Codanā-lakṣaṇo'rtho Dharmaḥ") because Jaimini says that "that which is signified by a direction and leads to a benefit is Dharma". When one is unable to find any Vedic authority for a rule, one must assume that the śruti-text is lost and it will come out if diligently searched for. The commentators like Medhātithi and Viśvarūpa show their skill in the discovery of such texts. Of course, when we are told that the Vedas are the highest authority on Dharma, we are not to understand that they lay down injunctions like the Smṛtis but they contain incidental references to all important matters of Hindu law and practically they form what is known as 'Artha-vāda' in the Mīmāṃsā system, allied syntactically with 'Vidhi's. Hence the Hindu jurists rely upon the Vedas as the first source of 'Dharma'. The Mīmāṃsā theory of ('Vikalpa') option holds good when there is a conflict between two Vedic texts but not when a smṛti-text clashes with a śruti-text because the latter overrides the former. However, the śruti-text which is at present lost may be restored against a smṛti-text in question. The Mīmāṃsist's view is that until such discovery is done, action in cases of conflict should be suspended.

The Mīmāṃsā holds that all conflicts of law are only apparent but not real because both the texts on artha and dharma school claim canonical authority. But Yāj.[1] holds the superiority of the Dharma text to the Artha-text. Nārada[2] says the same thing. ("Artha-śāstrāt tu valavad Dharma-śāstram-iti sthitiḥ"—Yāj. and "Artha-śāstroktam-utsṛjya Dharma-śāstroktamācaret"—Nār.). The theory of the infallibility of the Veda, the common source of both Dharma and Arthaśāstras justifies the conclusion that Śruti cannot be opposed to equity (nyāya). Vijñāneśvara on Yāj. (II. 21) does not like the idea of the superiority of Dharmaśāstra to Arthaśāstra, because he explains the Arthaśāstra not as wellknown works of Uśanas and others but as the Arthaśāstra contained in the Dharma-śāstras; and he thinks that if there is any conflict between two classes of rules within the Dharma-śāstra, the Dharma-rule will prevail. He cites two examples. Manu[3] says that an ātatāyīn must be killed at once, even if he be a learned brāhmaṇa. But this rule conflicts with another of Manu[4] where he says that there is no expiation for the intentional murder of a brahmin. The former is an Artha text which should be invalidated by the latter, a Dharma-rule. The reconciliation may be had if the reference to the learned brahmin ātatāyīn is taken only as a rhetorical expression, meant for laying stress on the injunction on the treatment of assassins and if the dictum is applied to cases other than those of brāhmaṇas. Again, Yāj.[5] enjoins the artha-law that the acquisition of a friend is superior to that of land and wealth and the Dharma-law in II. 1. that free from anger and covetousness the judge should decide according to the principles of Dharma-śāstra. If a rich suitor is to be unjustly favoured, the first rule is observed but it should not be, being an artha-rule opposed to the Dharma rule. In determining doubtful cases of law, the opinion of those conversant with law and usage must be accepted. ("Dharmajña-samayaḥ pramāṇam"). Manu[6] enjoins: "Anāmnāteṣu dharmeṣu kathaṃ syāditi ced-bhavet/Yaṃ śiṣṭāḥ brāhmaṇā Vruyuḥ sa 'Dharmaḥ syād-aśaṅkitaḥ//"—that is, in cases where the law is not known, the law should unhesitantly be taken to be what is approved by the cultured and holy men. Jayaswal[7] says that the Samiti or Pariṣad was to decide the disputed law in Vedic times. The Pariṣad continued in later days, of course, with thinned members. Manu says that in the absence of any Pariṣad, the opinion of even one 'excellent brāhmaṇa' will do. The members of the Pariṣad should be śiṣṭa-s (cultured—'akāmātmā'), equally sympathetic to all living beings, learned in the Vedas, believers in the validity of both Veda and perception (Śruti-pratyakṣa-hetavaḥ), skilled in logical inference, knowers of things in various periods of time and space, resourceful and of good character (sadācārāḥ). Śaṅkha-Likhita limit the scope of a brāhmaṇa-pariṣad to the determination of the correctness of Vedic texts, smṛti-texts, custom, usage and dharma; and this body of experts was convened for determining rules for judicial guidance. The Pariṣad ceases to exist after the 7th cent. A.D. and the Paṇḍita, corresponding to 'Vinaya-sthiti-sthāpaka'[8] of the Gupta inscriptions comes into prominence as a Legal Remembrancer.

REFERENCES

1. II. 21.
2. 1.90.
3. VIII. 350-351.
4. XI. 90.
5. I. 352.
6. XII. 108.
7. *Manu and Yājñavalkya*, p. 78.
8. *EI*, XI, 107 and *ASI, AR*, 1903-4.

Appendix B
The Purohita

The Purohita was one of 18 Tīrthas or administrative heads of ancient India. He was the king's advisor in matters, both religious and secular,[1] as evidenced by the Saṃhitā-s and Brāhmaṇas. He is described as the 'Rāṣṭra-gopa', the guardian of the realm.[2] Some scholar thinks of the origin of this institution after the establishment of the caste system in India, that is, by the period of composition of the latest portion of the *Ṛgveda*;[3] but the term 'purohita' is referred to also in the earlier portion of the *Ṛgveda*. Fick traces this office even from the pre-Vedic times.[4] However, the king and the purohita were like the twins of the same mother, the state. Sometimes one purohita is heard of as serving two or three kings.[5] Keith remarks rightly that "the Vedic purohita was the forerunner of the Brahmin statesmen who from time to time in India have shown conspicuous ability in the management of affairs and there is no reason to doubt that a Viśvāmitra or Vaśiṣṭha was a more important element of government of the early Vedic realm".[6] But the purohita was punished with death for his acts of treason, as attested by the *Pañcaviṃsa Brāh.* (XIV, 6.8).

The office of the Purohita is glorified in the *AŚ* of Kauṭilya and Kāmandaka and in the Dharmaśāstras. Dr. Ghoshal, however, argues that the Arthaśāstra rules out this post from the list of prominent factors of government.[7] But the commentator of the Kāmandaka, Śaṅkarārya speaks of the purohita as the special minister ("Viśeṣa amātya").

The Purohita is also heard of in the ancient South Indian polity, as confirmed by the commentary on the Śilappadikaram.[8] Kauṭ.[9] mentions the chief qualities for this office (cf. Yāj. 1.313). He[10] speaks of the Purohita as one of the advisors to the king ("mantri-purohita-sakhaḥ"), and allows him to be paid the highest pay like ministers etc. Bodhāyana and Manu seem to associate the Purohita not only with religious duties but with the affairs of the state as well. Bodhāyana says: "Let (the king) choose a domestic priest (who shall be) foremost in all (transactions)." Let him act according to his instructions".[11] The Purohita was according to the *Dhammaddhaja Jāt.* (I. p. 220), as an administrator of justice. He was practically the guiding force in the administration but he was also not above the law of the land. He was punished with imprisonment or banishment, if he swerved from his duty to the king or revolted against him.[12]

Manu enjoins: "But with the most distinguished of all (ministers), a learned Brāhmaṇa, let the king deliberate on the most important affairs which relate to the six measures of the royal policy". And "Let him appoint a domestic Purohita". This shows that Manu makes a brāhmaṇa other than the Purohita the chief advisor to the king. According to Kauṭilya the Purohita should be of unblemished family and character, well-educated in the Vedas and six aṅgas .... well-versed in the science of government and the king should follow him strictly, showing thereby that the Purohita was the advisor of the king on all state-affairs. Yāj.[13] was evidently inspired by Kauṭilya and according to him, the Purohita took important part in matters of administration and he was not directly a member of the cabinet but superior to the cabinet. Yāj.[14] speaks of a brāhmaṇa, learned in all laws, obviously both religious and secular ("Sarva-dharma-vit"), who was evidently a Purohita, acting as a judge in lieu of the king in co-operation with sabhya-s. Nārada mentions this post as that of a Prāḍ-vivāka.

The *Mbh.*[15] speaks of the exalted position of the Purohita with whose guidance the king prospers. Bhīṣma asks Yudhiṣṭhira to act in conjunction with his Purohita because he can help the king in protecting the righteous and suppressing the unrighteous.

The Dharma school insists that the king must act according to the instruction of the Purohita. The Purāṇas also mention the qualifications of the royal priest.[16] Daṇḍī, however, paints a real picture of avaricious priests who extracted gifts from the king through the help of special messengers, of course, giving them in return a secret share out of these gifts.[17]

Śukra[18] says that the Purohita is one of the highly paid officials[19] and the qualifications he must have, agree with those, recommended in the *Arthaśāstra.* Bṛhaspati speaks of the chief minister and the Purohita as the mother and father. ("Samau mātr-pitṛ-bhyām"). The place of the Purohita was taken under the Rāṣṭrakūṭa kings by an officer, appointed to exercise general supervision over religion and morality. The officer under Nanna-raja (708 A.D.) was known as "Dharmāṅkujśa".[20] Paṇḍita, the minister of morality and religion in *Śukranīti* seems to embody the tradition of 'Dharma-māhamātyas' of Aśoka, Samana-mahāmātyas of Andhras[21] and the Vinaya-sthiti-sthāpakas of the Guptas.

REFERENCES

1. *Vedic Index,* I, p. 113 and II, p. 90.
2. *RV,* VII, 18.13; *A V,* III, 18 and *Ait. Brāh.*, VIII, 24-25.
3. Alindisches Leben, ch. VI, pp. 195 ff.
4. Tr. by S.K. Mitra, p. 164.
5. *Śat. Brāh.*, II, 4.4.5.
6. *C.H.I.*, I, pp. 95-96.
7. *Hindu Political Theories,* pp. 88-89.
8. *Tamil Lexicon,* vol. I, pt. III, p. 579.
9. I, 9.
10. 1.10.
11. 1.18.7.8, "Sarvatodhuraṃ Purohitaṃ vṛṇuyāt, tasya śāsane varteta".
12. *AŚ,* IX, sec. 3.14; Manu, VIII. 335.
13. 1.313.
14. II. 3.
15. Ādi, CLXXXVI, 77-84.
16. *Garuḍa P.*, ch. CXII—and *Agni Purāṇa* - CXXXIX, 16-17.
17. *Daśakumāracaritam,* Uttara, Ucchvāsa, VIII.
18. II. 78-81.
19. II. 70-72.
20. *Ind. Ant.*, XVIII, p. 230.
21. Nasik Ins., *E.I.*, VIII, p. 91.

Bibliography

Original Sources (with abbreviations)

Ṛg-Veda (R.V.)
Atharva-veda (A.V.)
Śatapatha Brāhmana (Śat. Br.)
Taittirīya Brāhmana (Taitt. Br.)
Vājasaneya Saṃhitā (Vāj. Sam.)
Kāṭhaka Saṃhitā
Pañca-Viṃsa Saṃhitā
Bṛhadāraṇyaka Upaniṣad (Bṛh. Upa.)
Chandogya Upaniṣad (Chan. Upa.)
Pāṇini's Aśṭādhyāyī (Pāṇ.)
Patañjali's Mahābhāṣya (Patañ. Mahābh.)
Gautama's Dharma-sūtra (Gaut. Dh.S.) with Haradatta's comm.
Āpastamba's Dharma-sūtra (Āpas. Dh. S.)
Bodhāyana's Dharma-sūtra (Bodh. Dh.S.)
Jaimini's Sūtra
Rāmāyaṇa (Rāmā)
Mahābhārata (Mbh.)
Nīlakaṇṭha on Mbh.

Smṛti-Śāstras:

Manu, Vasiṣṭha
Viṣṇu
Yājñāvalkya (Yāj.)
Nārada (Nār.)
Bṛhaspati (Bṛh.)
Kātyāyana (Kātyā)
Śukra (tran. by Benoy K. Sarkar)
Kāmandaka
Vyāsa
Śaṅkha-Likhita
Paiṭhīṇasi
Parāśara
Hārīta
Pitāmaha
Sumantu
Atri
Yama
Devala

Commentaries and Digests on Smṛti-s

Kullūka-ṭīkā
Medhātithi-bhāṣya

Vijñáneśvara on Yāj. (Vijñān.)
Aparārka-on-Yāj.
Viśvarūpa on Yāj.
Nītiprakāśa
Abhilaṣitārtha-cintāmaṇi
Vyavahāra-Mayūkha
Vyavahāra-prakāśa
Parāśara-Mādhava
Daṇḍa-viveka, published in Gaikwad Oriental Series, 1930
Sarasvatī-vilāsa
Vyavahārāloka
Vyavahāra-mātṛkā (Calcutta)
Vivādārṇava-setu
Vīramitrodaya (Calcutta)
Asahāya on Nārada (Bib. Indica)
Vācaspati
Bālambhatti on the Mitākṣarā
Subodhinī on the Mitākṣarā
Vivāda-cintāmaṇi (Bombay)
Smṛti-candrikā
Vyavahāroddyata
Nibandhana-kāra

Other literary works:

of Aśvaghośa
of Kālidāsa (Raghu, Śakuntalā etc.)
of Daṇḍin—Daśakumāracharitam (Daśak.)
Mṛcchakaṭikam (Mṛccha.)
Gāthā-sapta-śatī
Kādambarī
Pañcatantra
Dhūrta-samāgamam
Prabandha-cintāmaṇi
Rāja-taraṅgiī (Raja-tar.)
Matsya-Purāṇa
Garuḍa-Purāṇa
Agni-Purāṇa

Skanda-Purāṇa
Mānasollāsa
Arthaśāstra of Kauṭilya—
trans. by R. Shamasastri, Bangalore, 1950
trans. by R.P. Kangle, Uni. of Bombay, 1963
Vedic Index - Macdonell

Buddhist Works
Jātaka
Com. on Dīgha-Nikāya, ed. Rhys Davids & J. Carpenter, (P.T.S.)
Divyāvadāna, ed. Cowell and Neil, Cambridge, 1886. (London)
Mahādukkha-suttanta.
Milinda-pañho
Mahāvaṁsa

Jaina sources
Daśavaikālikacūrṇī, Jinadasagani, Rutlam
Ācāra-cūrṇī, Rutlam, 1941
Āvaśyaka-curṇī, Rutlam, 1928
Bṛhatkalpabhāṣya
Uttarādhyayana-ṭīkā
Paṇṇavaṇā (Paṇha)—com. Malayagiri, Bombay, 1910-Guj.
trans. by Bhagvan Das, Ahmedabad, V.S. 1991.
Nāyādhammakahāo-ed. N.V.Vaidya, Poona
Vivāgasūya ed. by A.T. Upadhya, Belgaum, 1935

Journals and Inscriptions
Aśokan Inscriptions, ed. by R.G. Basak
Basārh Seals, ed. Bloch
Bombay Gazetteer
C.I.I.
Damodarpur C.P. Ins.
Epigraphica Indica - (*E.I.*)
E.I. Report - 1910-12.
Epi. Carnatica (*E.C.*)
Indian Antiquary (*I.A.*), Calcutta weekly notes.,
Journal of American Oriental Society (*JAOS*), XIII.
Journal of Bihar and Orissa Research Society (*JBORS*), XX
Journal of Criminology

Journal of Royal Asiatic Society of Bengal (*JRASB*), XVI.
Kāśhmīr Chronicle
Law Quarterly Review, Calcutta Law Journal
Madras Ins. Report
Maliya C.P. Ins.
Sir Āsutosh Mukherjee Silver Jubilee Volumes, Vol. I.
South Indian Inscriptions (*S.I.I.*)

Modern Works

Aiyaṅgar, K.V.A., *Some Aspects of Ancient Indian Politics.*
Alberuni's "Indica" trans. by Dr. S. Sachau in 2 vols. London, 1888.
Barnes, Mr. Harry. E., *Story of Punishment.*
Bandyopadhyaya, N.C. *Kauṭilya.*
Banerjee, P.N. *Public Administration of Ancient India.*
Beal on Yuan Chwang's report
Best on Evidence
Bloch, *Le Inscriptions l' Asoka.*
Brew, (Dr.) J.M. *In the Service of Youth.*
Das Gupta, R.P. *Crime and Punishment in Ancient India.*
Diksitar, V.R.R., *Hindu Administrative Institutions.*
Fick, R., *Social Organisation of N.E. India* in the time of Buddha, tr. by S. Mitra, Cal., 1920.
Ghosh, N.M. *Indo-Aryan Literature and Culture.*
Ghoshal, U.N. *Hindu Political Theories.*
Giles, *Travels of Fahien*
Hart (Dr.), *Way of Justice*
Hastings, *Encyclopaedia of Religion and Ethics* (*E.R.E.*) "Crime and Punishment" by Jolly
Holdsworth, *History of English Law*
Jayaswal, K.P., *Hindu Polity.*
———, *Manu and Yājñavalkya.*
Jolly, *Hindu Law and Customs,* trans. by B.K. Ghosh.
Johnes, *Institutes of Hindu Law.*
Kane, P.V., *History of Dharmá-Śāstras.*
Kern, *Der Buddhismus.*
Kingsmill, *Athenaeum.*
Kohler, *Philosophy of Law.*

Legge, *Fahien*
Maine, *Early Law and Custom.*
Majumdar, R.C. *Hindu Colonies in the Far East.*
McCrindle, *Megasthenes Frag.*
Monahan, *Early History of Bengal.*
Robson, *Civilisation and the Growth of Law.*
Rapson, *Cambridge History of India* (C.H.I.)

Sacred Books of the East
Sastri, N.K. *The Cholas.*
Sengupta, N.C. *Sources of Law and Society in Ancient India.*
—— ——, *Evolution of Ancient Indian Law.*
Sircar, D.C., *South Indian Coins.*
Thakur, Amareswara, *Hindu Law of Evidence,* C.U., 1933
Wilson, *Story of Judicial and Revenue Terms.*
Yazdani, *Early History of the Deccan.*

Tamil Lexicon.

Other Books on Law

Dhalla, M.N. *Zoroastrian Civilisation.*
Edwards, Chilperic *The Hammurabi Code.*
Ferri, Prof. *Criminal Sociology.*
Gondy, *Roman Law,* Muirhead, ed.
Jolly, *History of Hindu Law* (Tagore Law Lectures).
Kennedy, Charles R. *The Orations of Demosthenes,* trans. (1856), Vol. III with appendices containing a summary of Athenian Criminal Laws.
Ludwig Carl von Bar & others, tran. by Thomas S. Bell and others, *A History of Continental Criminal Law.*
Maine, *Ancient Law.*
Nelson, *Prospectus of a scientific study of Hindu Law.*
The Old Testament.
Outlines of Roman History, with translation of the Twelve Tables and the Institutes of Justinian.
Pollock, Sir Frederic and Frederic, William Maitland, *The History of English Law (before the time of Edward).*
Rylar, Archer *Commentaries of the Laws of England in 4 books with an analysis of the work,* by W. Blackstone, London, 1829.

Robertson, A.J. ed. & tr. *The Laws of the Kings of England from Edmund to Henry.*
Salmond, *Jurisprudence.*
Sastri, L.S. *Indian Penal Code.*
Sen , Dr. Priyanath *The General Principles of Hindu Jurisprudence,* (Tagore Law Lectures, 1909).
Stephen, *Digest of English Criminal Law.*
Stephens, J.F. *History of the Criminal Laws of England.*
Zend-Avesta (*S.B.E.*)

Index